高校英语选修课系列教材

COLLEGE ESSAY WRITING SKILLS

简明英语写作教程

张 慧 李珊珊 主编

清华大学出版社
北京

内容简介

本书旨在帮助学生了解英语短文的写作特点，掌握英语短文的写作方法，培养和加强学生的书面表达能力。本书共分四个部分：第一部分介绍短文写作的三个步骤，含三个单元；第二部分列举了八类写作方法，含九个单元；第三部分介绍大学生常用的写作范例，如文章摘要、读书报告、简历、求职信等，含六个单元；第四部分介绍英文标点和表达技巧，含两个单元。本书是一本系统的写作入门教材，书中所介绍的写作方法具有较强的实用性和可操作性。

本书既适用于英语写作的初学者，尤其是大学本科低年级学生，也适用于英语爱好者自学。

版权所有，侵权必究。举报：010-62782989，beiqinquan@tup.tsinghua.edu.cn。

图书在版编目（CIP）数据

简明英语写作教程 = College Essay Writing Skills / 张慧，李珊珊主编. —— 北京：清华大学出版社，2023.12
高校英语选修课系列教材
ISBN 978-7-302-64931-1

Ⅰ. ①简… Ⅱ. ①张… ②李… Ⅲ. ①英语—写作—高等学校—教材 Ⅳ. ①H319.36

中国国家版本馆 CIP 数据核字（2023）第 225903 号

责任编辑：徐博文
封面设计：平　原
责任校对：王凤芝
责任印制：丛怀宇

出版发行：清华大学出版社
网　　址：https://www.tup.com.cn, https://www.wqxuetang.com
地　　址：北京清华大学学研大厦 A 座　　邮　编：100084
社 总 机：010-83470000　　邮　购：010-62786544
投稿与读者服务：010-62776969, c-service@tup.tsinghua.edu.cn
质量反馈：010-62772015, zhiliang@tup.tsinghua.edu.cn

印 装 者：涿州汇美亿浓印刷有限公司
经　　销：全国新华书店
开　　本：185mm×260mm　　印　张：14.75　　字　数：365 千字
版　　次：2023 年 12 月第 1 版　　印　次：2023 年 12 月第 1 次印刷
定　　价：68.00 元

产品编号：099252-01

前　言

写作，尤其是议论文和说明文的写作，是大学英语学习一个非常重要的组成部分，写作能力和水平是体现学生综合能力的一个窗口。让中国学生写出地道的英语作文，并非易事。本书旨在帮助学生应对这一难题，掌握英语短文的写作方法，提升和培养英语书面表达的能力。写作技能是可以迁移的，写作的进步会对学生的整个学习产生深远影响。本书介绍的短文写作策略可以用在多种文体的写作中，帮助学生获得基本的写作技能，写出论点鲜明、论证充分、逻辑严密、结构合理的短文。

全书包括四个部分。第一部分介绍短文写作和写作的概念基础。该部分讲述了如何构思、起草和修改作文，如何建立和支撑自己的观点，如何做到论点一致、论据充分、语言连贯，如何在修改阶段与同伴合作互评以提高写作水平。第二部分列举了短文论证的八种方法，即描写、叙事、举例、过程、因果、对比、定义和分类，对于每一种方法，编者都选用了实例供分析、学习和模仿。第三部分针对大学生的需求，介绍大学阶段经常用到的专门体裁的写作，如文章摘要、读书报告、个人简历、求职信、个人陈述和报告等。第四部分介绍写作中常用的标点符号和表达技巧，这一部分可以用作学习过程中的参考。已经掌握了比较全面的英语语法知识的学生，可以将这部分的内容结合前面三部分的学习，贯穿到每一类作文的写作中。

本书的出版得到了清华大学出版社的大力支持。本书责任编辑徐博文女士在选题和内容编排方面提出了许多宝贵意见，感谢她为本书的出版付出的辛劳。由于时间仓促，学识有限，书中的不妥之处，望读者不吝赐教。

编　者

2023 年 5 月

Contents

Part One Short Essay Writing

Chapter 1 Planning Your Essay 3
Chapter 2 Writing Your Essay 25
Chapter 3 Revising Your Essay 67

Part Two Strategies of Essay Development

Chapter 4 Introduction to Essay Development 77
Chapter 5 Narration: Recounting Events 83
Chapter 6 Description: Portraying People, Places, and Things 91
Chapter 7 Exemplification: Explaining with Examples 97
Chapter 8 Process Analysis: Explaining How Something Works or Is Done ... 105
Chapter 9 Cause and Effect: Using Reasons and Results to Explain 113
Chapter 10 Comparison or Contrast: Showing Similarities or Differences 121
Chapter 11 Definition: Explaining What You Mean 135
Chapter 12 Division or Classification: Explaining Categories or Parts 143

Part Three Special Assignments

- Chapter 13 Writing a Summary 153
- Chapter 14 Writing a Book Report 161
- Chapter 15 Preparing a Multimedia Presentation 167
- Chapter 16 Writing a Personal Statement 173
- Chapter 17 Writing a Business Letter 177
- Chapter 18 Writing a Résumé and a Cover Letter 183

Part Four Punctuation and Expression

- Chapter 19 Punctuation 193
- Chapter 20 Expression 203

Part One

Short Essay Writing

Creating an essay in which there is an overall thesis statement and in which each of the supporting paragraphs begins with a topic sentence is more challenging than writing a free-form or an expressive paper. Such an essay obliges you to carefully sort out, think through, and organize your ideas. An excellent way to learn how to write clearly and logically is to practice the traditional college essay—a paper of about five hundred words that typically consists of an introductory paragraph, one to three supporting paragraphs, and a concluding paragraph. Mastering the traditional essay will make you a better writer.

Chapter 1

Planning Your Essay

Careful, thoughtful planning is vital. It will not only improve the structure of your essay, making it more coherent and logical, but make the business of writing a lot easier. By planning your essay to provide your readers with a sequence of obvious logical steps so that they can follow the train of thought, you give yourself an invaluable safety net: in many cases a weak or poorly defined point will gain strength and precision from being a step in a clear logical argument. The arguments will gain strength and clarity from the clear, well planned context in which they are developed.

1.1 Developing a Thesis Statement

The first step in planning is to discover what point you want to make and to write as a single sentence. There are two reasons for doing this: You want to know right from the start whether you have a clear and workable thesis. Also, you will be able to use the thesis as a guide while writing the essay. At any stage you can ask yourself: Does this support the thesis? With the thesis as a guide, the danger of drifting away from the point of the essay is greatly reduced.

The most important part of any essay is the thesis statement, or main idea. Just as the topic sentence expresses the controlling idea of a paragraph, a thesis statement explains the controlling idea of an essay. The thesis statement presents the writer's position and serves as the essay's mission statement. A thesis is not simply a narrowed topic—a thesis expresses a point of view. It is a declaration of purpose.

An effective thesis statement should:
- State the opinion on some subject related to the assignment;
- Assert one main idea;
- Have something worthwhile to say.

An effective thesis statement may also forecast how the essay will be organized. For example:

- Playing team sports, especially football and baseball, develops skills and qualities that can make you successful in life because these sports demand communication, teamwork, and responsibility.

When you write, think of a thesis statement as a promise to the reader. The rest of the essay delivers on the promise. The example thesis promises the audience, that by reading this essay, they will discover how football and baseball players learn communication, teamwork, and responsibility, and how these skills and qualities contribute to the players' success in life.

1. Elements of a Thesis Statement

Effective thesis statements share common elements:

- The thesis statement forms the core of the essay. It states the writer's most important idea.
- Thesis statements are usually stated in a single sentence. Thesis statements help limit the topic. Part of the job of a thesis statement is to focus the topic. The thesis statement "Speed dating is an effective way for busy professionals to meet each other" expresses a point of view and narrows the essay to a single method of meeting new people.
- Thesis statements organize supporting details. The thesis statement "Running burns calories, exercises the heart, and reduces stress" suggests that the body part of the essay will be divided into three paragraphs.
- Thesis statements indicate the kind of support that follows. The thesis statement "The airport must be expanded to reduce congestion" implies a cause-and-effect argument based on factual details.

2. Forming a Thesis Statement

Now that you know how thesis statements work, you can begin writing. To start, you need a topic that is neither too broad nor too narrow. Suppose, for example, that an instructor asks you to write a paper on marriage. Such a subject is too broad to cover in a five-hundred-word essay. You would have to write a book to support adequately any point you might make about the general subject of marriage. What you would need to do, then, is limit the subject. Narrow it down until you have a thesis that you can deal with specifically in about five hundred words. In the box that follows are: (1) several general subjects, (2) a limited version of each general subject, and (3) a thesis statement about each subject.

Part One Short Essay Writing

General Subjects	Narrowed Topics	Thesis Statements
marriage	honeymoon	A honeymoon is perhaps the worst way to begin a marriage.
children	disciplining of children	My husband and I have several effective ways of disciplining our children.
television	TV preachers	TV evangelists use sales techniques to promote their messages.
TV shows	reality shows	Reality shows are popular because they allow viewers to relate to people like themselves.
being a smart consumer	using credit cards wisely	Credit cards should be used for emergencies and necessities, not meals, fashion items, or impulse purposes.
job search	job interview skills	Job applicants can improve their chances of success through preparation, honesty, and persistence.
sports	players' salaries	Players' high salaries are bad for the game, for the fans, and for the values.

Working to create a sharp thesis can help you focus both the thinking and the writing. Here are three steps for moving from a topic to a thesis statement:

1) State your topic as a question. You may have an idea for a topic, such as "gasoline prices", "analysis of 'real women' ad campaigns", or "famine". Those may be good topics, but they're not thesis statements, primarily because none of them actually makes a statement. A good way to begin moving from topics to thesis statements is to turn your topic into a question.

For example:
- What causes fluctuations in gasoline prices?
- Are ads picturing "real women" who are not models effective?
- What can be done to prevent famine in East Africa?

2) Turn your question into a position. A thesis statement is an assertion—it takes a stand or makes a claim. Whether you're writing a report or an argument, you are saying, "This is the way I see...", "My research shows...", or "This is what I believe about...". the thesis statement announces your position on the question you are raising about the topic, so a relatively easy way of establishing a thesis is to answer your own question.

For example:
- Gasoline prices fluctuate for several reasons.

- Ads picturing "real women" instead of models are effective because women can easily identify with them.
- The most recent famine in Somalia could have been avoided if certain measures had been taken.

3) Narrow your thesis. A good thesis is specific, guiding and showing your audience exactly what the essay cover. The preceding thesis statements need to be qualified and focused—they need to be made more specific. A good way to narrow a thesis is to ask questions about: Why do gasoline prices fluctuate? How could the Somalia famine have been avoided? The answers will help you craft a narrow, focused thesis.

For example:

- Gasoline prices fluctuate because of production procedures, consumer demand, international politics, and oil companies' policies.
- Dove's "Campaign for Self-Esteem" and Cover Girl's ads featuring Queen Latifah work because consumers can admire the women's confidence in displaying them.
- The 2017 famine in Somalia could have been avoided if farmers had received training in more effective methods and had planted droughtresistant crops and if other nations had provided more aid quickly.

4) Qualify your thesis. Sometimes you want to make a strong argument and to state the thesis bluntly. Often, however, you need to acknowledge that the assertions may be challenged or may not be unconditionally true. In those cases, consider limiting the scope of the thesis by adding such terms as *may, could probably, apparently, very likely, sometimes,* and *often*.

For example:

- Gasoline prices **very likely** fluctuate because of production procedures, consumer demand, international politics, and oil companies' policies.
- Dove's and Cover Girl's ad campaigns featuring "real women" **may** work because consumers admire the women's confidence in displaying them.
- The 2017 famine in Somalia **could probably** have been avoided if farmers had received training in more effective methods and had planted drought-resistant crops and if other nations had provided more aid quickly.

Thesis statements are typically positioned at or near the end of a text's introduction, to let readers know at the outset what is being claimed and what the text will be aiming to prove. While a thesis often forecasts the organization, it doesn't necessarily do so; the organization may be more complex than the thesis itself. For example, a student's essay, "An Outbreak of the Irrational", contains this thesis statement:

Part One Short Essay Writing

- The movement to opt out of vaccinations is irrational and dangerous because individuals advocating for their right to exercise their personal freedom are looking in the wrong places for justification and ignoring the threat they present to society as a whole.

The essay that follows includes discussions of herd immunity; a socioeconomic profile of parents who choose not to vaccinate their children; outlines of the rationales those parents use to justify their choice, which include fear of autism, fear of causing other health problems, and political and ethical values; and a conclusion that parents who refuse to vaccinate their children are unreasonable and selfish. The paper delivers what the thesis promises but includes important information not mentioned in the thesis itself.

Practice

Subjects in Lists 1-4 reflect several stages that writers go through from a general subject to a narrow thesis statement. For each list, number the stages from 1 to 5, with 1 marking the broadest one, and 5 marking the narrow thesis statement.

List 1
_____ Major league baseball players
_____ Athletes
_____ Major league pitchers' salaries too high
_____ Professional athletes
_____ Major league pitchers

List 2
_____ John Philip Souza
_____ American composers
_____ Music 101 taught me to appreciate Souza's band music.
_____ Music
_____ Band music

List 3
_____ Retail companies
_____ Supermarkets
_____ Dealing with customers
_____ Working in a supermarket
_____ How to handle unpleasant supermarket customers

List 4

_____ Camping
_____ First camping trip
_____ Summer vacation
_____ My first camping trip was a disastrous experience
_____ Vacations

3. Writing an Effective Thesis Statement

A thesis statement can be modified at almost any time in the process of writing. Some writers can develop a thesis statement when they have a good stock of ideas, to give a definite sense of direction. Some writers will work with their thesis question at least through drafting to keep options open. And no matter when it's drafted, a thesis statement can change during the writing process, as the writer discovers ideas and expresses them in sentences. Use the following guidelines to write an effective thesis statement or to evaluate and revise your working thesis.

1) An effective thesis makes an assertion. Rather than stating a fact, a thesis should take a position, express a viewpoint, or suggest your approach toward the topic.

For example:

- Hollywood movies, like *127 Hours and Jersey Boys*, are frequently based on true stories.
- The subject of this essay will be soccer fans.
- Some Vancouver high schools could close as soon as this fall.
- Video gaming is the concern of this essay.
- This new product brought in over $300,000 last year.

Do these sentences challenge you to think about their topics? If not, they are not thesis statements. They just announce the topics; they do not engage you on any level because they do not make any point about the topics. Below, each of those announcements has been revised so that it is a reasonable thesis statement.

For example:

- Hollywood movies, like *127 Hours and Jersey Boys*, manipulate true stories to cater to the tastes of the audience.
- Hooliganism, riots, and racism are extreme aspects of soccer fans' outrageous loyalty.
- Possible closures of some Vancouver high schools will result in less-prepared students.
- Players develop useful skills from time spent on video gaming.
- This new product succeeded because of its innovative marketing campaign, including widespread press coverage, in-store entertainment, and a consumer newsletter.

Part One Short Essay Writing

Practice

Determine which of the following is a statement of fact (F) and which is an assertion (A). Then revise each statement of fact, making it an assertion that could be an effective thesis statement.

(1) By budgeting time and money, students can avoid stress and enjoy the holidays. (   )

(2) The poem is about motherhood. (   )

(3) Levying a fine on college students who cheat on an assignment might help improve academic integrity. (   )

(4) Taking a class online can be convenient, but succeeding in online classes requires self-discipline and motivation. (   )

(5) As a result of taking care of her family's dog, Adrian developed a strong desire to rescue abandoned pit bulls. (   )

(6) Personal electronics that are popular with students is the subject of this essay. (   )

(7) This essay's concern is near-death experiences reported by accident victims. (   )

(8) A discussion of planning errors in the downtown area forms the core of this paper. (   )

(9) The topic to be considered is loneliness. (   )

(10) This essay will concern itself with career-planning strategies. (   )

2) An effective thesis is specific. It claims something specific and significant about the subject, and it is a claim that requires support. An effective thesis statement focuses on just one central point or issue. Suppose you prepare the following thesis statement for a short essay:

- Centerville College should re-examine its policies on open admissions, vocational programs, and aid to students.

This sprawling statement would commit you to grapple with three separate issues. At best, you could make only a few general remarks about each one. To correct matters, consider each issue carefully in light of how much it interests you and how much you know about it. Then make your choice and draft a narrower statement. The following thesis statement would do nicely for a brief paper. It shows clearly that the writer should focus on just one issue:

- *Because of the rising demand among high school graduates for job-related training, Centerville College should expand its vocational offerings.*

A good thesis statement also tailors the scope of the issue to the length of the paper. No writer could deal adequately with "Many first-year college students face crucial adjustment problems" in two or three pages. The idea is too broad to yield more than a smattering of poorly supported general statements. Paring it down to "Free time is a responsibility that challenges many first-year college students" however, results in an idea that could probably be developed adequately. Can you argue and accurately support any of these following statements in a short essay?

- Disease has shaped human history.
- Insects are fascinating creatures.
- Since the beginning of time, men and women have been very different.
- She learned a great deal from her experiences as a teenage parent.
- Televised sports are different from live sports.
- People should not go on fad diets.

Where would you begin with vast subjects such as *disease, insects,* and *the differences between men and women*? These are sweeping, often meaningless, concepts that you cannot explain to readers—the thesis controls the range of the essay's points; it sets the limits of the argument. Do not promise more than you can deliver. Avoid beginning any thesis statement with phrases such as, "All over the world..." or "People everywhere...". The following sentences based on the topics above represent possible thesis statements:

- Plane travel has made local diseases global problems.
- Strength, organization, and communication make ants one of nature's most successful insects.
- Men and women are often treated very differently in entry-level positions.
- From her experiences as a teenage parent, she learned to accept responsibility for her own life and for that of her son.
- Although television cannot transmit all the excitement of a live game, its close-ups and slow motion replays reveal much about the players and the strategy of the game.
- Fad diets can be dangerous when they deprive the body of essential nutrients or rely excessively on potentially harmful foods.

Practice

Determine which of the following thesis statements are too general. Then narrow the overly general thesis statements for a brief college-level writing assignment.

(1) Unfortunately, discrimination exists in many forms in today's society.
(2) The demands of my job undermined my relationship with my family.
(3) Manners are a kind of social glue.
(4) The religion of Islam is widely misunderstood in the United States.

(5) The experience of living in a dorm provides students with opportunities to develop valuable people skills that will serve them well throughout their lives.
(6) Violent storms can have devastating effects on communities.
(7) Although it seemed unwise at the time, postponing college was one of the wisest decisions I ever made.
(8) Contagious diseases are global problems.
(9) The media distort every issue concerning young people.
(10) Parenthood is the most important job there is.

3) An effective thesis statement is not too narrow. It is the one that you can support and develop in an essay.

For example:
- There are speed bumps in the north end of Winnipeg.
- In March 2009 there was a moderate earthquake just outside of Leamington, Ontario.
- The main road into town is lined with fast-food outlets.
- The speed limit near my home is sixty-five miles per hour.
- A hurricane hit southern Florida last summer.
- A person must be at least thirty-five years old to be elected president of the United States.

Are you challenged by any of these statements? Can you think of ways to support any of them? These sentences, in fact, are simple statements of fact that do not present a viewpoint or require any support. They are often called "dead-end" statements. Remember, a thesis statement must be broad enough to require support in an essay. The following sentences, based on those above, represent successful thesis statements.

For example:
- Speed bumps in north Winnipeg fuel drivers' tempers, increase noise pollution, and add to greenhouse gases in the air.
- Towns in most parts of Ontario, like Leamington, are unprepared for earthquakes.
- Town councils should regulate the number of fast-food operations on entrance roads.
- The speed limit near my home should be lowered to fifty-five miles per hour for several reasons.
- Federal officials made a number of mistakes in their response to the recent Florida hurricane.
- The requirement that a US president must be at least thirty-five years old is unfair and unreasonable.

Practice

Revise the following narrow or dead-end statements so that each makes a point that could be developed into a five-paragraph essay.

(1) Volunteer positions are available at local retirement homes.
(2) Film courses are always popular with students.
(3) The bicycle lanes on campus are new this year.
(4) The average karate student simulates competition fighting.
(5) Libraries provide access to computers and study spaces.

Practice

For each pair of statements, write "TN" before the one that is too narrow to be developed into an essay, and write "OK" for that is a clear, limited point.

(1) _____ a. I had squash, tomatoes, and corn in my garden last summer.
    _____ b. Vegetable gardening can be a frustrating hobby.
(2) _____ a. The main road into our town is lined with billboards.
    _____ b. For several reasons, billboards should be abolished.
(3) _____ a. The addition of a fifty-seat computer lab at our college has made it possible to expand the computer-science, mathematics, and English curricula.
    _____ b. Our college just added a fifty-seat computer lab.
(4) _____ a. Nathaniel Hawthorne's novel *The Scarlet Letter* is about the Puritans.
    _____ b. Nathaniel Hawthorne's novel *The Scarlet Letter* criticizes Puritan morality.
(5) _____ a. Americans are living longer than before because of better diets, a cleaner environment, and advanced medical care.
    _____ b. The average American can now expect to live longer than before.

4) An effective thesis statement narrows the subject to a single, central idea.

For example:

- Studying with others has several benefits, but it also has drawbacks and can be difficult to schedule.
- The "baby boom" generation has had many advantages, but it also faces many problems.
- Waste prevention is the key to waste management; in developing countries, though, waste management creates jobs and community participation.
- This college should improve its tutoring services, sponsor more activities of interest to Latino students, and speed up the registration process for students.
- Cell phones can be convenient, but they can also be dangerous.

How many ideas are in each of these thesis statements? "Studying with others has several benefits..." is one topic and one viewpoint, and "... it also has drawbacks and can be difficult to schedule" is another. The thesis statements above all present more than one idea; they push readers in two separate directions. The point of a short essay is to communicate a single main idea to readers. To be as clear as possible, then, try to limit the thesis statement to the single key idea you want readers to know. The following sentences, based on each of the examples above, represent more effective thesis statements.

For example:
- Studying with others requires careful planning, as well as cooperation and discipline on everyone's part.
- The "baby boom" generation has enjoyed many advantages, including sheer numbers and wealth.
- Community-based approaches to waste management can lead to waste prevention and productive use of waste.
- To better represent the student population it serves, this college should sponsor more activities of interest to Latino students.
- The convenience of cell phones does not justify the risks of driving while talking or texting.

Practice

The following thesis statements focus on more than one central point. Revise them so that each focuses clearly on only one point.

(1) In order to be more successful in college, students must learn time management strategies, curtail their social life during the week, and learn to balance work and school obligations so that they are able to enjoy all parts of their life.

(2) The Internet has revolutionized the way friends communicate, but it has also made children more sedentary, which has had negative health effects, and it has also made people in the workforce more solitary, which has undermined teamwork.

(3) Movie theaters continue to attract viewers to new releases although many of them are simply remakes of older movies and ones that appeal only to those who like graphic violence.

(4) Although the tornado destroyed the entire town and seriously injured hundreds of people, the local townspeople grew closer as they tended to the injured, helped to rebuild houses, and shared their financial resources with one another.

(5) Although the company has made strides in repairing its reputation in the community, it still needs to pay its employees a fair salary, restructure management, and conduct business with more reputable vendors.

(6) Although infomercials are misleading, sometimes they are quite informative.

(7) Movies with computer-generated backgrounds look spectacular, but they are not as appealing as those shot on location.

(8) Shopping online is easy and fun, although it is not always secure.

5) An effective thesis statement sometimes needs to establish your voice, suggesting your attitude toward the subject and the role you assume with readers.

For example:

Lacks Voice: Television viewing can reduce loneliness, cause laughter, and teach children.

Revised: Despite its many faults, television has at least one strong virtue: It provides replacement voices that can ease loneliness, spark healthful laughter, and even educate young children.

6) An effective thesis statement offers an original perspective and an interesting angle on the topic. If your thesis seems dull or ordinary, it probably needs revision.

For example:

Too Ordinary: Many traffic accidents are a result of carelessness.

Better: An automobile accident can change a driver's entire approach to driving.

Poor: The four children in my family have completely different personalities. (This statement may be true, but would anyone other than the children's parents really be fascinated by this topic?)

Better: Birth order can influence children's personalities in startling ways. (The writer is wiser to offer this controversial statement, which is of more interest to readers than the preceding one because many readers have brothers and sisters of their own. The writer can then illustrate her claims with examples from her own family, and from other families, if she wishes.)

Poor: I don't like to take courses that are held in big lecture classes at this school. (Why should the reader care one way or another about your class preference?)

Better: Large lecture classes provide a poor environment for the student who learns best through interaction with both teachers and peers. (This thesis will allow the writer to present personal examples that the reader may identify with or challenge, without writing an essay that is exclusively personal.)

7) An effective thesis statement avoids making an announcement. Don't use phrases such as "This essay will discuss..." or "The subject of my paper is...". Instead, state the main point directly.

For example:

Announcement: The baby-boom generation is the concern of this essay.

Revised: The baby-boom generation has changed American society in key ways.

Announcement: The point I am trying to make is that people should not be allowed to smoke on campus.

Revised: The college should prohibit smoking on campus.

8) An effective thesis statement indicates the organization of the essay. Consider using your thesis to mention the two or three key concepts on which the essay will focus, in the order in which you will discuss them.

For example:

- Playing team sports, especially football and baseball, develops skills and qualities that can make you successful in life because these sports demand communication, teamwork, and responsibility.

This thesis indicates that communication, teamwork and responsibility will be the three key concepts in the discussion of the essay.

Note: You may sometimes need more than one sentence for the thesis statement, particularly if it requires some buildup. However, don't use this possibility to produce a wordy, general, or disunified statement. The two (or more) sentences must build on each other, and the final sentence must present the key assertion of the paper.

For example:

- Modern English, especially written English, is full of bad habits that interfere with clear thinking. Getting rid of these habits is a first step to political regeneration.

Practice

For each pair of statements, write "A" beside the sentence that is an announcement rather than a thesis statement. Write "OK" for that is a clear, limited point.

(1) _____ a. I want to discuss what it means to be a good citizen.

_____ b. Being a good citizen means becoming informed about important social, environmental, and political issues.

(2) _____ a. I made several mistakes in the process of trying to win the respect and affection of my teenage stepson.

_____ b. My thesis in this paper is relationships between stepparents and stepchildren.

(3) _____ a. Successful teamwork requires focusing on the group's goals, not your own.

_____ b. This paper explains how to work well in a team.

(4) _____ a. This paper will be about sharing housework.

_____ b. Deciding who will perform certain unpleasant household chores can be the crisis that makes or breaks a marriage.

(5) _____ a. I want to show how cardiology has changed in the last 20 years.

_____ b. The advances in cardiology in the last 20 years have been miraculous.

Practice

Working in a group of two or three students, discuss what is wrong with each of the following thesis statements. Then revise them to be more effective.

(1) In this paper, I will discuss the causes of asthma, which include exposure to smoke, chemicals, and allergic reactions.
(2) Jogging is an enjoyable aerobic sport.
(3) The crime rate is increasing in US cities.
(4) Living in an apartment has many advantages.
(5) Children's toys can be dangerous, instructional, or creative.
(6) Aggression usually leads to violence, injury, and even death, and we should use it constructively.
(7) One episode of a radio talk show amply illustrates both the appeal of such shows and their silliness.
(8) Credit cards are a necessity everywhere in the world.
(9) The use of service dogs in catastrophes and emergency situations is the subject of this essay.
(10) Severe exhaustion is a chronic condition for some students.

Practice

Write a thesis according to each of the five supporting statements to understand the logical relationship between a thesis and its supporting details.

(1) Thesis: _____

A. My first car was a rebellious-looking one that matched the way I felt and acted as a teenager.

B. My next car reflected my more mature and practical adult self.

C. My latest car seems to tell me that I'm aging; it shows my growing concern with comfort and safety.

(2) Thesis: _____
   A. All the course credits that are accumulated can be transferred to a four-year school.
   B. Going to a two-year college can save a great deal of money in tuition and other fees.
   C. If the college is nearby, there are also significant savings in everyday living expenses.

(3) Thesis: _____
   A. First, I tried simply avoiding the snacks aisle of the supermarket.
   B. Then I started limiting myself to only five units of any given snack.
   C. Finally, in desperation, I began keeping the cellophane bags of snacks in a padlocked cupboard.

(4) Thesis: _____
   A. Thomas Jefferson wrote *the Declaration of Independence* and helped lead the American Revolution.
   B. As third president of the United States, he negotiated the Louisiana Purchase, which doubled the size of the country.
   C. He donated the first books in the Library of Congress.

(5) Thesis: _____
   A. Many students who intend to go to law school major in English.
   B. Studying writing and literature is excellent preparation for a career in teaching.
   C. After earning undergraduate degrees in English, some students pursue a master's degree in business administration.

1.2 Organizing Ideas

Deciding how to organize a large amount of information into a unified and coherent paragraph is one of the most difficult aspects of the writing process. An effective essay has a recognizable shape—an arrangement of parts that guides readers, helping them see how ideas and details relate to each other and contribute to the whole. You may sometimes let an effective organization emerge over one or more drafts. But many writers find that organizing ideas to some extent before drafting can provide a helpful sense of direction. If you feel uncertain about the course, the essay should follow or have a complicated topic with many parts, devising a shape for the material can clarify your options. This section helps you to organize your ideas.

1. Distinguishing the general and the specific

To organize material for an essay, you need to distinguish general and specific ideas and see the relations between ideas. General and specific refer to the number of instances or objects included in a group signified by a word. The "ladder" below illustrates a general-to-specific hierarchy.

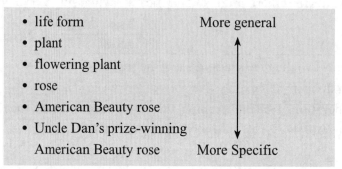

Here are some tips for arranging the ideas in your preliminary writing:

- Underline, boldface, or circle the most general ideas. These are the ideas that offer the main support for the thesis statement. They will be more general than the evidence that supports them.
- Make connections between each general idea and the more specific details that support it. Write each general idea down with space beneath it, and add specific information in the appropriate spaces.
- Respect the meanings of ideas. Think through the implications of ideas as you sort them. Otherwise, your hierarchies could become jumbled, with rose, for instance, illogically subordinated to animal, or life form somehow subordinated to rose.
- Remove information that doesn't fit. If you worry about losing deleted information, transfer the notes to a separate sheet of paper.
- Fill holes where support seems skimpy. If you recognize a hole but don't know what to fill it with, try using a discovery technique such as brainstorming or drawing, or go back to the research sources.
- Experiment with various arrangements of general ideas and supporting information. Seek an order that presents your material clearly and logically.

Practice

Here are four lists from the general topic to the specific topic. For each topic in Lists 1-4, number them from "1" to "4" ("1" indicating the most general topic, and "4" marking the most specific topic).

Part One Short Essay Writing

List 1	List 2
_____ Class sizes	_____ Bicycles
_____ Education	_____ Dangers of bike riding
_____ Lectures and tutorials	_____ Transportation
_____ Small-group learning	_____ Personal vehicles

List 3	List 4
_____ Retail companies	_____ Genetic studies
_____ Supermarkets	_____ Genetically modified vegetables
_____ Dealing with customers	_____ Science
_____ Working in a supermarket	_____ Biology

2. Choosing an Organizing Tool

Many writers use outlines not only before but also after drafting—to check the underlying structure of the draft when revising it. No matter when it's made, though, an outline can be changed to reflect changes in the thinking. View any outline you make as a tentative sketch, not as a fixed diagram. There are different kinds of outlines, some more flexible than others. All of them can enlarge and clarify your thinking, showing the patterns of general and specific, suggesting proportions, and highlighting gaps or overlaps in coverage.

3. A Scratch or Informal Outline

For many essays, especially those with a fairly straightforward structure, a simple listing of ideas and perhaps their support may provide adequate direction for your writing. A scratch outline lists the key points of the paper in the order they will be covered. Here are Katy Moreno's thesis statement and scratch outline for her essay on the global job market:

> Thesis statement
> My mother's experience of having her job outsourced teaches a lesson that Thomas L. Friedman overlooks: Technical training by itself can be too narrow to produce the communicators and problem solvers needed by contemporary businesses.
>
> Scratch outline
> Mom's outsourcing experience
>   Excellent tech skills
>   Salary too high compared to overseas tech workers
>   Lack of planning + communication skills, unlike managers who kept jobs
>   Well-rounded education to protect vs. outsourcing
>   Tech training, as Friedman says
>   Also, experience in communication, problem solving, other management skills

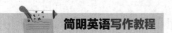

An informal outline is usually more detailed than a scratch outline, including key general points as well as the specific evidence for them. A student's thesis statement and informal outline appear below.

Thesis statement

After Home Inc.'s hiring practices were exposed in the media, the company avoided a scandal with policy changes and a well-publicized outreach to employees and consumers.

Informal outline

Background on scandal
    Previous hiring practices
    Media exposure and public response (brief)
Policy changes
    Application forms
    Interviewing procedures
    Training of personnel
Outreach to employees
    Signs and letters
    Meetings and workshops
Outreach to consumers
    Press conference
    Store signs
    Advertising—print and radio

4. A Formal Outline

For complex topics requiring complex arrangements of ideas and support, you may want or be required to construct a formal outline. More rigidly arranged and more detailed than other outlines, a formal outline not only lays out main ideas and the support but also shows the relative importance of all the essay's elements and how they connect with one another. Because of its structure, a formal outline can be an excellent tool for planning a revision. You might use an outline to check whether the organization is logical. For example, Katy Moreno created the formal outline to plan expansions and other changes suggested by readers of her first draft.

Thesis statement

My mother's experience of having her job outsourced teaches a lesson that Thomas L. Friedman overlooks: Technical training by itself can be too narrow to produce the communicators and problem solvers needed by contemporary businesses.

> **Formal outline**
> I. Summary of Friedman's article
>   1. Reasons for outsourcing
>   1) Improved technology and access
>   2) Well-educated workers
>   3) Productive workers
>   4) Lower wages
>   2. Need for improved technical training in US
> II. Experience of my mother
>   1. Outsourcing of job
>   1) Mother's education, experience, performance
>   2) Employer's cost savings
>   2. Retention of managers' jobs
>   1) Planning skills
>   2) Communication skills
> III. Conclusions about ideal education
>   1. Needs of US businesses
>   1) Technical skills
>   2) Management skills
>   (1) Communication
>   (2) Problem solving
>   (3) Versatility
>   2. Consideration of personal goals
>   1) Technical training
>   2) English and history courses for management skills
> IV. Conclusions about ideal education
>   1. Business needs for technical skills
>   2. Needs for management skills such as communication and problem solving
>   3. Personal goal of technical training
>   4. Additional courses for management skills

Moreno's outline illustrates several principles of outlining that can help ensure completeness, balance, and clear relationships. These principles largely depend on distinguishing between the general and the specific.

5. Principles of Writing a Formal Outline

- All the outline's parts are systematically indented and labeled. Roman numerals (I,

II) label primary divisions of the essay, followed by numbers 1 and 2 for secondary divisions, 1) and 2) for principal supporting points, and (1) and (2) for details. Each succeeding level contains more specific information than the one before it.
- The outline divides the material into several groups. A list needs tighter, more logical groups to show the relationships between 1 and 2 and between 3 and 4.
- Within each part of the outline, distinct topics of equal generality appear in parallel headings, with the same indention and numbering or lettering.
- All subdivided headings in the outline break into at least two or more parts because a topic cannot logically be divided into only one part. Any single subdivision should be matched with another subdivision, combined with the heading above it, or rechecked for its relevance to the heading.
- All headings are expressed in parallel grammatical form. Moreno's draft is a topic outline, in which the headings consist of a noun (*summary, reasons, technology and access,* and the like) with modifiers (*of Friedman's article, improved, well-educated,* and the like).

Principles of the formal outline
- Labels and indentions indicate order and relative importance;
- Sections and subsections reflect logical relationships;
- Topics of equal generality appear in parallel headings;
- Each subdivision has at least two parts;
- Headings are expressed in parallel grammatical form.

6. Choosing a Structure

Reading somebody else's work is like entering an unfamiliar city: You can get lost easily, you're dependent upon others to give directions, and even worse, you really don't know why you're there in the first place, unless somebody else tells you. A well-arranged structure of the essay, therefore, represents the city map, the introduction, and the thesis statement. The topic sentence at the beginning of each paragraph are the writer's attempt to let readers know where they are being taken, which turnings they will be taking along the way, and why.

Structure is one of the features that distinguish genres of writing. For instance, a social-science research report generally has distinct sections in an established order: abstract, introduction, method, results, and discussion. Many academic genres, particularly those in the humanities, do not come with such a detailed plan, but they still share a basic shape: the introduction-body-conclusion pattern. The central idea—the thesis statement appears in the introductory paragraph, and the specific support for the thesis appears in the paragraphs that follow. The supporting paragraphs allow for a

Part One Short Essay Writing

fuller treatment of the evidence that backs up the central point than would be possible in a single-paragraph paper.

- Introductory paragraph captures and focuses readers' attention. At a minimum, it announces and clarifies the topic. Often it ends with the thesis statement, making a commitment that the rest of the work delivers on.
- The body paragraphs of the essay develop the thesis and thus fulfill the commitment of the introduction. The paragraphs in the body develop the general points that support the thesis—the items that would be labeled with Roman numerals and capital letters in a formal outline like the formal outline written by Katy Moreno. These general points are like the legs of a table supporting the top, the thesis. Each general point may take a paragraph or more, with the bulk of the content providing the details, examples, and reasons (the wood of each table leg) to support the general point and thus the thesis.
- The concluding paragraph gives readers something to take away from the writing — a summary of ideas, for instance, or a suggested course of action.

An essay should have a beginning, a middle, and an end, that is, an introduction, a body, and a conclusion. The introduction sparks interest and acquaints the reader with what is to come. The body delivers the main message and exhibits a clear connection between ideas so that the reader can easily follow your thoughts. The conclusion ends the discussion so the reader feels satisfied rather than suddenly cut off. Overall, your essay should follow a pattern that is suited to its content.

Practice

Essay "Coping with Old Age" has no indentations starting new paragraphs. Read it carefully and divide the whole essay into three paragraphs. Then double-underline the thesis and single-underline the topic sentence. Write the numbers of those sentences in the spaces provided at the end.

Coping with Old Age

¹ I recently read about an area of the former Soviet Union where many people live to be well over a hundred years old. ² Being 115 or even 125 isn't considered unusual there, and these old people continue to do productive work right up until they die. ³ The United States, however, isn't such a healthy place for older people. ⁴ Since I retired from my job, I've had to cope with the physical, mental, and emotional stresses of being "old". ⁵ For one thing, I've had to adjust to physical changes. ⁶ Now that I'm over sixty, the trusty body that carried me around for years has turned

traitor. ⁷Aside from the deepening wrinkles on my face and neck, and the wiry gray hairs that have replaced my brown hair, I face more frightening changes. ⁸I don't have the energy I used to. ⁹My eyes get tired. ¹⁰Once in a while, I miss something that's said to me. ¹¹My once faithful feet seem to have lost their comfortable soles, and I sometimes feel I'm walking on marbles. ¹²In order to fight against this slow decay, I exercise whenever I can. ¹³I walk, I stretch, and I climb stairs. ¹⁴I battle constantly to keep as fit as possible. ¹⁵I'm also trying to cope with mental changes. ¹⁶My mind was once as quick and sure as a champion gymnast. ¹⁷I never found it difficult to memorize answers in school or to remember the names of people I met. ¹⁸Now, I occasionally have to search my mind for the name of a close neighbor or favorite television show. ¹⁹Because my mind needs exercise, too, I challenge it as much as I can. ²⁰Taking a college course like this English class, for example, forces me to concentrate. ²¹The mental gymnast may be a little slow and out of shape, but he can still do a backflip or turn a somersault when he has to. ²²Finally, I must deal with the emotional impact of being old. ²³Our society typecasts old people. ²⁴We're supposed to be unattractive, senile, useless leftovers. ²⁵We're supposed to be the crazy drivers and the cranky customers. ²⁶At first, I was angry and frustrated that I was considered old at all. ²⁷And I knew that people were wrong to stereotype me. ²⁸Then I got depressed. ²⁹I even started to think that maybe I was a castoff, one of those old animals that slow down the rest of the herd. ³⁰But I have now decided to rebel against these negative feelings. ³¹I try to have friends of all ages and to keep up with what's going on in the world. ³²I try to remember that I'm still the same person who sat at a first-grade desk, who fell in love, who comforted a child, who got a raise at work. ³³I'm not "just" an old person. ³⁴Coping with the changes of old age has become my latest full-time job. ³⁵Even though it's a job I never applied for, and one for which I had no experience, I'm trying to do the best I can.

Thesis statement: _____
Topic sentence of first supporting paragraph: _____
Topic sentence of second supporting paragraph: _____
Topic sentence of third supporting paragraph: _____
Conclusion: _____

Chapter 2

Writing Your Essay

After outlining your essay, even if it is an informal list of topics jotted down on the back of an envelope, you have decided where to start. It's time to write the first draft.

2.1 Body Paragraphs

The body paragraphs make up the largest part of the essay and present the evidence and commentary that show the thesis statement to be valid. Each paragraph has two jobs:
- to develop one important point in support of the thesis statement;
- to show how that point furthers the argument of the essay.

Body paragraphs open with a topic sentence and include evidence and a clear link between the paragraph's subject matter and the thesis claim. Besides, the focus of the body paragraphs is to support the thesis statement, and there is a dependent relationship established between the body paragraphs and the thesis statement. Writing a well-developed paragraph can be easy once you understand the structure that is expected. Think of each paragraph as a mini-essay: a topic sentence that functions like the thesis statement followed by supporting evidence for that topic sentence. Keep in mind that the topic sentence and evidence have to support the essay's thesis statement. This is why it is best to construct an outline or a writing plan focused on the proof of the thesis statement before beginning a draft.

1. The Structure of a Body Paragraph

A paragraph is a group of connected sentences that develop a single idea about a topic. Each paragraph in your essay should support the thesis and contribute to the overall

meaning and effectiveness of the essay.

Well-developed body paragraphs contain:
- a well-focused topic sentence;
- specific supporting details (definitions, examples, facts and statistics, explanations, or other evidence);
- transitions and strategic repetition that show how the ideas are related, within and across paragraphs.

For a paragraph to develop a single idea, it must have unity: It must stay focused on one idea, without switching or wandering from topic to topic. A paragraph also should be of a reasonable length, neither too short nor too long. Short paragraphs are often underdeveloped; long paragraphs may be difficult for readers to follow. Note that what is an appropriate length may change across genres of writing—scholarly articles usually have longer paragraphs than college essays. Here is a sample paragraph with its parts labeled.

- Audiences gather with varying degrees of willingness to hear a speaker. Some are anxious to hear the speaker, and may even have paid a substantial admission price. The "lecture circuit", **for example**, is a most lucrative aspect of public life. **But** whereas some audiences are willing to pay to hear a speaker, others don't seem to care one way or the other. **Other** audiences need to be persuaded to listen (or at least to sit in the audience). **Still other** audiences gather because they have to. **For example**, negotiations on a union contract may require members to attend meetings where officers give speeches.

The first sentence in this paragraph is a topic sentence. The words in bold face are guideposts. Notice also how the writer repeats the words *audience(s)* and *speaker*, along with the synonyms *lecture* and *speeches*, to help tie the paragraph to the idea in the topic sentence. To visualize the structure of a well-developed paragraph, see the following table.

Topic Sentence	• Identifies what the paragraph is about • Makes a point about the topic • Connects to the previous paragraph
Supporting Details	• Explain the topic sentence • Support the topic sentence with evidence, such as examples, facts, statistics, personal experience, and definitions
Concluding or Transitional Sentence	• Draws the paragraph to a close, or • Leads to the next paragraph

2. Paragraph Writing Step One: Develop a Topic Sentence

After creating an outline, you have a good sense of the ideas that support the topic and viewpoint. The supporting points will form the topic sentences for the body paragraphs in the essay. As you have created the outline, turn each supporting-point word or phrase into a topic sentence. A topic sentence should make clear what the paragraph is about (its topic) and express a view or make a point about the topic.

For example:

- <u>Shocking behavior by fans, including rudeness and violent language,</u> <u>has become</u>
  topic

  <u>common at many sporting events.</u>
  point about topic

It should use specific and detailed language to tell readers what the paragraph is about. Avoid vague, general, or unfocused statements. A good topic sentence should include either of the following:

- one clear topic

  weak: *It's important to have friends, and also to do well in school.*

  strong: *I don't think I will ever have a better friend than Heather.*

- an opinion or idea about the topic

  weak: *I have been studying karate.*

  strong: *Studying karate has given me strength and self-confidence.*

A good topic sentence should not be:

- too broad (too much to write about)

  weak: *Australia is an interesting country.*

  strong: *On my visit to Australia, I saw many unusual animals.*

- too narrow (not enough to write about / is just a fact)

  weak: *School starts at 8:30 am.*

  strong: *Getting ready for school in the morning is more difficult than any of my classes.*

To summarize, just as a thesis announces the main point of an essay, a topic sentence states the main point of a paragraph. In addition, each topic sentence must in some way explain the thesis or show why the thesis is believable or correct. An effective topic sentence should be focused, support the thesis, and be placed appropriately (usually at the beginning of the paragraph).

Revise each of the following topic sentences to make it focused and specific. At

least two of your revised topic sentences should also preview the organization of the paragraph.

(1) In society today, there is always a new fad or fashion in clothing.

(2) People watch television talk shows because they find them irresistible.

(3) Tattoos are a popular trend.

(4) Procrastinating can have a negative effect on your success in college.

(5) In America, the lottery is a big issue.

Practice

For each of the following thesis statements, identify the topic sentence that does not support the thesis.

(1) To make a marriage work, a couple must build trust, communication, and understanding.

    A. Knowing why a spouse behaves as he or she does can improve a relationship.

    B. People get married for reasons other than love.

    C. The ability to talk about feelings, problems, likes, and dislikes should grow as a marriage develops.

    D. Marital partners must rely on each other to make sensible decisions that benefit both of them.

(2) Internet sales are capturing a larger market share relative to in-store sales.

    A. Internet retailers that target a specific audience tend to be most successful.

    B. The convenience of ordering any time of day or night accounts, in part, for increased Internet sales.

    C. Many customers use PayPal for online purchases.

    D. Websites that locate and compare prices for a specified item make comparison shopping easier on the Internet than in retail stores.

3. Paragraph Writing Step Two: Support the Topic Sentence with Evidence

After you have written a working topic sentence, the next step is to develop evidence that supports it. Evidence is any type of information, such as examples and anecdotes, facts and statistics, or expert opinion, that will convince readers that the topic sentence is reasonable or correct. You can advance supporting evidence in these ways:

- Explain: Provide important facts, details, and examples;
- Narrate: Share a brief story or recreate an experience to illustrate an idea;
- Describe: Tell in details how someone appears or how something works;
- Define: Identify or clarify the meaning of a specific term or idea;
- Analyze: Examine the parts of something to better understand the whole;

- Compare: Provide examples to show how two things are alike or different;
- Argue: Use logic and evidence to prove that something is true;
- Reflect: Express your thoughts or feelings about something;
- Cite authorities: Add expert analysis or personal commentary.

These evidence, organized into well-developed paragraphs, make up the body of your essay.

Supporting evidence must suit the essay-writing situation. Depending on the type of essay and the subject about which you are writing, different forms of supporting evidence will be appropriate. Generally, as you begin college or university, early essay assignments will require details that are a mixture of your own thoughts and ideas derived from other sources. For most kinds of academic writing, certain types of evidence are preferred over others. In general, your personal experiences and opinions are not considered as useful as more objective evidence such as facts, statistics, historical background, and expert testimony. Suppose you are writing an academic paper on the effects of global warming, your observations about climate changes in your city would not be considered adequate or appropriate evidence to support the idea of climatic change as an effect of global warming. To support the thesis, you would need to provide facts, statistics, and expert testimony on climatic change in a wide geographic area and demonstrate their relationship to global warming.

4. Evidence in Body Paragraphs: Supporting Detail

Possibly the most serious—and most common—weakness of all essays by novice writers is the lack of effectively developed body paragraphs. The information in each paragraph must adequately explain, exemplify, define, or in some other way support the topic sentence. Therefore, you must include enough supporting information or evidence in each paragraph to make readers understand the topic sentence. Moreover, you must make the information in the paragraph clear and specific enough for the readers to accept your ideas. Supporting details are examples, precise descriptions of items, facts or statistics, quotations, or even brief anecdotes. To be specific, supporting details include:

- Some examples: *situations, people, character types, places, events, or objects that illustrate a supporting point.*
- Descriptions: *careful word pictures of objects, situations, or beings that make ideas concrete to readers.*
- Facts: *items of information about things that exist or have existed—they can be confirmed by other sources; statistics are verifiable information that is represented numerically.*

- Quotations: *the exact words of some other person. Note that person must be credited, and the quotation must appear in double quotation marks.*
- Anecdotes: *short accounts of true incidents used to illustrate or provide evidence for a point.*

Your writing situation—that is the purpose, audience, point of view, genre, and medium—will determine which types of evidence will be most effective. The table below lists various types of evidence and gives examples of how each type could be used to support a working thesis on acupuncture.

Types of Evidence Used to Support a Thesis	
Working Thesis: Acupuncture, a form of alternative medicine, is becoming more widely accepted in the United States.	
Types of Evidence	**Examples**
Definitions	*Explain that in acupuncture, needles are inserted into specific points of the body to control pain or relieve symptoms.*
Historical background	*Explain that acupuncture is a medical treatment that originated in ancient China.*
Explanation of a process	*Explain the principles on which acupuncture is based and how scientists think it works.*
Factual details	*Explain who uses acupuncture, on what parts of the body it is used, and under what circumstances it is applied.*
Descriptive details	*Explain what acupuncture needles look and feel like.*
Narrative story	*Relate a personal experience that illustrates the use of acupuncture.*
Causes or effects	*Discuss one or two theories that explain why acupuncture works. Offer reasons for its increasing popularity.*
Classification	*Explain types of acupuncture treatments.*
Comparison and contrast	*Compare acupuncture with other forms of alternative medicine, such as massage and herbal medicines. Explain how acupuncture differs from these other treatments.*
Advantages and disadvantages	*Describe the pros (nonsurgical, relatively painless) and cons (fear of needles) of acupuncture.*
Examples	*Describe situations in which acupuncture has been used successfully — by dentists, in treating alcoholism, for pain control.*

Types of Evidence	Examples
Problems	*Explain that acupuncture is not always practiced by medical doctors; licensing and oversight of acupuncturists may thus be lax.*
Statistics	*Indicate how many acupuncturists practice in the United States.*
Quotations	*Quote medical experts who attest to the effectiveness of acupuncture as well as those who question its value.*

5. The Importance of Specific Details

Just as a thesis must be developed with supporting points, each topic sentence must be developed with specific details. Specific details are valuable in two key ways. First, details excite the reader's interest. They make writing a pleasure to read, for we all enjoy learning particulars about people, places, and things. Second, details serve to explain a writer's points. They give the evidence needed for us to see and understand general ideas.

Students may try to disguise unsupported paragraphs through repetition and generalities. Do not fall into this "wordiness trap". All too often, the body paragraphs in essays contain only vague generalities, rather than the specific supporting details that are needed to engage and convince a reader. Be prepared to do the plain hard work needed to ensure that each paragraph has solid support. Having a well-developed paragraph is more than a matter of adding material, however. The information in each paragraph must effectively explain or support the topic sentence. Vague generalities or repetitious ideas are not convincing. In the following paragraph, the writer offers only generalities.

- We ought to ban the use of cell phones in moving vehicles. Some people who have them think that's a really good idea, but a lot of us don't agree. Using a phone while driving causes too many dangerous accidents to happen, and even if there's no terrible accident, people using them have been known to do some really stupid things in traffic. Drivers using phones are constantly causing problems for other drivers; pedestrians are in big trouble from these people, too. I think this is getting to be a really dangerous situation, and we ought to do something about it soon.

This paragraph is weak because it is composed of repetitious general statements using vague, unclear language. None of its general statements is supported with specific evidence. Why is phone use when driving not a "good" idea? How can it cause accidents? What are the "problems" and "trouble" the writer refers to? What exactly does "do something about it" mean? The writer obviously have some ideas in mind, but these ideas are not clear to the reader because they are not adequately developed with specific evidence and language. By adding supporting examples and details, the writer might revise the paragraph this way.

- Although cell phones are a time-saving convenience for busy people, they are too distracting for use by drivers of moving vehicles, whose lack of full attention poses a serious threat to other drivers and to pedestrians. The simple act of answering a phone, for example, may take a driver's eyes away from traffic signals or other cars. Moreover, involvement in a complex or emotional conversation could slow a driver's response time just when fast action is needed to avoid an accident. Last week, I drove behind a man using his phone. As he drove and talked, I could see him gesturing wildly, obviously agitated with the other caller. His speed repeatedly slowed and then picked up, slowed and increased, and his car drifted more than once on a street frequently crossed by schoolchildren. Because the man was clearly not in full, conscious control of his driving, he was dangerous. My experience is not isolated: a recent study by the Foundation for Traffic Safety maintains that using a cell phone is more distracting to drivers than listening to the radio or talking to a rider. With additional studies in progress, voters in our state should soon demand legislation to restrict phone use to passengers or to drivers when the vehicles are in motion.

The reader now has a better idea why the writer feels such cell phone use is distracting and, consequently, dangerous. By using two hypothetical examples (*looking away, slowed response time*), one personal experience (*observing the agitated man*), and one reference to research (*the safety study*), the writer offers the reader three kinds of supporting evidence for the paragraph's claim. Below is another example, a student's writing on the topic "Something that distracts you".

- Although my roommate is a helpful companion at times, she is a distracting nuisance whenever I try to study. Throughout the evening, her CD player blares in my ears. Even worse, she insists on smacking her gum. She also interrupts me with questions that have nothing to do with homework. At any other time, my roommate is a friend, but while I'm studying, she's my greatest enemy.

Instead of presenting a list of things her roommate does to distract her, she could have written something that actually did happen at a particular time and a particular place. In other words, she could have written about one specific study period; she could have told us not just that her CD player was going—but what CD she was playing. She could have told us what kind of gum she was chewing, and also what specific "dumb" questions she asked her. She has revised the paragraph.

- Although my roommate is a helpful companion at times, she is a distracting nuisance whenever I try to study. Just last Wednesday night, Anna decided to spend the evening playing her "classic" Bob Dylan CDs. While I was trying desperately to integrate a math function, all I could hear was that the answer was somewhere "blowin' in the wind". Even worse, the entire time Dylan was rasping away, Anna accompanied him by smacking and popping her Bazooka bubble gum. I'd finally given up on math and started my struggle with chemistry when she abruptly asked (loudly, of course, so I could hear her over the music), "Do you think any Cokes are left in the Coke machine?" My stomach started rumbling and my throat suddenly felt dry—even drier than the chemistry text I was trying to read. As I dropped the change into the Coke machine, I realized that although Anna is usually a friend, while I'm studying she is my greatest enemy.

Now we can picture her, and Anna, and all those distractions. She's told us the story (a narrative example) of her evening trying to study, helping us to see her and feel her frustration. In the strong paragraph, sharp details capture our interest and enable us to share the writer's experience. They provide pictures that make us feel we are there. The particulars also enable us to understand clearly the writer's point. Therefore, aim to make your own writing convincing by providing detailed support.

Practice

Write "S" before the one that provide specific evidence to support the opening point; write "X" before that is followed by vague, general, wordy sentences.

_____ (1) The tree house my father and I built was a masterpiece. It had three floors, each of which was about 75 square feet. There were two windows made of real glass on each floor, allowing sunlight to flood in and making the place pleasant and cheerful. The walls were made of sweet-smelling cedar planks Dad and I salvaged from a landfill. On the bottom floor was a small cast-iron stove, which gave off enough heat to keep us toasty on the coldest winter day. The second floor had an old rocking chair on which I read my favorite comics every summer afternoon. On the top floor, Dad had set up a telescope from which we observed the glories of the night sky.

_____ (2) Our first camping trip in Keystone State Forest was disappointing. Many of the animals we had hoped to see on our walk just weren't there. Some smaller animals were, but we had seen them before in our backyards. The forest was rather quiet. It was not what we had expected. The weather didn't cooperate either. It was dreadful for most of our stay. Then there were the bugs! We had planned for the trip well, spending a lot of money on provisions and special equipment. But much of it was a waste because we left much earlier than we had intended. We came home frustrated and soured on the whole idea of camping.

_____ (3) Some things are worse when they're "improved". A good cheesecake, for one thing, is perfect. It doesn't need pineapple, cherries, blueberries, or whipped cream smeared all over it. Plain old American blue jeans, the ones with five pockets and copper rivets, are perfect too. Manufacturers only made them worse when they added flared legs, took away the pockets, tightened the fit, and plastered white logos and designers' names all over them.

_____ (4) Pets can be more trouble than children. My dog, unlike my children, has never been completely housebroken. When he's excited or nervous, he still has an occasional problem. My dog, unlike my children, has never learned how to take care of himself when we're away, despite the fact that we've given him plenty of time to do so. We don't have to worry about our grown children anymore. However, we still have to hire a dog-sitter.

6. The Importance of Adequate Details

One of the most common and most serious problems in students' writing is inadequate development. You must provide enough specific details to fully support the point in body paragraphs of an essay. You could not, for example, include in a paragraph about a friend's unreliability and provide only a one- or two-sentence example. You would have to extend the example or add several other examples showing your friend as an unreliable person. Without such additional support, the paragraph would be underdeveloped. The following paragraph is underdeveloped because it offers reasons but no specific examples or details to support its claims.

- Living with my ex-roommate was unbearable. First, she thought everything she owned was the best. Second, she possessed numerous filthy habits. Finally, she constantly exhibited immature behavior.

The writer might provide more evidence this way:
For example:
- Living with my ex-roommate was unbearable. First, she thought everything she owned, from clothes to cosmetics, was the best. If someone complimented my pants, she'd point out that her designer jeans looked better and would last longer because they were made of better material. If she borrowed my shampoo, she'd let me know that it didn't get her hair as clean and shiny as hers did. My hand cream wasn't as smooth; my suntan lotion wasn't as protective; not even my wire clothes hangers

Part One Short Essay Writing

were as good as her padded ones! But despite her pickiness about products, she had numerous filthy habits. Her dirty dishes remained in the sink for days before she felt the need to wash them. Piles of the "best" brand of tissues were regularly discarded from her upper bunk and strewn about the floor. Her desk and closets overflowed with heaps of dirty clothes, books, cosmetics, and whatever else she owned, and she rarely brushed her teeth (when she did brush, she left oozes of toothpaste in the sink). Finally, she constantly acted immaturely by throwing tantrums when things didn't go her way. A poor grade on an exam or paper, for example, meant books, shoes, or any other small object within her reach would hit the wall flying. Living with such a person taught me some valuable lessons about how not to win friends or keep roommates.

By adding more supporting evidence—specific examples and details—to this paragraph, the writer has a better chance of convincing the reader of the roommate's real character. Readers cannot "see what you see" in your mind, so the words do the work of showing your thoughts to them. This is where providing enough specifics is essential. When you offer enough details to properly clarify a supporting point, you show readers what makes that point true for you. If the supporting points are not adequately developed—that is, if there are not enough details to illustrate or prove the point of a paragraph—then you are forcing the reader to figure out why the point is valid. That is not the reader's job; it is your job as a writer. You could not, for instance, write a paragraph about the importance of a good resumé and provide only one reason, even if you use five sentences to write that reason. Without additional support, the paragraph is underdeveloped and readers will not accept the point or the knowledge of it. Because audiences are most drawn to the specifics in your support, and are most attentive to details, they will judge your writing on how logically the supporting details follow from the claims made by the topic sentences, how reasonable and defensible the details are, and how precise and credible those details are. You meet the audience with the support you choose—an essay stands or falls on the quality of its support. Always ask yourself the following:

- Are my ideas based on reasoning, or am I just stating an opinion that I cannot back up logically?
- Do my ideas and details show bias or unfair judgments? Could I defend them on any basis other than emotion, or liking or disliking them?
- Are any of my details just generalities, unfocused statements that do not add to my argument?
- How do I know my points and details are true? Why should readers find them credible?

Practice

The following body paragraphs are from students' essays. Two of the paragraphs provide sufficient details to support the topic sentences. Write "AD" for adequate development for these two. For the last three paragraphs using vague, wordy, general, or irrelevant information, write "U" for underdeveloped beside them.

_____ (1) Another consideration in adopting a dog is the cost. Initial fees for shots and a license might add up to $50. Annual visits to the vet for heartworm pills, rabies and distemper shots, and general checkups could cost $100 or more. Then there is the cost of food. A twenty-five-pound bag of dry food (the cheapest kind) costs around $15. A large dog can eat that much in a couple of weeks.

_____ (2) People can be cruel to pets simply by being thoughtless. They don't think about a pet's needs, or they simply ignore those needs. It never occurs to them that their pet can be experiencing a great deal of discomfort as a result of their failure to be sensitive. The cruelty is a result of the basic lack of attention and concern—qualities that should be there, but aren't.

_____ (3) If I were in charge of the nighttime programming on a TV network, I would make changes. I would completely eliminate some shows. In fact, all the shows that proved to be of little interest would be canceled. Commercials would also change so that it would be possible to watch them without wanting to turn off the TV. I would expand the good shows so that people would come away with an even better experience. My ideal network would be a great improvement over the average lineup we see today on any of the major networks.

_____ (4) A friend's rudeness is much more damaging than a stranger's. When a friend says sharply, "I don't have time to talk to you just now," you feel hurt instead of angry. When a friend shows up late for lunch or a shopping trip, with no good reason, you feel that you're being taken for granted. Worst, though, is when a friend pretends to be listening to you but his or her wandering eyes show a lack of attention. Then you feel betrayed. Friends, after all, are supposed to make up for the thoughtless cruelties of strangers.

_____ (5) Giving my first shampoo and set to a real person, after weeks of practicing on wigs, was a nerve-racking experience. The customer was a woman who acted very sure about what she came for. She tried to describe what she wanted, and I tried without much success to understand what she had in mind. Every time I did something, she seemed to be indicating in one way or another that it was not what she wanted. I got more and more nervous as I worked on her hair, and the nervousness showed. The worst part of the ordeal happened at the very end, when I added the final touches. Nothing, to this woman, had turned out right.

7. Choosing the Evidence

In collecting evidence in support of a thesis, you will probably generate more than you need. Consequently, you will need to identify the evidence that best supports the thesis and best suits your purpose and audience. The following guidelines will help you select the types of evidence that will best support the thesis.

1) **Make sure the evidence is relevant**. All of your evidence must clearly and directly support the thesis. Irrelevant evidence will distract and puzzle (or annoy) readers. If the thesis is "acupuncture is useful for controlling pain", you would not need to describe other alternative therapies.

2) **Provide specific evidence**. Avoid general statements that will not help you make a convincing case for the thesis. For instance, to support the thesis "acupuncture is becoming more widely accepted by patients in the United States", citing statistics that demonstrate an increase in the number of practicing acupuncturists in the United States over the past five years would be most convincing.

3) **Offer a variety of evidence**. Using different kinds of evidence increases the likelihood that the evidence will convince readers. If you provide only four examples of people who have found acupuncture helpful, for instance, readers may conclude that four people's experiences do not mean that acupuncture is becoming more popular nationally. If you also provide statistics and quotations from experts, however, more readers will be likely to accept the thesis. Using different types of evidence also enhances your credibility, showing readers you are well informed about the topic.

4) **Provide a sufficient amount of evidence**. The amount of evidence you need varies according to the audience and the topic. To discover whether you have provided enough evidence, ask a classmate to read the essay and tell you whether he or she is convinced. If your reader is not convinced, ask him or her what additional evidence is needed.

5) **Provide representative evidence**. Do not provide unusual, rare, or exceptional situations as evidence. Suppose the thesis is "acupuncture is widely used for various types of surgery", that an example of one person who underwent painless heart surgery using only acupuncture will not support your thesis unless the use of acupuncture in heart surgery

is common. Including such an example would mislead the reader and may bring your credibility into question.

6) **Provide accurate evidence from reliable sources**. Do not make vague statements, guess at statistics, or make estimates. For example, do not simply say that many medical doctors are licensed to practice acupuncture in the United States or estimate the number. Instead, find out exactly how many US physicians are licensed for this practice.

Practice

Read the following paragraph. Each sentence contains one of the detail types listed below from A to G. Mark the letter in the blank for the type of information in the sentence.

A. Unsupportable personal opinion

B. Personal statements based on bias, emotional response

C. Common knowledge

D. Hearsay/anecdotal evidence

E. Expert evidence, correctly cited

F. Unsupported fact

G. Unfocused generalization

_____ (1) Success is something most people never attain. _____ (2) It is an illusion that everyone should stop chasing. _____ (3) The price of success is dedication and hard work. _____ (4) In fact, some say that successful folks never notice that they are working; their work is their life. _____ (5) Jim Pattison, for example, the Vancouver-based entrepreneur, is said never to stop working. _____ (6) His pleasure is expanding his business empire, buying another team or TV station. _____ (7) People like that are unfair examples to the average person, though, because not everyone can work that hard. _____ (8) Many do not have the physical energy and the willpower. _____ (9) And most people do not have the luxury of working for their own businesses; they have to work for others. _____ (10) Therefore, it is hard to agree with Thoreau, who said, "We were born to succeed, not to fail."

Practice

Write a paragraph in the third person point of view supporting the thesis: "Managing time is a student's biggest problem". Afterward, share it with other students. When writing in the "invisible" third person point of view, close attention to specific details is even more essential.

2.2 Introductory Paragraph

Whenever we pick up something to read, we generally start by looking at the first few words or sentences to see if they grab our attention, and based on them we decide whether to keep reading. Beginnings, then, are important, both attracting readers and giving them some information about what's to come. A good introduction welcomes readers, makes them comfortable with the subject, states the thesis, and leads on to the first body paragraph. While the first paragraph must be unified and coherent, like the other paragraphs, it performs a lot of specialized tasks that body paragraphs do not. Because you must know what the essay will say, and why and how it will say it. Before you try to interest readers, you may find it awkward or wasteful to write a full introduction with the first draft. In fact, many writers compose their introductory paragraph after writing the body of the essay. It is easier to work on the opening paragraph after revising the first draft.

1. Functions of the Introduction

A well-written introductory paragraph usually satisfies several requirements:
- It attracts the readers' interest, encouraging them to continue reading the essay;
- It supplies any background information that may be needed to understand the essay;
- It presents a thesis statement that usually appears near the end of the introductory paragraph.

2. General Approaches to the Introduction

There are three basic approaches to writing an introduction, and there are specific methods based on each approach. Think first in general terms about how you wish to introduce yourself to readers.

1) **Idea-Focused Openings**. If you are writing an essay that explains or argues a concept that you would like readers to consider within a larger context, introduce readers to that larger context first. Then move logically through the development section of the introduction by narrowing that general opening context to a more specific level, finally ending with the very specific thesis statement. Introduce the audience gradually, in logical and increasingly specific terms, to the thesis. You may also proceed from ideas the audience knows to ideas that are less familiar or unknown to them. Idea-focused openings are suitable for essays on literature, essays in the humanities, and essays in the sciences.

2) **Striking or Dramatic Openings**. Openings designed to spark reader's interest start with a very specific idea or technique. Idea-focused approaches are gradual; striking openings, as the name suggests, are direct. Ask a surprising question related to the thesis, relate a short anecdote, or choose an interesting quotation. These are familiar techniques, known to most people from marketing and advertising, but used well, they are highly effective in provoking readers' interest or even catching readers a bit off base. Be careful that there is a clear line of development between the opening strategy and the thesis—a question unrelated to the point of the essay will do nothing but annoy readers. This category of openings works well with persuasive or argumentative essays.

3) **Emotional-Appeal Openings**. If you choose to open with an appeal to the emotions of readers, open with statements designed to hit a chord of sympathy with them. You may open with a vivid description of some incident: for instance, a traffic accident—such an opening attention-getter speaks to readers' emotions and bypasses logic. These openings must be based on predictable responses so that audiences are likely to share the feeling you evoke. Knowing the audience as well as possible is essential when you choose to appeal to emotion; if your appeal misses or offends, you lose the reader. If used carefully, the appeal to emotions can be appropriate for persuasive essays about social issues, but at a postsecondary level it is less useful than other types of introductions.

3. Methods of Introduction

These methods are grouped by the approach they are based on, to help you think about what sort of introduction would be appropriate to the purpose, audience, thesis, and perhaps your tone. If your purpose is to explain the seriousness of an issue, and you are uncertain how much the audience understands about its gravity or how it relates to them, avoid a general opening and proceed immediately to establish this issue's relevance to readers. Alternatively, if the topic suits a light approach, you could take a humorous tone and begin with an amusing anecdote or question.

4. Idea-Focused Methods

1) **Begin with a somewhat general statement of the topic, and narrow it down to the thesis statement: a funnel opening.** General statements ease the reader into the thesis statement by first introducing the topic. However, avoid sweeping statements such as "the world these days", or "humanity's problems". No writer could handle such huge concepts in a short essay. In the example below, the writer talks generally about diets and then narrows down to comments on a specific diet.

- Bookstore shelves today are crammed with dozens of different diet books. The Canadian public seems willing to try any sort of diet, especially the ones that promise instant, miraculous results. As well, authors are more than willing to invent new fad diets to cash in on this craze. Unfortunately, some of these fad diets are ineffective or even unsafe. One of the worst fad diets is the Zone Diet. It is expensive, doesn't achieve the results it claims, and is a sure route to poor nutrition.

2) **Supply background information or context.** Much of your future writing and many assignments will be based on subject matter unfamiliar to general readers. Therefore, this introductory approach is relevant and useful. Whenever you write about a subject that is not considered "general knowledge" or "common interest", use this method.

   For example:
   - *The Spanish influenza (flu) was a pandemic that, between 1918 and 1920, reached every corner of the earth, including the Arctic and the most remote Pacific islands. Unlike most other flu, this one attacked healthy young men and women primarily, not the very old or the very young. Scientists estimate that the disease killed 50 to 100 million people worldwide. Even more significantly, the Spanish influenza was caused by a strain of the H1N1 virus that threatens the world today.*

3) **Begin with familiar, known information or situations, and move to the lesser known or unfamiliar.** This is sometimes called a "comparison" or analogy introduction because it makes use of the way humans learn about most things: by comparing them to something people already know. This is a form of logic readers understand immediately. Typically, if the thesis or topic is relatively unknown to readers or is complex, this is a good alternative to the funnel or background context opening.

   For example:
   - People call each other all sorts of animal names. Kittens, dogs, pigs, bunnies, vultures: each of these animals represents some aspect, positive or negative, of humanity. But the animal whose name is an insult everywhere is surprisingly one of the most similar to human beings. The first similarity is that both rats and humans are omnivorous—they eat everything...

4) **Explain the importance of the topic to the reader.** If you can convince readers that the subject applies to them, or is something they should know more about, they will want to keep reading.

   For example:
   - Diseases such as scarlet fever and whooping cough used to kill more young children than any other illness. Today, however, child mortality due to disease has been

almost completely eliminated by medical science in first-world countries. Instead, car accidents are the number one killer of children. Most children fatally injured in car accidents were not protected by car seats, belts, or restraints of any kind. Several steps must be taken to reduce the serious dangers car accidents pose to children.

5) **Define key terms or concepts.** The success of an argument often hinges on how key terms are defined. You may wish to provide definitions up front, as an advocacy website does in a report on the hazards of fragrances in health-care facilities:

For example:

- To many people, the word "fragrance" means something that smells nice, such as perfume. We don't often stop to think that scents are chemicals. Fragrance chemicals are organic compounds that volatilize, or vaporize into the air—that's why we can smell them. They are added to products to give them a scent or to mask the odor of other ingredients. The volatile organic chemicals (VOCs) emitted by fragrance products can contribute to poor indoor air quality (IAQ) and are associated with a variety of adverse health effects.

6) **Use a definition.** You can use definitions either to confirm the thesis's point or to contrast with it. Definitions are good specific hooks and guide readers straight into the content but avoid the clichéd "According to Oxford (Webster, Gage...)"; readers can open the dictionary for themselves. If you quote or paraphrase a definition, be sure to cite it correctly.

For example:

- In *What Is Liberal Education?* Leo Strauss asserts that "Liberal education is the ladder by which we try to ascend from mass democracy as originally meant". While liberal education may indeed have been used for such a purpose, it has an intrinsic value and should be accessible to all. In a free, democratic society citizens do have a choice. Liberal education gives people the tools to make informed choices.

5. Striking or Dramatic Approaches

1) **Start with an idea or situation that is the opposite of the one you will develop.** This approach, sometimes called the "contrast" introduction, works because readers will be surprised, and then intrigued, by the contrast between the opening idea and the thesis that follows it.

For example:

- Technology is the enemy of art. The keyboard and mouse are no substitutes for the artist's hand and eye. Screens are not galleries. Or so traditionalists would say. But what about displaying the artist's work or getting feedback on it? Here, the emergence of online art communities has been a blessing for anyone looking to share their craft and garner critiques from fellow artists. PHP Scripting has created user-friendly interfaces containing easy-to-upload personal galleries, comment features, and message boards. Millions of users can submit art pieces every minute for show and/or critique. With sites boasting a wide range of categories including digital art, photography, analog painting, and more, artists are bound to find similar creators in their genre to inspire them and commune with.

2) **Use an incident or brief story.** Stories are naturally interesting. They appeal to a reader's curiosity. In the introduction, an anecdote will grab the reader's attention right away. The story should be brief and should be related to the main idea. The incident in the story can be something that happened to you or something you have heard or read about. Students who must write reports for courses in business and social-services disciplines find anecdotal introductions useful.

For example:
- Writer and witty critic Dorothy Parker was once assigned a remote, out-of-the-way office. According to the story, she became so lonely, so desperate for company, that she ultimately painted "Gentlemen" on the door. Although this university is large, no one on this campus needs to feel as isolated as Parker obviously did: our excellent Student Activity Office offers numerous clubs, programs, and volunteer groups to involve students of all interests.

3) **Ask one or more questions.** You may simply want the reader to think about possible answers, or you may plan to answer the questions yourself later in the paper. Questions provoke responses, and the reader responds by paying attention.

For example:
- What is love? How do we know that we are really in love? When we meet that special person, how can we tell that our feelings are genuine and not merely infatuation? If they are genuine, will these feelings last? Love, as we all know, is difficult to define. Yet most people agree that true and lasting love involves far more than mere physical attraction. Love involves mutual respect, the desire to give rather than take, and the feeling of being wholly at ease.

4) **Use a quotation.** A quotation can be something you have read in a book or article. It can also be something that you have heard: a popular saying or proverb ("never give advice to a friend"), a current or recent advertising slogan, or a favourite expression used by friends or family. Remember to give the source for the quotation because you are adding someone else's voice to your own.

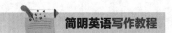

For example:
- "Fish and visitors", wrote Benjamin Franklin, "begin to smell after three days." Last summer, when my sister and her family came to spend their two-week vacation with us, I became convinced that Franklin was right. After only three days of my family's visit, I was thoroughly sick of my brother-in-law's lame jokes, my sister's endless complaints about her boss, and their children's constant invasions of our privacy.

5) **Connect the subject to readers' interests or values.** You'll always want to establish common ground with readers, and sometimes you may wish to do so immediately, in the introduction, as in the following:

For example:
- We all want to feel safe. Most Americans lock their doors at night, lock their cars in parking lots, try to park near buildings or under lights, and wear seat belts. Many invest in expensive security systems, carry pepper spray or a stun gun, keep guns in their homes, or take self-defense classes. Obviously, safety and security are important issues in American life.

6. Emotional-Appeal Approaches

1) **Write a vivid description of an emotionally powerful incident or scenario.** If you are certain of the direct relationship between the scene you describe and the thesis, then you may try this approach. Keep the description to about three sentences, so it does not overshadow the development of the thesis.

For example:
- Fruit flies never seem much of a menace in themselves, but when they cluster outside back doors and in alleys in a haze of hot, stomach-turning stench, they seem like messengers of disease and disorder. Much of Canada's largest city was in the grip of a fruit-fly infestation; this was the result in part of the six-week city workers' strike that gave rise to mountains of rotting trash in temporary dump sites throughout the metropolis.

2) **Make a claim for the sympathy of readers.** Many successful claims for sympathy are written in a "reportorial" way, as if you are bringing news of the topic to readers without obvious commentary. Following this formula lessens the risk of suffocating or battering readers by trying to force them to feel something.

For example:
- There is a man in Nova Scotia who wears his life on his face. His skin is deeply creased, and each of these creases has a story to tell about growing up in the East. He is every man and woman who grew up on hard biscuit and grease, who started

smoking too young, who lived in decrepit houses in dying communities. He came down to Toronto for a while to make a better living, but got lonely and drank too much. Now he sits outside the old hotel, waiting for nothing but his welfare cheque. This is the human face of the Maritimes' economic failure.

The box below summarizes a range of strategies for the opening paragraph:

- State an opinion related to the thesis;
- Outline the argument the thesis refutes;
- Provide background;
- Offer a surprising statistic or other fact;
- Create a visual image that represents the subject;
- Make a historical comparison or contrast;
- Outline a problem or dilemma;
- Define a word central to the subject;
- Ask a question;
- Relate an incident;
- Use a vivid quotation;
- Narrate an anecdote;
- In some business or technical writing, summarize the paper;
- Draft the rest of the essay and use the conclusion you drafted as the introduction; then write a new conclusion.

The box below lists things to avoid in an introductory paragraph:

- Opening with a flat explanation of what you intend to cover in the paper: "This essay is about..." or "I am going to inform you..." or "In this essay I will argue that..."
- A reference to the essay's title. Don't refer to the title of the essay in the first sentence—for example, "This is a big problem" or "This book is about the history of the guitar."
- Meaningless platitudes: "Violence is undesirable in our society. Therefore..." or "Man has always searched for..."
- Empty statements: "Everyone knows that drinking milk is good for you."
- Broad and sweeping statements: "Since the beginning of time..." or "Humans everywhere seek..." or "Of all studies ever done..."
- Using a casual, overly familiar, or chatty tone, especially in academic writing. Openings such as "You'll never in a million years believe what happened..." are generally not appropriate for college essays.
- Opening with the thesis statement, unless the introduction is very brief (say, for a timed writing). When the thesis statement opens the paper, the temptation is to give more information about the thesis claim, to begin summarizing points or clarifying ideas. If the

reader is shown most of the points that will be discussed in the paper in the first paragraph of the paper, what incentive is there to read the paper? It is best to place the thesis after the context of the paper is established.

- An apology. Don't fault the opinion or the knowledge with "I'm not sure if I'm right, but..."; "I don't know much about this, but..."; or a similar line.

The first few sentences of the essay are particularly important; first impressions, as you know, are often lasting ones. The beginning of the essay, then, must catch readers' attention and make them want to keep reading. Consequently, you must pay particular attention to making those first lines especially interesting and well written.

Practice

The followings are six kinds of introductions. Read the intoduetory paragraphs, mark each one with the correspondent letter.

A. General to narrow

B. Starting with an opposite

C. Stating importance of topic

D. Incident or story

E. Questions

F. Quotation

_____ (1) The ad, in full color on a glossy magazine page, shows a beautiful kitchen with gleaming counters. In the foreground, on one of the counters, stands a shiny new food processor. Usually, a feminine hand is touching it lovingly. Around the main picture are other, smaller shots. They show mounds of perfectly sliced onion rings, thin rounds of juicy tomatoes, heaps of matchstick-sized potatoes, and piles of golden, evenly grated cheese. The ad copy tells you how wonderful, how easy, food preparation will be with a processor. Don't believe it. My processor turned out to be expensive, difficult to operate, and very limited in its use.

_____ (2) My father stubbornly says, "You can often tell a book by its cover," and when it comes to certain paperbacks, he's right. When you're browsing in the drugstore or supermarket and you see a paperback featuring an attractive young woman in a low-cut dress fleeing from a handsome dark figure in a shadowy castle, you know exactly what you're getting. Every romance novel has the same elements: an innocent heroine, an exotic setting, and a cruel but fascinating hero.

_____ (3) We Americans are incredibly lazy. Instead of cooking a simple, nourishing meal, we pop a frozen dinner into the oven. Instead of studying a daily newspaper, we are contented with the capsule summaries on the network news. Worst of all, instead of walking even a few blocks to the local convenience store, we jump into our cars. This dependence on the automobile, even for short trips, has robbed us of a valuable experience—alking. If we drove less and walked more, we would save money, become healthier, and discover fascinating things about our surroundings.

2.3 Concluding Paragraph

When we get to the end of a text, we expect to be left with a sense of closure, of satisfaction—that the story is complete, our questions have been answered, the argument has been made. So endings are important, too. The concluding paragraph is the chance to remind the reader of the thesis and bring the essay to a satisfactory end. The conclusion will normally consist of:
- a summary of the main ideas (related to the importance to the topic);
- a summary of the evidence (with the evaluation of it);
- the overall conclusion / the answer to the question.

1. Functions of Concluding Paragraph

Conclusions should never wander, and they should never introduce new ideas or examples. You are closing off your conversation with the reader, not starting a new one. The conclusion will be more specific than the introduction, as you will already have mentioned the ideas you are commenting on. Do not add any new evidence or ideas: if you have more to say, then this should be done in the body of the text. Conclusions should be proportional to the essay's length and argument. For a short essay, a two-sentence concluding paragraph is probably too brief, but a lengthy ten-sentence concluding paragraph would likely lose readers' attention. Like the introduction, the conclusion is likely to contain no more than 10 percent of the word count. As you look over the first draft's final paragraph, consider, once again, the purpose, the essay's content, the audience, and also the impression or effect you would like to leave with readers. Do you want readers to smile, to think seriously, or to take some action? Whichever concluding approach you choose, remind readers of where they began—the thesis statement. They will recognize

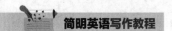

this return to the beginning as a signal of completion and will appreciate the effort to close the essay in a satisfying way.

2. Methods of Conclusion

There are two basic methods for concluding the thesis's argument: close the circle after proving the point or leave an "open door" by challenging or recommending that readers see the point in a larger perspective. There are, in turn, two approaches to using each method.

3. Closing the Circle

There are two approaches to "closing the door"; each is based on reassuring readers that you have met the challenge that the thesis posed to readers.

1) **End with a summary and final thought.** When army instructors train new recruits, each of their lessons follows a three-step formula:
   - Tell them what you're going to tell them;
   - Tell them;
   - Tell them what you've told them.

An essay that ends with a summary is not very different. After you have stated the thesis ("Tell them what you're going to tell them") and supported it ("Tell them"), you restate the thesis and supporting points ("Tell them what you've told them"). However, don't use the exact wording you used before.

For example:
   - Online shopping at home, then, has several advantages. Such shopping is convenient, saves you money, and saves you time. It is not surprising that growing numbers of people are doing the majority of their shopping on the Internet, for everything from turnip seeds to televisions.

Note: the summary is accompanied by a final comment that rounds off the essay and brings the discussion to a close. This combination of a summary and a final thought is the most common method of concluding an essay.

2) **Answer any questions the lead-in or introduction asked.** Use a restatement of the thesis to answer a lead-in question you posed; doing so gives readers a sense of closure and reinforces the notion that you have proved the point.

For example:
   - What do fans hope to see at an NHL or NFL game? They hope to see brutal competition, fierce fighting, and stars winning out over all. Anything else is not worth the ticket price—the excitement comes from the brutal values that pro sports

are built on. Unfortunately, those are the same values that North Americans put into practice every day of their lives.

Opening the Door

There are two approaches to leading readers back out into a wider context of thinking, as you do when you "open the door" with the conclusion.

1) **Include a thought-provoking question or short series of questions.** A question grabs the reader's attention. It is a direct appeal to the reader to think further about what you have written. It may involve:
   - Why the subject of the essay is important?
   - What might happen in the future?
   - What should be done about this subject, or;
   - Which choice should be made?

   In any case, be sure that the question is closely related to the thesis.

   For example:
   - What, then, will happen when most of the population will be over sixty years old? Retirement policies could change dramatically, with the age sixty-five testimonial dinner and gold watch postponed for five or ten years. Even television would change as the Red Bull generation replaces the Pepsi generation. Glamorous gray-haired models would sell everything from toilet paper to televisions. New soap operas and situation comedies would reveal the secrets of the "sunset years". It will be a different world indeed when the young find themselves outnumbered.

2) **End with a prediction or recommendation to act.** Questions, predictions and recommendations also involve readers. A prediction states what may happen in the future.

   For example:
   - If people stopped to think before acquiring pets, there would be fewer instances of cruelty to animals. Many times, it is the people who adopt pets without considering the expense and responsibility involved who mistreat and neglect their animals. Pets are living creatures. They do not deserve to be treated as carelessly as one would treat a stuffed toy.

   A recommendation suggests some action that should be taken about a situation or problem.

   For example:
   - Stereotypes such as the helpless homemaker, harried female executive, and dotty grandma are insulting enough to begin with. In magazine ads or television

commercials, they become even more insulting. Such hackneyed caricatures of women are not just the objects of derisive humour; these stereotypes now pitch a range of products to an unsuspecting public. Consumers should boycott companies whose advertising continues to use such stereotype.

The box below summarizes some strategies for closing paragraphs:

- End with a summary of the thesis and the essay's major points;
- End with an evaluation of the importance of the essay's subject;
- End with a quotation from an authority or someone whose insight emphasizes the main point;
- Show how the argument you have made affirms an argument or issue raised by someone else;
- Go back to an idea or detail from the introduction and bring the essay full circle;
- End by talking about the implications and/or significance of the argument;
- Allude to a historical idea or mythological figure to place the topic in a larger framework;
- End by calling for further research;
- End by urging readers to follow the recommendation with action;
- End with an anecdote or a brief example that emphasizes or sums up the point of the essay;
- End with an emotional statement that appeals to readers' pity, sense of justice, hopes, or fears;
- End with a rhetorical question that makes the reader think about the essay's main point.

The box below lists things to avoid in a conclusion:

- A repeat of the introduction. Don't simply replay the introduction. The conclusion should capture what the paragraphs of the body have added to the introduction.
- A new direction. Don't introduce a subject that is different from the one the essay has been about. If you arrive at a new idea, this may be a signal to start fresh with that idea as the thesis.
- A sweeping generalization. Don't conclude more than you reasonably can from the evidence you have given. If the essay is about the frustrating experience trying to clear a parking ticket, you cannot reasonably conclude that all local police forces are tied up in red tape.
- Apologizing, softening, or reversing your position. Don't cast doubt on the essay. Don't say, for example, "Even though I'm no expert" or "This may not be convincing, but I believe it's true" or "Although I am only twenty-one...". Don't back down after criticizing someone by saying "After all, she's only human". Rather, to win your readers' confidence, display confidence.
- Offending the reader by making arrogant and absolute pronouncements about what you have said or proven, or coming on too strong or using an unproductive tone.
- Making an announcement or a restatement of the thesis directly. Statements like "In my essay I have shown..." are dull and mechanical.

Remember that the concluding paragraph is the last chance to convince the reader. As one cynical but realistic student pointed out, the conclusion may be the last part of the essay the teacher reads before putting a grade on your paper. Therefore, make your conclusion count.

Practice

Note how each concluding paragraph ends. Write "S" for the summary and final thought; write "P/R" for the prediction or recommendation and "Q" for a question.

_____ (1) Disappointments are unwelcome, but regular, visitors in everyone's life. We can feel depressed about them, or we can try to escape from them. The best thing, though, is to accept a disappointment and then try to use it somehow: step over the unwelcome visitor and then get on with life.

_____ (2) Saving the environment is up to each of us. Levels of harmful emissions would drop dramatically if we chose to carpool or take public transportation more often. Conserving fuel and electricity at home by sealing up leaky windows and using energy-saving light bulbs would help too. What will you do to conserve?

_____ (3) Some people dream of starring roles, their names in lights, and their pictures on the cover of *People* magazine. I'm not one of them, though. A famous person gives up private life, feels pressured all the time, and is never completely safe. So let someone else have that cover story. I'd rather lead an ordinary, but calm, life than a stress-filled one.

_____ (4) Holidays, it is clear, are often not the fulfilling experiences they are supposed to be. They can, in fact, be very stressful. But would we rather have a holiday-free calendar?

_____ (5) People's dreams of stardom, of seeing their names in lights and their pictures on the covers of magazines, are based on illusions. The celebrities whose lives are documented for all to see give up their private lives, endure constant pressure, and are never completely safe. The price of fame is too high, and never worth its cost.

2.4 The Title

A title serves various purposes, naming a text and providing clues to the content. It also helps readers decide whether they want to read further, so it's worth when you

come up with a title that attracts interest. Some titles include subtitles. You generally have considerable freedom in choosing a title, but always you'll want to be sure your title serves the purpose and appeals to the audience you want to reach.

A descriptive title—is almost always appropriate and is often expected for academic writing. It announces the topic clearly, accurately, and as briefly as possible. The title of Katy Moreno's essay (refer to the section "Choosing an Organizing Tool") is an example: "Can We Compete? College Education for the Global Economy". Other examples include "Images of Lost Identity in *North by Northwest*," "An Experiment in Small Group Dynamics", and "Why Lincoln Delayed Emancipating the Slaves", etc.

A suggestive title—the kind often found in popular magazines—may be appropriate for more informal writing. Examples include "Making Peace" (for an essay on the Peace Corps) and Thomas L. Friedman's "It's a Flat World, after All" (on the global job market). For a more suggestive title, Moreno might have chosen "Training for the New World" or "Education for a Flat World" (echoing Friedman's title). A suggestive title conveys the writer's attitude and main concerns but not the precise topic, thereby pulling readers into the essay to learn more. A source for such a title may be a familiar phrase, a fresh image, or a significant expression from the essay itself. A title tells readers how big the topic is. For Moreno's essay, the title "Globalization and Jobs" or "Competing in Today's Job Market" would have been too broad, whereas "Outsourcing Our Jobs" or "The Importance of a Broad Education" would have been too narrow because each deals with only part of the paper's content.

1. Features of Titles

Writers use a variety of titles. A well-written title may take a variety of forms, depending on an essay's purpose, audience, and tone. Essays aimed at informing readers often display titles that are highly condensed summaries of their content.

For example:

- *A College Diploma: The Ticket to Success?*

Academic essays in many disciplines use titles that describe the content succinctly:

- *Soap Operas and Festivals: A Comparative Analysis*

Some titles simply announce the subject of the text:

- *Why Colleges Shower Their Students with A's*
- *Does Texting Affect Writing?*

Some titles provoke readers or otherwise entice them to read:

- *Kill 'Em! Crush 'Em! Eat 'Em Raw!*

- *Thank God for the Atom Bomb*

Sometimes writers craft a title that presents a word or phrase followed by a colon introducing a definition, a revealing image, a question, or some other kind of explanatory material to interest the reader.

For example:
- *It's in Our Genes: The Biological Basis of Human Mating Behavior*
- *From Realism to Virtual Reality: Images of America's Wars*
- *Intervention in Iran: A Recipe for Disaster*
- *Yoga: Does Twisting Like a Pretzel Really Help?*

A humorous essay should have a title that fits its tone, suggesting that what follows will entertain its readers. Creative titles and questions should be avoided in research papers and formal business reports but can be very effective to generate attention in personal essays. For academic essays, write straightforward titles that accurately describe the topic and approach. For other writing situations—depending on the purpose, audience, stance, genre, and medium—the title may be direct, informative, witty, intriguing, or a combination of these.

For example:
- **Ask a question that your essay answers.**
  Who Plays the Lottery?
- **Use alliteration. Repeating initial sounds often produces a catchy title.**
  Lotteries: Dreaming about Dollars
- **Use a play on words or a catchy or humorous expression (This technique may work well for less formal essays).**
  Playing to Lose
- **Use a brief quotation (mention the quotation in the essay and indicate there who said it and where).**
  The Lottery: "A Surtax on Desperation"?

Titles may be specialized to suit patterns of essay development as well:
- Exemplification or Illustration with Examples: *Adjustment Issues of Mature Students*
- Process: *How Photosynthesis Works*
- Classification and Division: *Forms of Workplace Discrimination*
- Definition: *What Fitness Means*
- Cause and Effect: *Rage Addiction: Effects on the Family*
- Comparison/Contrast: *Energy Drinks Versus Nutritious Meals*
- Argumentation: *Why English Is Such a Challenge*

2. When to Consider a Title

Titles play a vital role in creating effective essays. A strong title announces what the essay is about, attracts attention, expresses a thesis, and prepares readers to accept ideas. You will generally want the title to entice audiences to read the essay. Don't think you have to decide on a title right away. As in the case of opening paragraph, the title may be written at any time, but many writers prefer to finish the essays before naming them. As you write, you may discover an interesting word or phrase that captures the essence of the essay and can serve as an effective title. In fact, the revision stage is a good time to consider a title. After drafting, you have a clearer sense of the direction, and the attempt to sum up the essay in a title phrase can help you focus sharply on the topic, purpose, and audience.

3. Capitalization in Titles and Subtitles

Capitalize all the words in a title except the following: articles (*a, an, the*), *to* in infinitives, coordinating conjunctions (*and, but*, etc.), and prepositions (*with, between*, etc.). Capitalize also these words when they are the first or last word in a title or when they fall after a colon or semicolon.

For example:
- *An Architecture for Democracy: The Bellmont Civic Center*
- *How a Knowledge of English Has Helped Me in My Studies and Work*
- *Is Money Everything?*
- *Why I Want a Wife*
- *Grant and Lee: A Study in Contrasts*
- *Rules to Abide By*
- *Hemingway and A Farewell to Arms*

Always capitalize the prefix or first word in a hyphenated word within a title. Capitalize the second word only if it is a noun or an adjective or is as important as the first word.

For example:
- A Substitute for the H-Bomb
- Hit-and-Run Accidents
- The One-Minute Grammarian
- The Social History of the Jack-in-the-Box
- Applying Stage Make-up
- The Pre-Raphaelites
- Through the Looking-Glass

Part One Short Essay Writing

Practice

Write an appropriate title for each of the following introductory paragraphs.

(1) I'm not just a consumer—I'm a victim. If I order a product, it is sure to arrive in the wrong color, size, or quantity. If I hire people to do repairs, they never arrive on the day scheduled. If I owe a bill, the computer is bound to overcharge me. Therefore, in selfdefense, I have developed the following consumer's guide to complaining effectively.
Title: _____

(2) Schools divide people into categories. From first grade on up, students are labeled "advanced" or "remedial". Students pigeonhole their fellow students, too. We've all known the "brain", the "jock", and the "dummy". In most cases, these narrow labels are misleading and inaccurate. But there is one label for a certain type of college students that says it all: "zombie".
Title: _____

(3) Having the ideal job doesn't depend only on the amount of money it pays, the working conditions, or the opportunities for advancement. It also has to do with one's fellow employees and, of course, the boss. While most people realize that bosses need to exercise careful supervision over the workplace and the employees, they prefer bosses who socialize with workers, make few demands, and look the other way when they don't perform well. Unfortunately, such supervisors too often turn out to be inefficient, disorganized, and unpredictable. A better alternative is someone who enforces rules predictably and demands that workers meet reasonable expectations.
Title: _____

(4) When people see rock-concert audiences only on television or in newspaper photos, the audiences at these events may all seem to be excited teenagers. However, attending a few rock shows would show people that several kinds of ticket buyers make up the crowd. At any concert, there are usually the typical fan, the out-of-place person, and the troublemaker.
Title: _____

(5) Are you sitting in a messy room right now? Are piles of papers or heaps of clothes tilting at weird angles and leaning on towers of magazines, boxes, and bags all around you? You are not alone, and you should not feel ashamed. Messes are just the natural overflow of our personalities. Messes say that we are too busy, too interesting to spend time cleaning, organizing, and turning into obsessive organizers. Most of all, a good mess is full of potential treasures. A mess is a safety zone, a sign of an active life, and a source of inspiration.
Title: _____

2.5 Unity and Coherence

In writing the essay, you should be aware of two qualities of effective writing that relate to organization: unity and coherence. When you perceive that someone's writing "flows well", you are probably appreciating these two qualities. **Unity** means *oneness*. For an essay to have unity, it must have oneness. Specifically, an essay has unity if all its parts relate to and support the thesis statement. Check for unity with these questions:

- Is each main section relevant to the main idea (thesis) of the essay?
- Within main sections, does each example or detail support the principal idea of that section?

An essay has **coherence** if readers can see the relations among parts and move easily from one thought to the next. Check for coherence with these questions:

- Do the ideas follow in a clear sequence?
- Are the parts of the essay logically connected?
- Are the connections clear and smooth?

1. Maintaining Unity

Just as readers expect paragraphs to relate clearly to an essay's central idea, they also generally expect each paragraph to explore a single idea. They will be alert for that idea and will patiently follow its development. In other words, they will seek and appreciate paragraph unity: clear identification and clear elaboration of one idea and of that idea only. In an essay the thesis statement often asserts the main idea as a commitment to readers. In a paragraph a topic sentence often alerts readers to the essence of the paragraph by asserting the central idea and expressing the writer's attitude toward it. In a brief essay each body paragraph will likely treat one main point supporting the essay's thesis statement; the topic sentences simply elaborate on parts of the thesis. In longer essays paragraphs tend to work in groups, each group treating one main point. Then the topic sentences will tie into that main point, and all the points together will support the thesis.

Practice

The following paragraphs contain ideas or details that do not support the central idea. Identify the topic sentences in the paragraphs and delete the unrelated information.

(1) Just as history repeats itself, fashions have a tendency to do the same. (2) In the late 1960s, for example, women wore miniskirts that came several inches above the knee;

some forty years later, the fashion magazines are featuring this same type of dress, and many teenagers are wearing them. (3) The miniskirt has always been flattering on slender women. (4) I wonder if the fashion industry deliberately recycles fashions. (5) Men wore their hair long in the hippie period of the late 1960s and 1970s. (6) Today, some men are again letting their hair grow. (7) Beards, considered "in" during the 1970s, have once again made an appearance.

(1) In the southern part of the state, some people still live much as they did a century ago. (2) They use coal- or wood-burning stoves for heating and cooking. (3) Their homes do not have electricity or indoor bathrooms or running water. (4) The towns they live in don't receive adequate funding from the state and federal governments, so the schools are poor and in bad shape. (5) Beside most homes there is a garden where fresh vegetables are gathered for canning. (6) Small pastures nearby support livestock, including cattle, pigs, horses, and chickens. (7) Most of the people have cars or trucks, but the vehicles are old and beat-up from traveling on unpaved roads.

(1) Living in a college dorm is a good way to meet people. (2) There are activities every weekend, such as game night and parties where one can get acquainted with all kinds of students. (3) Even just sitting by someone in the cafeteria during a meal can start a friendship. (4) Making new friends from foreign countries can teach students more about international relations. (5) A girl on my dorm floor, for example, is from Peru, and I've learned a lot about the customs and culture in her country. (6) She's also helping me with my study of Spanish. (7) I hope to visit her in Peru some day.

 Practice

Choose a paper you've written and examine the body paragraphs for unity. Do they have clear topic sentences? If not, are the paragraphs' central ideas still clear? Are the paragraphs unified around the central idea? Should any details be deleted for unity? Should other more relevant details be added?

2. Creating Coherence

Coherence means literally "sticking together". When you create coherence, you show a smooth, clear sequence from sentence to sentence and paragraph to paragraph. When you decide on a principle of organization for the essay, you learn the value of "signal words", or transitions, to guide readers. You are, in fact, already preparing to make the essay coherent.

1) Means of achieving coherence

Coherence is the product of choices you make in the outlining, drafting, and revising stages of the writing process. First, as you outline and draft, you organize the entire essay according to time, emphasis, or spatial placement, as appropriate to the subject and purpose. Second, as you write and revise the rough draft, you connect paragraphs and sentences with appropriate methods of transition.

2) Transitions in general

Transitions are not "ornaments" or additional words to be plugged in mechanically at certain points in an essay. For the audience, transitional words, phrases, and sentences are essential parts of how you show the essay's movement from one idea to the next in a logical way. You may know the direction in which you are going as you write, but the audience likely does not. Transitions are the audience's guides to a clear understanding of every level of the essay. Transitions have two functions:

- Transitions signal the direction of a writer's thought;
- Transitions are links or "bridges" between paragraphs, sentences, and thoughts— they signal connections to the audience.

To achieve coherence, you will organize and connect all three levels of the essay with the use of transitions, transitional sentences, and other transitional structures. Below are techniques for achieving coherence at the essay level, paragraph level, and sentence level. Refer to these points as you work on the drafts.

(1) To Create Coherence at the Essay Level

- Write an effective thesis statement with clear, logically derived supporting points.
- Indicate the order for the supporting points of the thesis, and sustain that order through the topic sentence and body paragraphs.

(2) To Create Coherence at the Paragraph Level

- Write topic sentences that refer clearly to the thesis point covered by that paragraph.
- Write topic sentences that cover all details and examples found in each body paragraph.
- Reinforce, with transitional phrases or structures, the order established in the thesis in each body paragraph's topic sentence.
- Use transitions in each body paragraph's topic sentence that remind the reader of the ending of the previous paragraph.
- Use transitional phrases or structures in each body paragraph's closing sentence that connect that paragraph with the one that follows.
- Use concluding or summarizing phrases to signal the concluding paragraph.

(3) To Create Coherence at the Sentence Level

- Within each paragraph of the essay, use transitional phrases or devices to show relationships between sentences and to mark changes of direction, meaning, or emphasis.

3) Sentence- and paragraph-level transition words and phrases

All transitions show readers what you mean more accurately. When you use transitions to guide readers through the logical pattern behind the arrangement of the sentences, you create coherence at the audience's closest point of connection with you: at sentence level within the paragraphs. In the box below are some common transitions, grouped by the type of expression or according to the kind of signal they give to readers. Note that certain words provide more than one kind of signal.

> **Addition signals:** *again, besides, for one thing, then, one, first of all, second, the third reason, also, next, another, and, in addition, moreover, furthermore, finally, last of all*
> **Cause or effect:** *since, because, therefore, thus, hence, for the reason that, so, accordingly, otherwise, if, then*
> **Conceding or allowing a point:** *indeed, although, admittedly, it is true that, no doubt, naturally, to be sure, though*
> **Time signals:** *first, then, next, after, after that, afterward, as, at that time, at the moment, before, currently, presently, earlier, while, meanwhile, soon, now, during, while, eventually, gradually, immediately, finally, in the future, in the past, one day, so far*
> **Emphasis:** *assuredly, decidedly, more, most, just, better, best, certainly, especially, even, undoubtedly, clearly, mainly, principally, above all, least (most) of all, indeed, of course, in effect*
> **Space signals:** *above, behind, beyond, beside, next to, across, on one (the other) side, on the opposite side, to (on) the left, to (on) the right, closer in, farther out, below, on the top (bottom), near(by), north, south, east, west*
> **Change-of-direction or contrast signals:** *but, however, instead, nevertheless, yet, in contrast, although, otherwise, still, on the contrary, on the other hand*
> **Illustration signals:** *for example, for instance, specifically, as an illustration, (in) that way, once, such as, in other words*
> **Conclusion signals:** *therefore, consequently, thus, then, as a result, in summary, to conclude, last of all, finally*

Remember, your sentences are the closest and most constant points of contact with readers. So if the writing flows from sentence to sentence, it eases the audience's way through the pointing out when a change of direction, an example, or an ending is coming.

Practice

1) Choose time signals from what you have just learned to fill in the blanks.

_____ you've snagged the job of TV sports reporter, you have to begin working on the details of the image. _____, invest in two or three truly loud sports jackets. Look for gigantic plaid patterns in odd colour combinations like purple and green or orange and blue; the role model is Don Cherry. These should become familiar enough to viewers that they will associate that crazy jacket with that dynamic sportscaster. _____, try to cultivate a distinctive voice that will be just annoying enough to be memorable. A nasal whine or a gravelly growl will do it. _____ be sure to speak only in tough, punchy sentences that seem to be punctuated with imaginary exclamation points. _____, you must share lots of pompous, obnoxious opinions with the viewers. The tone of voice must convey the hidden message, "I dare anyone to disagree with me."

2) *Choose space signals and one emphatic transition from what you have just learned to fill in the following blank.*

The vegetable bin of the refrigerator contained an assortment of weird-looking items. _____ a shrivelled, white-coated lemon was a pair of oranges covered with blue fuzz. _____ the oranges was a bunch of carrots that had begun to sprout points, spikes, knobs, and tendrils. The carrots drooped limply over a bundle of celery. _____ the carrots was a net bag of onions; each onion had sent curling shoots through the net until the whole thing resembled a mass of green spaghetti. _____ item, though, was a head of lettuce that had turned into a pool of brown goo. It had seeped out of its bag and coated the bottom of the bin with a sticky, evil-smelling liquid.

4) Other transitional structures for sentence- and paragraph-level coherence

In addition to transitional words and expressions, you can use other kinds of connecting words and phrases to tie together the specific evidence in an essay: repeated words, variations on key words, parallel structure, pronouns, and synonyms. Use these to connect one sentence to another, and to make sentences in a paragraph flow more smoothly. Repeat words. Are you taught never to repeat yourself when you write? Well, occasionally repeating key words helps readers tie together the flow of thought in an essay. Here, repetition reminds readers of the selection's central idea.

For example:

- *One reason for studying psychology is to help parents deal with children. Perhaps a young daughter refuses to go to bed when parents want her to and bursts into tears at the least mention of "lights out". A little knowledge of psychology comes in handy. Offer her a choice of staying up until 7:30 pm with her parents or going upstairs and playing until 8:00 pm. Since she gets to make the choice, she does not feel so powerless and will not resist. Psychology is also useful in rewarding a child for a job well done. Instead of telling a ten-year-old son what a good boy he is when he makes his own bed, tell him how neat it looks, how pleasing it is, and how proud of him you are for doing it by himself. The psychology books all say that being a good boy is much harder to live up to than doing one job well.*

There is no rigid rule about how much repetition is bad, and how much is useful; the purpose and the needs of the audience can help you see where repeating a word is useful. Often, if a term is important to the reader's understanding material, repeating it is effective; it helps audiences home in on what is important and helps them process the information.

Try some variations on key words, rather than simple repetition. This technique prevents possible monotony. Variations on words are similar but not identical to synonyms, another transitional structure.

For example:

- *People have mixed reactions to the amount of money spent on the Canadian space program. Typically, the public tends to think that space exploration and space technology, like the Canadarm, just cost too much. Jerman Mayzelle, an Ottawa federal employee, says, "The Canadian dollars going into space, based on our GNP and economy, are out of line. The money could be better spent elsewhere." However, when an item of space technology is successful, the general public is thought to approve of our country's accomplishments.*

Parallel structure. Parallel structure is word repetition at a higher level. You create parallel structure with the repetition of phrases, clauses, and sentences. Repeating a phrase or sentence creates a rhythm, similar to that in the chorus of a song. The rhythm of the repeated text tells readers that the ideas in the parallel structures are related. Their minds say, "If that sentence started with 'The pursuit of happiness...' and this one does too, then the ideas in the last parts of both sentences are probably related." As with basic repetition, the overuse of parallel structure can result in monotony. But within a paragraph, where there will be ideas and details related to the topic sentence, parallel structure is appropriate. The effectiveness of parallel structure is based on how the parallel phrases sound when spoken silently by audiences as they read. Great public speakers have always used parallel structure to add emphasis and coherence to their texts. Martin Luther King Jr.'s "I Have a Dream" speech is a well-known example:

- *I have a dream that one day this nation will rise up and live out the true meaning of its creed: "We hold these truths to be self-evident, that all men are created equal."*
  I have a dream that one day on the red hills of Georgia, the sons of former slaves and the sons of former slave owners will be able to sit down together at the table of brotherhood.
  I have a dream that one day even the state of Mississippi, a state sweltering with the

heat of injustice, sweltering with the heat of oppression, will be transformed into an oasis of freedom and justice.

I have a dream that my four little children will one day live in a nation where they will not be judged by the color of their skin but by the content of their character. *I have a dream* today!

Pronouns. Pronouns (*he, she, it, you, they*) are another way to connect ideas. Also, using pronouns in place of other words can help you avoid needless repetition. (Note, however, that pronouns should be used with care to avoid problems such as unclear pronoun reference.) Here is a selection that makes use of pronouns to continue the reference to *people*:

- Another way for people to economize at an amusement park is to bring their own food. If they pack a nourishing, well-balanced lunch of cold chicken, carrot sticks, and fruit, they will avoid having to pay high prices for hamburgers and hot dogs. They won't eat as many calories. Also, instead of filling up on soft drinks, they should bring a thermos of iced tea. Iced tea is more refreshing than pop, and it is a great deal cheaper. Every dollar that is not spent at a refreshment stand is one that can be spent on another ride.

Pronouns also have a "summing up" function for readers; they connect ideas naturally because pronouns almost always refer you to something you or they read earlier in a passage. When you read "This is true because...", you automatically think about what *this* could mean. The pronoun *this* causes you to add up, quickly and without thinking, all the ideas that *this* stands for before going on to the *because* part of the sentence.

Synonyms. Using synonyms (words alike in meaning) can also help move readers clearly from one thought to the next. In addition, just as when you use variations on words, when you use synonyms, you increase variety and readers' interest in the text by avoiding needless repetition. To strengthen the vocabulary and widen the knowledge of synonyms, you may use a thesaurus. Alternate words or phrases or synonyms are not exact substitute words, though. No thesaurus can understand the shadings of meaning a synonym presents. Only you know the exact meaning you intend. Always have a dictionary at hand when you use either type of thesaurus; check the meaning of any word presented to you as a synonym. Note the synonyms for method in the following selection:

- There are several methods of fundraising that work well with small organizations. One technique is to hold an auction, with everyone either contributing an item from home or obtaining a donation from a sympathetic local merchant. Because all the merchandise and the services of the auctioneer have been donated, the entire proceeds can be placed in the organization's treasury. A second fundraising procedure is a car wash. Club members and their children get together on a Saturday and wash all the cars in the neighbourhood for a few dollars apiece. A final, time-tested way to raise money is to hold a bake sale, with each family contributing homemade cookies, brownies, layer cakes, or cupcakes. Sold by the piece or by the box, these baked goods will satisfyingly fill both the stomach and the pocketbook.

Practice

The two following essays about "Positive or negative effects of television" are both unified and supported. However, one communicates more clearly and effectively. Discuss with your classmates to tell which one and why.

Essay 1

Harmful Effects of Watching Television

(1) In a recent cartoon, one character said to another, "When you think of the awesome power of television to educate, aren't you glad it?" It's true that television has the power to educate and to entertain, but unfortunately, these benefits are outweighed by the harm it does to dedicated viewers. Television is harmful because it creates passivity, discourages communication, and presents a false picture of reality.

(2) Television makes viewers passive. Children who have an electronic babysitter spend most of their waking hours in a semiconscious state. Older viewers watch tennis matches and basketball games with none of the excitement of being in the stands. Even if children are watching *Sesame Street* or *Barney & Friends*, they are being educated passively. The child actors are going on nature walks, building crafts projects, playing with animals, and participating in games, but the little viewers are simply watching. Older viewers watch guests discuss issues with Oprah Winfrey, but no one will turn to the home viewers to ask their opinion.

(3) Worst of all, TV presents a false picture of reality that leaves viewers frustrated because they don't have the beauty or wealth of the characters on television. Viewers absorb the idea that everyone else in the United States owns a lavish apartment, a suburban house, a sleek car, and an expensive wardrobe. Every detective, police officer, oil baron, and lawyer, male or female, is suitable for a pinup poster. The material possessions on TV shows and commercials contribute to the false image of reality. News anchors and reporters, with their perfect hair and makeup, must fit television's standard of beauty. From their modest homes or cramped apartments, many viewers tune in daily to the upper-middle-class world that TV glorifies.

(4) Television discourages communication. Families watching television do very little talking except for brief exchanges during commercials. If Uncle Bernie or the next-door neighbors drop in for a visit, the most comfortable activity for everyone may be not conversation but watching ESPN. The family may not even be watching the same set; instead, in some households, all the family members head for their own rooms to watch their own sets. At

dinner, plates are plopped on the coffee table in front of the set, and the meal is wolfed down during NBC Nightly News. During commercials, the only communication a family has all night may consist of questions like "Do we have any popcorn?" and "Where's TV Guide?"

(5) Television, like cigarettes or saccharin, is harmful to our health. We are becoming isolated, passive, and frustrated. And, most frightening, the average viewer now spends more time watching television than ever before.

Essay 2

The Benefits of Television

(1) We hear a lot about the negative effects of television on the viewer. Obviously, television can be harmful if it is watched constantly to the exclusion of other activities. It would be just as harmful to listen to CDs all the time or to eat constantly. However, when television is watched in moderation, it is extremely valuable, as it provides relaxation, entertainment, and education.

(2) First of all, watching TV has the value of sheer relaxation. Watching television can be soothing and restful after an eight-hour day of pressure, challenges, or concentration. After working hard all day, people look forward to a new episode of a favorite show or yet another showing of *Casablanca* or *Anchorman*. This period of relaxation leaves viewers refreshed and ready to take on the world again. Watching TV also seems to reduce stress in some people. This benefit of television is just beginning to be recognized. One doctor, for example, advises his patients with high blood pressure to relax in the evening with a few hours of television.

(3) In addition to being relaxing, television is entertaining. Along with the standard comedies, dramas, and game shows that provide enjoyment to viewers, television offers a variety of movies and sports events. Moreover, viewers can pay a monthly fee and receive special cable programming or Direct TV. Viewers can watch first-run movies, rock and classical music concerts, and specialized sports events, like international soccer and Grand Prix racing. Viewers can also buy or rent movies and TV shows on DVD. Still another growing area of TV entertainment is video games. PlayStation, Xbox, and Nintendo consoles allow the owner to have a video-game arcade in the living room.

(4) Most important, television is educational. Preschoolers learn colors, numbers, and letters from public television programs, like *Sesame Street*, that use animation and puppets to make learning fun. On the Discovery Channel, science shows for older children go on location to analyze everything from volcanoes to rocket launches. Adults, too, can get an education (college credits included) from courses given on television. Also, television widens our knowledge by covering important events and current news. Viewers can see and hear presidents' speeches, state funerals, natural disasters, and election results as they are happening.

(5) Perhaps because television is such a powerful force, we like to criticize it and search for its flaws. However, the benefits of television should not be ignored. We can use television to relax, to have fun, and to make ourselves smarter. This electronic wonder, then, is a servant, not a master.

Chapter 3

Revising Your Essay

Drafting is to find and convey meaning through the act of writing. If you fear making mistakes while drafting, that fear will choke your ideas. You draft only for yourself, so errors do not matter. Write freely until you have worked out what you want to say; then revise—focus on any mistakes you may have made.

3.1 Revising

Revision literally means "re-seeing"—looking anew at ideas and details, their relationships and arrangement, the degree to which they work or don't work for the thesis. While drafting, you focus inwardly, concentrating on pulling the topic out of yourself. In revising, you look out to readers, trying to anticipate how they will see your work. You adopt a critical perspective toward your work, examining it as an athlete or dancer would examine a video of his or her performance. A thorough, thoughtful revision can change a C paper to an A paper! Revising can make a significant difference in how well your paper achieves the purpose and expresses the ideas to the intended audience. This difference is why most professional writers—and successful student writers—revise frequently and thoroughly.

1. Revising and Editing

Revising is not a process of correcting surface errors, such as spelling mistakes or punctuation errors. Rather, it is a process of looking at your ideas and finding ways to make them clearer and easier to understand. This may mean adding, eliminating, or reorganizing key elements within the essay, even revising the thesis statement and refocusing the entire essay.

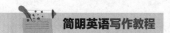

Think of revision and editing as separate stages: in revision you deal with the underlying meaning and structure of the essay; in editing you deal with the surface, with the manner of expression, clarity, and correctness. By making separate drafts beyond the first—a revised one and then an edited one—you'll be less likely to waste time tinkering with sentences that you end up cutting, and you'll avoid the temptation to substitute editing for more substantial revision. Often the process of revising requires you to rethink the purpose, clarify the thesis statement, develop more ideas, or reorganize. Save editing and proofreading until you are satisfied with the overall focus, development, and shape of the draft.

2. Revising Your Own Work

Reading your own work critically can be difficult. Changing or even deleting material that you've worked hard to express can be still more difficult. The key is to gain some objectivity toward the writing. The following techniques may help:

- Take a break after finishing the draft. A few hours may be enough; a whole night or day is preferable. The break will clear your mind, relax you, and give you some objectivity.
- Read the draft in a new medium. Typing a handwritten draft or printing out a word-processed draft can reveal weaknesses that you didn't see in the original.
- Outline your draft. Highlight the main points supporting the thesis, and write these sentences down separately in outline form. Then examine the outline you've made for logical order, gaps, and digressions. A formal outline can be especially illuminating because of its careful structure.
- Use a revision checklist. Don't try to re-see everything in the draft at once. Use a checklist like the one that follows, making a separate pass through the draft for each item.

Checklist for Revision

Thesis
What is the thesis of the writing? Where does it become clear? Does any part of the paper stray from the thesis? Does the paper fulfill the commitment of the thesis?

Organization
What are the main points of the paper? (List them.) How well does each support the thesis? How effective is their arrangement for the paper's purpose?

Development (Support)
How well do details, examples, and other evidence support each main point? Where, if at all, might readers find support skimpy or have trouble understanding the content?

> **Unity**
> What does each sentence and paragraph contribute to the thesis? Where, if at all, do digressions occur? Should they be cut, or can they be rewritten to support the thesis?
>
> **Coherence**
> How clearly and smoothly does the paper flow? Where does it seem rough or awkward? Can any transitions be improved?
>
> **Title, introduction, conclusion**
> How accurately and interestingly does the title reflect the essay's content? How well does the introduction engage and focus readers' attention? How effective is the conclusion in providing a sense of completion?

Generally, you have four bases to consider in revising an essay: unity, support, coherence, and effective sentence skills. If you write clear and error-free sentences, you are demonstrating effective sentence skills; if you advance a single point and stick logically to that point, you are on your way to unity; as you develop and refine the support so that it is specific, appropriate, and abundant, you are working toward the goal of effective support; as you organize the supporting ideas and sentences so that they cohere (stick together)—they transition smoothly from one bit of supporting information to the next, you are working to establish the coherence.

3.2 Peer Review

Your instructor may schedule a workshop in the classroom, or you may choose to set one up on your own with one or more peers. During a peer review workshop, you exchange essay drafts with another student in the class and read one another's work for the purpose of assessing its strengths and weaknesses. It's an important stage in writing process to share the writing with your classmates. You can see how other writers like you handled the same assignment, and you can get some good ideas from them. You can also see how well someone else understands the ideas. When you meet with other students in pairs or small groups to respond to one another's work, you have the opportunity to get feedback on the work from several readers who can help you plan revisions. At the same time, you learn from reading others' work how they approached the writing task. Some students wonder why class time is being taken up by peer response, assuming that their instructor's opinion is the only one that counts, but seeing the work of others and learning how others see the work can help you improve the clarity and depth of your writing.

The goal of peer review is to have someone else read the essay while it is still a work-in-progress. You and someone else who is working on a similar project, a peer, can get together to exchange ideas about each other's writing. This can guide the process of your revision work. As a writer, consider that readers are responding to the draft or even the final paper more as an exploration of ideas than as the last word on the subject; then you may be more receptive to readers' suggestions. As a reader, know that the tactful questions and suggestions about focus, content, and organization will usually be considered appropriate.

1. Benefiting from Comments on Your Writing

When you are the writer, you should feel like you can speak freely in a peer review workshop, without having to filter or make excuses for the thoughts or ideas. The more you can talk about the ideas, the clearer they will become both to you and to the listener. Instead of seeing yourself in a position where you're being judged, try to picture yourself as an instructor explaining a complicated idea to the listener. Also try not to be defensive if the listener misunderstands the ideas, doesn't give you a lot of praise, or disagrees with you about the value of a point. We learn from our critics. Although you may not agree with the listener right away, further thought about an idea may find you agreeing at a later date. Be as gracious and open-minded as you can during the peer review session and wait until you are actually doing the work of revision back at the computer to make final decisions about the feedback you receive. It might help to remember that this is your paper, and you are the final arbiter of what goes into it and what does not. However, if one reader is confused or misunderstands a passage or a point, chances are that other readers will feel the same way. Even if you think the essay is as convincing as possible, the fact that one or more readers miss certain points is important for you to consider, especially when the goal is to write a persuasive paper. To sum up, you will benefit from practicing the following suggestions:

- Think of the readers as counselors or coaches. They can help you see the virtues and flaws in your work and sharpen your awareness of readers' needs.
- Read or listen to comments closely. Know what the critic is saying.
- Don't become defensive. Letting comments offend you will only erect a barrier to improvement in the writing. As one writing teacher advises, "Leave your ego at the door."
- Revise the work in response to appropriate comments. You will learn more from the act of revision than from just thinking about changes.
- Remember that you are the final authority on the work. You should be open to suggestions, but you are free to decline advice when you think it is inappropriate.

- Keep track of both the strengths and the weaknesses others identify. Then in later assignments you can build on your successes and give special attention to problem areas. You'll gain the most from collaboration if you carry your learning from one assignment into the next.

2. Commenting on Others' Writing

The job of the reviewer in a peer review workshop is to ask questions, listen or read carefully, and take notes. Imagine that you are going to be tested on this material. Listen or read as fully as possible and make sure you understand completely. Ask questions regarding those things you don't understand. Write down key terms and engage in discussion about the writer's ideas. Imagine the kind of advice that would be useful to you in polishing your own essay as you begin to comment on your peer's essay. Find a way to speak with courtesy and honesty; don't just rubber stamp or praise everything the writer says. If you have a doubt about something you are hearing but are not sure that you are right, say it anyway. You and the writer can always explore the doubt and either dispel it or turn it into something productive for the writer. Your tenacity in gently urging the writer to think more critically and precisely can make the difference between a successful paper and a weak and underdeveloped one. Therefore, as a reviewer, you should:

- Read your peer review partner's draft first from beginning to end as an interested reader, trying to understand the information and ideas. Read your partner's drafts in the same spirit that you want yours to be read.
- Read the draft through twice before making any judgments or comments. Be sure you know what the writer is saying. If necessary, summarize the paper to understand its content.
- Address only the most significant concerns with the work. Focus on the deep issues in other writers' drafts, especially early drafts: thesis, purpose, audience, organization, and support for the thesis. Use a checklist for revision as a guide to what is significant. Unless you have other instructions, ignore mistakes in grammar, punctuation, spelling, and the like. Editing tips are fine, too, but because workshops encourage authors to rewrite large portions of their prose, attention to minor details may be less valuable early on than feedback on ideas, organization, and development.
- Remember that you are the reader, not the writer. Don't edit sentences, add details, or otherwise assume responsibility for the paper.
- Phrase the comments carefully. Avoid misunderstandings by making sure comments are both clear and respectful. If you are responding on paper or online, not face to face with the writer, remember that the writer has nothing but the

written words to go on. He or she can't ask you for immediate clarification and can't infer your attitudes from gestures, facial expressions, and tone of voice.

- Be specific. For instance, instead of saying that more examples are needed, tell the writer which ideas in which paragraphs are unclear or unconvincing without examples. If something confuses you, say *why*. If you disagree with a conclusion, say *why*.
- Be supportive as well as honest. Tell the writer what you like about the paper. Phrase the comments positively: instead of *This paragraph doesn't interest me*, say *You have an interesting detail here that I almost missed*. Question the writer in a way that emphasizes the effect of the work on you, the reader: *This paragraph confuses me because* ... And avoid measuring the work against a set of external standards, as in *This essay is poorly organized* or *The thesis statement is inadequate*.
- While reading, make the comments in writing. Even if you will be delivering the comments in person later on, the written record will help you recall what you thought.
- Link comments to specific parts of a paper. Especially if you are reading the paper on a computer, be clear about what in the paper each comment relates to. You can use a word processor's Comment function, which annotates documents.

After the activity is finished, think about what you have learned. Every group discussion is a lesson created to improve your thinking, writing, and reading skills. Ask yourself what ideas and strategies you can apply to your own writing to make it more effective—and then revise the work accordingly. Once you have studied the draft with a critical eye and gotten responses from other readers, it's time to revise again. Major changes may be necessary, and you may need to generate new material or do some rewriting. But assume that the draft is good raw material that you can revise to achieve your purposes. Revision should take place on several levels, from global (whole-text issues) to particular (the details). Work on the draft in that order, starting with the elements that are global in nature and gradually moving to smaller, more particular aspects. This allows you to use your time most efficiently and take care of bigger issues first. In fact, as you deal with the larger aspects of the writing, many of the smaller ones will be taken care of along the way. As you revise, assume that nothing is sacred. Bring a critical eye to all parts of a draft, not only to those parts pointed out by the reviewers. Content, organization, sentence patterns, individual words—all are subject to improvement. Be aware that a change in one part of the text may require changes in other parts. At the same time, don't waste energy struggling with writing that simply doesn't work; you can always discard it. Look for the parts of the draft that do work—the parts that match the purpose and say what you want to say. Focus your efforts on those bright spots, expanding and developing them.

3.3 Editing the Revised Draft

Editing for style, clarity, and correctness may come second to more fundamental revision, but it is still very important. A carefully developed essay will fall flat with readers if you overlook awkwardness and errors.

1. Discovering What Needs Editing

After you've read and reread a draft to revise it, finding awkwardness and errors can be difficult. Try the following approaches to spot possible flaws in the revised draft:

- Take a break, even fifteen or twenty minutes, to clear your head.
- Read the draft slowly, and read what you actually see. Otherwise, you're likely to read what you intended to write but didn't. (If you have trouble slowing down, try reading the draft from back to front, sentence by sentence.)
- Read as if you are encountering the draft for the first time. Put yourself in the reader's place.
- Have a classmate, friend, or relative read your work. Make sure you understand and consider the reader's suggestions, even if eventually you decide not to take them.
- Read the draft aloud or, even better, record it. Listen for awkward rhythms, repetitive sentence patterns, and missing or clumsy transitions.
- Learn from your own experience. Keep a record of the problems that others have pointed out in your writing.

2. Using an Editing Checklist

After revising sentences in a paper so that they flow smoothly and clearly, you need to edit the paper for mistakes in grammar, punctuation, mechanics, usage, and spelling. Even if a paper is otherwise well written, it will make an unfavorable impression on readers if it contains such mistakes. To edit a paper, check it against the agreed-upon rules, or conventions, of written English. The following checklist emphasizes students' most common editing challenges. In your editing, work first for clear and effective sentences that flow smoothly. Then check the sentences for correct spelling, grammar, and punctuation. Use the checklist's questions to guide the editing, making several passes through the draft.

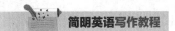

Checklist for Editing

Are sentences clear?
Do words and sentences mean what I intend to mean? Is anything confusing?
Check especially for these:
Exact language;
Parallelism;
Clear modifiers;
Clear reference of pronouns;
Complete sentences;
Sentences separated correctly.
Are sentences effective?
How well do words and sentences engage and hold readers' attention? How appropriate and effective is the voice created by words and sentences? Where does the writing seem wordy, choppy, or dull?
Check especially for these:
Expression of voice;
Emphasis of main ideas;
Smooth and informative transitions;
Variety in sentence length and structure;
Appropriate language;
Concise sentences.
Do sentences contain errors?
Where do surface errors interfere with the clarity and effectiveness of sentences?
Check especially for these:
Spelling errors;
Sentence fragments;
Comma splices;
Verb errors:
Verb forms, especially -s and -ed endings, correct forms of irregular verbs;
Verb tenses, especially consistency;
Agreement between subjects and verbs, especially when words come between them or the subject is *each*, *everyone*, or a similar word.
Pronoun errors:
Pronoun forms, especially subjective (*he, she, they, who*) vs. objective (*him, her, them, whom*)
Agreement between pronouns and antecedents, especially when the antecedent contains *or* or the antecedent is *each, everyone, person*, or a similar word.
Punctuation errors:
Commas, especially with comma splices, with *and* or *but*, with introductory elements, with nonessential elements, and with series.
Apostrophes in possessives but not plural nouns (*Dave's/witches*) and in contractions but not possessive personal pronouns (*it's/its*)

Part Two

Strategies of Essay Development

You will learn some of the strategies of development that will enable you to write the kinds of prose most frequently demanded in college and professional work. Mastering the most common prose strategies in their simplest forms will help you successfully assess and organize any kind of complex writing assignment you may face in the future.

Chapter 4

Introduction to Essay Development

4.1 Types of Essays

Narration and description are basic to all writing. Each time you relate a series of events, you are creating a narrative line, a trail for readers to follow. When you try to show readers how something looks, feels, or works, you are "drawing with words", or using description.

Exposition refers to different patterns of presenting the supporting points in the body of the essay. Usually, you will find that the topic of the essay, the purpose, and the audience's knowledge of the topic will determine which pattern of development, or combination of patterns, is most appropriate. Strategies of expository development are shown as follows.

- **Illustration by examples**: essays that present specific facts, observations, or scenarios to make the points and details concrete for readers. Every pattern of essay development makes use of examples in this way.
- **Process analysis**: essays that demonstrate or break down a process to instruct or show readers how something works, or how something happens.
- **Cause and effect**: essays that show or analyze causes and effects to break down and explain either the reasons (causes) for or the consequences (effects) of some situation or issue.
- **Comparison and/or contrast**: essays that compare or contrast to show the similarities and/or differences between two subjects or two aspects of one topic.
- **Definition**: essays that mainly define or explore various meanings of a word or concept.

- **Classification and division**: essays that classify or divide (break a topic down) into categories to help readers grasp different aspects of that subject.

Argumentation or persuasion naturally occurs in many well-supported essays as the thesis point is carefully explained and defended.

- Essays whose main goal is arguing a point use specific tactics either to gain support for a potentially contentious idea or to defend a position about which there might be differences of opinion.
- Essays whose main goal is persuasion are intended to alter the thinking of the reading audience, or to move readers' emotions in the direction of the writer's position. Persuasion is meant to lead to action on the reader's part—or at least to an openness to change. Persuasion, unlike argumentation, will rarely openly challenge a reader; instead, it will offer a series of appeals, based on knowledge of the audience. Essays that argue or persuade will often make use of several strategies of development to make their point.

1. Facts about Essay Writing and Methods of Development

Although we commonly refer to exposition, argumentation, description, and narration as the basic types of prose, in reality it is difficult to find any one mode in a pure form. In fact, almost all essays are combinations of two or more modes; it would be virtually impossible, for instance, to write a story—narration—without including description or to argue without also giving some information. Nevertheless, by determining a writer's main purpose, we can usually identify an essay or prose piece as primarily exposition, argumentation, description, or narration. In other words, an article may include a brief description of a new mousetrap, but if the writer's main intention is to explain how the trap works, then we may designate the essay as exposition. In most cases, the primary mode of any essay will be readily apparent to the reader.

1) **Essays generally use primary and secondary patterns of development.** You will practise writing essays that mainly follow a single pattern for supporting the point. However, more often than not, you will also, consciously or unconsciously, use secondary or subordinate methods to explain the points. You will probably use at least an example or two, whether you write about a process or trace the causes of some problem. Most essays, like the following sample written by Derrick Jensen, show primary and secondary patterns of development, and you will be prompted to identify them so you can understand why the authors might have chosen more than a single pattern to write about their topics.

2) **Essays generally involve presenting an argument.** No matter which pattern you choose for the subject, the essay will often present some form of argument or

persuasion; basically, essay structure that opens with a thesis and provides support argues or takes a position. Your essay's overriding purpose is to persuade the reader that the argument/point you advance is valid. While some authors write essays that adopt mainly a single method, many others create essays with paragraphs in a variety of development patterns, choosing among the patterns that will best help them achieve their goals. In the following essay, note how the author effectively combines multiple methods of organization.

Sample Essay

Derrick Jensen writes about environmental issues for a number of publications. The following article originally appeared in *Orion* (July/August 2013). According to the magazine's mission statement, "It is *Orion*'s fundamental conviction that humans are morally responsible for the world in which we live and that the individual comes to sense this responsibility as he or she develops a personal bond with nature." As you read, examine how the author combines strategies of development to persuade readers that declining baselines is a serious problem and convince them that something needs to be done about it.

Against Forgetting: Where Have All the Animals Gone?

Last night a host of nonhuman neighbors paid me a visit. First, two gray foxes sauntered up, including an older female who lost her tail to a leghold trap six or seven years ago. They trotted back into a thicker part of the forest, and a few minutes later a raccoon ambled forward. After he left I saw the two foxes again. Later, they went around the right side of a redwood tree as a black bear approached around the left. He sat on the porch for a while, and then walked off into the night. Then the foxes returned, hung out, and, when I looked away for a moment then looked back, they were gone. It wasn't too long before the bear returned to lie on the porch. After a brief nap, he went away. The raccoon came back and brought two friends. When they left the foxes returned, and after the foxes came the bear. The evening was like a French farce: As one character exited stage left, another entered stage right.	Narration: Tells a story in chronological order, to establish baseline

Description: Uses concrete details to help readers picture animal parade |
| Although I see some of these nonhuman neighbors daily, I was entranced and delighted to see so many of them over the span of just one evening. I remained delighted until sometime the next day, when I remembered reading that, prior to conquest by the Europeans, people in this region could expect to see a grizzly bear every 15 minutes. | Comparison-contrast: Contrasts number of animals today with number in the past |

This phenomenon is something we all encounter daily, even if some of us rarely notice it. It happens often enough to have a name: declining baselines. The phrase describes the process of becoming accustomed to and accepting as normal worsening conditions. Along with normalization can come a forgetting that things were not always this way. And this can lead to further acceptance and further normalization, which leads to further amnesia, and so on. Meanwhile the world is killed, species by species, biome by biome. And we are happy when we see the ever-dwindling number of survivors.	Definition: Provides definition of key term to be used in his thesis/argument
Cause-effect: Explains a chain of causes and effects to explain declining baselines
I've gone on the salmon-spawning tours that local environmentalists give, and I'm not the only person who by the end is openly weeping. If we're lucky, we see 15 fish. Prior to conquest there were so many fish the rivers were described as "black and roiling". And it's not just salmon. Only five years ago, whenever I'd pick up a piece of firewood, I'd have to take off a half-dozen sowbugs. It's taken me all winter this year to see as many. And I used to go on spider patrol before I took a shower, in order to remove them to safety before the deluge. I still go on spider patrol, but now it's mostly pro forma. The spiders are gone. My mother used to put up five hummingbird feeders, and the birds would fight over those. Now she puts up two, and as often as not the sugar ferments before anyone eats it. I used to routinely see bats in the summer. Last year I saw one.	Comparison-contrast: Contrasts number of animals today with number at various times in the past to dramatize declining
You can transpose this story to wherever you live and whatever members of the nonhuman community live there with you. I was horrified a few years ago to read that many songbird populations on the Atlantic Seaboard have collapsed by up to 80 percent over the last 40 years. But, and this is precisely the point, I was even more horrified when I realized that *Silent Spring* came out more than 40 years ago, so this 80 percent decline followed an already huge decline caused by pesticides, which followed another undoubtedly huge decline caused by the deforestation, conversion to agriculture, and urbanization that followed conquest.	Process analysis: Shows process of decline in songbird populations
Cause-effect: Shows causes of huge declines in songbird populations (effects)
My great-grandmother grew up in a sod house in Nebraska. When she was a tiny girl—in other words, only four human generations ago—there were still enough wild bison on the Plains that she was afraid lightning storms would spook them and they would trample her home. Who in Nebraska today worries about being trampled by bison? For that matter, who in Nebraska today even thinks about bison on a monthly, much less daily, basis?	Comparison-contrast: Contrasts number of animals today with number at various times in the past to dramatize declining

Part Two | Strategies of Essay Development

This state of affairs is problematic for many reasons, not the least of which is that it's harder to fight for what you don't love than for what you do, and it's hard to love what you don't know you're missing. It's harder still to fight an injustice you do not perceive as an injustice but rather as just the way things are. How can you fight an injustice you never think about because it never occurs to you that things have ever been any different?

Declining baselines apply not only to the environment but to many fields. Take surveillance. Back in the 1930s, there were people who freaked out at the notion of being assigned a Social Security number, as it was "a number that will follow you from cradle to grave." But since 9/11, according to former National Security Agency official William Binney, the US government has been retaining every e-mail sent, in case any of us ever does anything the government doesn't like. How many people complain about that? And it's not just the government. I received spam birthday greetings this year from all sorts of commercial websites. How and why does ESPN.com have my birth date? And remember the fight about GMOs? They were perceived as scary (because they are), and now they're all over the place, but most people don't know or don't care. The same goes for nanotechnology.

Yesterday I ate a strawberry. Or rather, I ate a strawberry-shaped object that didn't have much taste. When did we stop noticing that strawberries/plums/ tomatoes no longer taste like what they resemble? In my 20s I rented a house where a previous resident's cat had pooped all over the dirt basement, which happened to be where the air intakes for the furnace were located. The house smelled like cat feces. After I'd been there a few months, I wrote to a friend, "At first the smell really got to me, but then, as with everything, I got used to the stench and it just doesn't bother me anymore."

This is a process we need to stop. Milan Kundera famously wrote, "The struggle of man against power is the struggle of memory against forgetting." Everything in this culture is aimed at helping to distract us from—or better, help us to forget—the injustices, the pain. And it is completely normal for us to want to be distracted from or to forget pain. Pain hurts. That is why on every level from somatic reflex to socially constructed means of denial we have pathways to avoid it.

Cause-effect: Effects of declining baselines

Illustration: Examples to help readers understand how baselines decline

Comparison-contrast: Contrasts responses today with responses previously

Argument: States author's position

Cause-effect

81

But here is what I want you to do: I want you to go outside. I want you to listen to the (disappearing) frogs, to watch the (disappearing) fireflies. Even if you're in a city—especially if you're in a city — I want you to picture the land as it was before the land was built over. I want you to research who lived there. I want you to feel how it was then, feel how it wants to be. I want you to begin keeping a calendar of who you see and when: the first day each year you see buttercups, the first day frogs start singing, the last day you see robins in the fall, the first day for grasshoppers. In short, I want you to pay attention. If you do this, your baseline will stop declining, because you'll have a record of what's being lost.	Argument: Uses repetition to persuade readers to take steps

Cause-effect |
| Do not go numb in the face of this data. Do not turn away. I want you to feel the pain. Keep it like a coal inside your coat, a coal that burns and burns. I want all of us to do this, because we should all want the pain of injustice to stop. We should want this pain to stop not because we get used to it and it just doesn't bother us anymore, but because we stop the injustices and destruction that are causing the pain in the first place. I want us to feel how awful the destruction is, and then act from this feeling. | Argument: Uses comparison to persuade readers to take steps |
| And I promise you two things. One: Feeling this pain won't kill you. And two: Not feeling this pain, continuing to go numb and avoid it, will. | |

Chapter 5

Narration: Recounting Events

Narrating or telling stories is a basic human activity; we experience things every day and we want to tell others what happened. Like the great myths and legends, narrative stories teach humanity's lessons. This chapter is concerned with writing nonfiction expository narratives, stories that are used to explain or prove a point. Through narration, we make a statement clear by relating in detail something that has happened to us. In the story we tell, we present the details in the order in which they happened. A person might say, for example, "I was really embarrassed the day I took my driver's test," and then go on to develop that statement with an account of the experience. If the story is sharply detailed, we will be able to see and understand just why the speaker felt that way.

5.1 Developing a Narrative Essay

The main purpose of a narrative essay is to make a point by telling the audience a story. Colorful details and interesting events that build up to a point of some kind make narrative essays enjoyable for readers and writers alike. At one time or another, you have probably listened to someone tell a rambling story that didn't seem to go anywhere. You might have impatiently wondered, "Where is this story going?" or "Is there a point here?" Keep such questions in mind as you think about your own narrative essay. To satisfy the audience, the story must have some overall purpose and point. Also keep in mind that the story should deal with an event or a topic that will appeal to the audience. A group of young children, for example, would probably be bored by a narrative essay about your first job interview. They might, however, be very interested if you wrote about a time you were chased by a pack of mean dogs or when you stood up to a bully in your school.

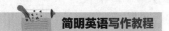

In general, narrative essays that involve human conflict—internal or external—are entertaining to readers of all ages.

While some narrative essays have the feel of a story, their structure is that of an essay. When you write a fictional story, you may not reveal a clear point at all; the story's point may be woven throughout it, or it may be in the characters' actions or feelings. But in a narrative essay you make a point and incorporate one central story or several brief stories as support. To be specific, when you write a narrative essay, your job is to make your point in the thesis, then to select events, scenes, and emotions that will maintain the readers' interest as they see your meaning shown in the supporting details.

1. Writing a Thesis Statement for a Narrative Essay

Narrative essays may be about conflict, change, or discovery. As non-fiction narratives, these essays lead readers to new states of awareness or alter their views of themselves or their lives in some way. The narrative essay's thesis can be some general truth that the conflict or discovery reveals. The narrative essay illustrates how you have come to understand the thesis. Whether the thesis explains a change or a human truth, it is the point or "lesson" of the essay.

A thesis for a narrative essay focused on change might be similar to the following:

- That turn in the road was a genuine turning point for Yonggi.

A thesis based on an easily understood human truth could be something like this:

- The value of family is, and should be, an unforgettable lesson.

When you work on a thesis statement for a narrative essay, ask yourself, "What specific moment or event changed me?" or "What truth did I learn from learning this?"—whether "this" is something you experienced directly or from research. That moment, event, or learning experience will be the topic and what you learned as a result of that pivotal experience will be the viewpoint that shapes the thesis statement.

2. Tips for Narrative Essays

1) Narrative essays always have a clear thesis, and present events, scenes, or records of the writer's reactions to support that thesis. Narrative essays present their point or thesis in the first paragraph.
2) Narrative essays are told from one of two points of view, first person or third person. Either viewpoint must be consistently maintained.
3) Narrative essays follow chronological order only. They recount a narrative line only in the order in which it occurred, and reinforce this order with careful use of time transitions and transitional phrases.

4) Narrative essays, to be successful, "show" their audiences what the writer feels or means with the use of careful descriptions and word choices. Such essays depend for their quality on the vividness with which the writer can "bring to life" situations and emotions, with the use of strong verbs, adjectives, and adverbs.

5) Narrative essays do often show a conflict or turning point as pivotal to a lesson learned by the writer, and display their support in the sequence in which events happened. Like stories, narrative essays may include dialogue to bring events and situations to life for audiences.

3. Function of Narration Essay

You can write a narrative on some topics, using the techniques of narration, to:

1) **Express your ideas**. You can write a narrative about an incident or experience that you see differently now than you did when it happened.
2) **Inform your reader**. You can write an essay informing your reader about the habits of successful (or unsuccessful) students, using a narrative to support one or more of your main points.
3) **Persuade your reader**. You can write an essay persuading the reader to take a particular stand on an issue of your choice, using a story from your experience to support your position or tell how you arrived at it.

5.2 Integrating Narration into an Essay

Although most of your college essays will not be primarily narrative, you can use stories—to illustrate a point, clarify an idea, support an argument, or capture readers' interest—in essays that mainly use another method of development or use several methods. Narration works with other methods of development. You expand on and explain events in a narrative with examples; you could use process analysis to set out the steps by which you reached some moment of change, and you will often compare or contrast one person or situation with another to clarify your point in a narrative. Narration is often part of essays using other mehtods of development. Short narratives can serve as supporting details in the form of examples: a brief anecdote will often illuminate one side of a comparison or contrast, and stories about people and events will help to persuade readers of the truth of the thesis. Here are a few suggestions for combining narration effectively with other mehtods of development:

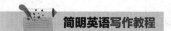

1) **Use a story**. It should illustrate the main point (or thesis) accurately and well (not just because it's funny or interesting).
2) **Keep the narrative short**. Include only the details readers need to understand the events you are describing.
3) **Introduce the story with a transitional sentence or clause**. It should indicate that you are about to shift to a narrative and make clear the connection between the story and the point it illustrates.
4) **Use descriptive language, dialogue, and action**. These will make the narrative vivid, lively, and interesting.

Sample Essay

In this narrative essay, the writer uses a story about a sick but fierce dog to show how he learned a valuable lesson in his job as a veterinarian's assistant. Notice the writer's good use of vivid details that make this well-paced story both clear and interesting.

Never Underestimate the Little Things	
When I went to work as a veterinarian's assistant for Dr. Sam Holt and Dr. Jack Gunn last summer, I was under the false impression that the hardest part of veterinary surgery would be the actual performance of an operation. The small chores demanded before this feat didn't occur to me as being of any importance. As it happened, I had been in the veterinary clinic only a total of four hours before I met a little animal who convinced me that the operation itself was probably the easiest part of treatment. This animal, to whom I owe thanks for so enlightening me, was a chocolate-colored chihuahua of tiny size and immense perversity named Smokey.	Introduction: A misconception

Thesis: Small preliminary details can be as important as the major action |
| Smokey could have very easily passed for some creature from another planet. It wasn't so much his gaunt little frame and overly large head, or his bony paws with nearly saberlike claws, as it was his grossly infected eyes. Those once-shining eyes were now distorted and swollen into grotesque balls of septic, sightless flesh. The only vague similarity they had to what we'd normally think of as the organs of vision was a slightly upraised dot, all that was left of the pupil, in the center of a pink and purply marble. As if that were not enough, Smokey had a temper to match his ugly sight. He also had surprisingly good aim, considering his largely | Description of the main character: His appearance |

diminished vision, toward any moving object that happened to place itself unwisely before his ever-inquisitive nose; with sudden and wholly vicious intent, he would snap and snarl at whatever blocked the little light that could filter through his swollen and ruptured blood vessels. Truly, in many respects, Smokey was a fearful dog to behold.

Such an appearance and personality did nothing to encourage my already flagging confidence in my capabilities as a vet's assistant. How was I supposed to get that little demon out of his cage? Jack had casually requested that I bring Smokey to the surgery room, but did he really expect me to put my hands into the cage of that devil dog? I suppose it must have been my anxious expression that saved me, for as I turned uncertainly toward the kennel, Jack chuckled nonchalantly and accompanied me to demonstrate how professionals in his line of work dealt with professionals in Smokey's. He took a small rope about four feet long with a no-choke noose at one end and unlatched Smokey's cage. Then cautiously he reached in and dangled the noose before the dog's snarling jaws. Since Smokey could only barely see what he was biting at, his attacks were directed haphazardly in a semicircle around his body. The tiny area of his cage led to his capture, for during one of Smokey's forward lunges, Jack dropped the noose over his head and moved the struggling creature out onto the floor. The fight had only just begun for Smokey, however, and he braced his feet against the slippery linoleum tiling and forced us to drag him, like a little pull toy on a string, to the surgery.

Once Smokey was in the surgery, however, the question that hung before our eyes like a veritable presence was how to get the dog from the floor to the table. Simply picking him up and plopping him down was out of the question. One glance at the quivering little figure emitting ominous and throaty warnings was enough to assure us of that. Realizing that the game was over, Jack grimly handed me the rope and reached for a muzzle. It was a doomed attempt from the start: the closer Jack dangled the tiny leather cup to the dog's nose, the more violent did Smokey's contortions and rage-filled cries become and the more frantic our efforts became to try to keep our feet and fingers clear of the angry jaws. Deciding that a firmer method had to be used, Jack instructed me to raise the rope up high enough so that Smokey would have to stand on his hind legs.

> His personality
>
> The difficulty of moving the dog to the surgery room
>
> The difficulty of moving the dog to the table

This greatly reduced his maneuverability but served to increase his tenacity, for at this the little dog nearly went into paroxysms of frustration and rage. In his struggles, however, Smokey caught his forepaw on his swollen eye, and the blood that had been building up pressure behind the fragile cornea burst out and dripped to the floor. In the midst of our surprise and the twinge of panic startling the three of us, Jack saw his chance and swiftly muzzled the animal and lifted him to the operating table.	
Even at that point it wasn't easy to put the now terrified dog to sleep. He fought the local anesthesia and caused Jack to curse as he was forced to give Smokey more of the drug than should have been necessary for such a small beast. After what seemed an eternity, Smokey lay prone on the table, breathing deeply and emitting soft snores and gentle whines. We also breathed deeply in relief, and I relaxed to watch fascinated, while Jack performed a very delicate operation quite smoothly and without mishap.	The difficulty of putting the dog to sleep before the surgery
Such was my harrowing induction into the life of a veterinary surgeon. But Smokey did teach me a valuable lesson that has proven its importance to me many times since: wherever animals are concerned, even the smallest detail is important and should never be taken for granted.	Conclusion: The lesson she learned

Practice

Think of an experience in your life that supports one of the following statements. Then, using that statement as your thesis, write a narrative essay about that experience.

(1) The chains of habit are too weak to be felt until they are too strong to be broken. —Samuel Johnson

(2) Words in mouth, no load upon head. —Jamaican proverb

(3) Don't grieve. Anything you lose comes round in another form. —Djalâl ad-Dîn Rûmî

(4) Stories can conquer fear, you know. They can make the heart bigger. —Ben Okri

(5) It is better to walk than curse the road. —Senegalese proverb

(6) A little learning is a dangerous thing. —Alexander Pope

(7) Anger is just a cowardly extension of sadness. —Alanis Morissette

(8) Man needs his difficulties because they are necessary to enjoy success. —Abdul Kalam

(9) We lie loudest when we lie to ourselves. —Eric Hoffer

Practice

Write a narrative essay about an experience that had a significant effect that changed your views in some important way. Choose an experience that:
(1) Taught you something about yourself;
(2) Revealed the true character of someone you know;
(3) Helped you discover a principle to live by;
(4) Helped you appreciate the beauty of something;
(5) Has become a family legend (one that reveals the character of a family member or illustrates a clash of generations or cultures), and;
(6) Explains the personal significance of a particular object.

Chapter 6

Description: Portraying People, Places, and Things

When you describe someone or something, you give readers a picture in words. To make the word picture as vivid and real as possible, you must observe and record specific details that appeal to readers' senses (sight, hearing, taste, smell, and touch). More than any other type of essay, a descriptive essay needs sharp, colorful details. Here is a description with almost no appeal to the senses: "In the window was a fan." In contrast, here is a description rich in sense impressions: "The blades of the rusty window fan clattered and whirled as they blew out a stream of warm, soggy air." Sense impressions in this second example include sight (*rusty window fan, whirled*), hearing (*clattered*), and touch (*warm, soggy air*). The vividness and sharpness of the sensory details give you a clear picture of the fan and enable you to share the writer's experience. Description and narration work together; they are uniquely suited to help you express what you see and feel. Narration gives your readers a line to follow and description shows readers what you see and experience. Description is the key tool in explaining what you see in the world.

6.1 Developing a Descriptive Essay

The main purpose of a descriptive essay is to make readers see—or hear, taste, smell, or feel—what you are writing about. Vivid details are the key to descriptive essays, enabling your audience to picture and, in a way, experience what you describe. There are two basic forms of description: subjective/impressionistic and objective. When you write vivid descriptions, you not only make the writing livelier and more interesting but also indicate your attitude toward the subject through the choice of words and details.

Description appears in the writing for a particular reason: to help you inform, clarify, persuade, or create a mood. In some essays you will want the description as objective as you can make it; for example, you might describe a scientific experiment or a business transaction in straight factual detail. Other times, however, you will want to convey a particular attitude toward the subject. Note the differences between the following two descriptions of a tall, thin boy: the objective writer sticks to the facts by saying, "The eighteen-year-old boy was 6'1" and weighed 155 pounds," whereas the subjective writer gives an impressionistic description: "The young boy was as tall and scrawny as a birch tree in winter." Before you begin describing anything, you must first decide your purpose and whether it calls for objective or subjective reporting.

As you start to think about your own descriptive essay, choose a topic that appeals strongly to at least one of your senses. It's possible to write a descriptive essay, maybe even a good one, about a boiled potato. But it would be easier (not to mention more fun) to describe a bowl of potato salad, with its contrasting textures of soft potato, crisp celery, and spongy hardboiled egg: the crunch of the diced onion, the biting taste of the bits of pickle, the salad's creamy dressing and its tangy seasonings. The more senses you involve, the more likely your audience is to enjoy your paper. Also, when selecting your topic, consider how much your audience already knows about it. If your topic is a familiar one—for instance, potato salad—you can assume your audience already understands the general idea. However, if you are presenting something new or unfamiliar to your readers—perhaps a description of one of your relatives or a place where you've lived— you must provide background information.

Once you have selected the topic, focus on the goal or purpose of the essay. What message do you hope to convey to the audience? For instance, if you chose as the topic a playground you used to visit as a child, decide what dominant impression you want to communicate. Is your goal to make readers see the park as a pleasant play area, or do you want them to see it as a dangerous place? If you choose the second option, focus on conveying that sense of danger to the audience. Then jot down any details that support that idea. You might describe broken beer bottles on the asphalt, graffiti sprayed on the metal jungle gym, or a pack of loud teenagers gathered on a nearby street corner. In this case, the details support the overall purpose, creating a threatening picture that the audience can see and understand.

1. Writing a Thesis Statement for a Descriptive Essay

When you work on a thesis statement for a descriptive essay based on something you have experienced, or someone you know, ask yourself, "What do I feel (or think of) when I see (my topic) in my mind?" or "What words come to mind when I think about (my topic)?" In a personal/expressive descriptive essay, your thesis (or point) is the overall response to something or someone, the dominant impression that this person, place, or thing makes on you. Your dominant impression must be broad enough to cover all the aspects of, and all the observations about the item or person that you will include in the essay. The thesis statement, then, sums up and previews for the reader the range of emotions, sensations, observations, and/or responses that you will describe in the essay. Your descriptive essay will go on to break down that dominant impression into the key reactions you have to the topic. A thesis for a descriptive essay about a motorcycle trip could be something like this:

- The trip that was such a thrilling idea was, in reality, gruelling days of bone-chilling wind and stinging rain.

Descriptive essays or reports for more objective writing situations—descriptions of places, people or animals, processes, or situations—call for a different version of a dominant impression as their thesis statements. If you write scientific or objective descriptions, for example, the dominant impression will be a kind of preview statement, of the subject. In objective descriptions, the goal is not to present your emotional response to the subject, but to offer an overview of the scope of what you will describe. Here is a thesis by an environmental geography student. He is writing a description of land types on the north shore of Lake Erie:

- Eight main areas represent important communities on Pelee and Middle Islands; the community types range from forests and savannas to alvars and wetlands.

2. Descriptive Essays

When you write an expressive or personal descriptive essay in which you want to share the impressions of a place or person, your aim is to evoke in readers not just an image of the place or person, but of the feelings or experience of it as well. To do so, the word choices are keys to the success in the writing task. Use nouns, verbs, modifiers, and figures of speech that appeal to readers' senses. When you are assigned a more objective descriptive essay, share or reproduce the image of the object, person, or place described as accurately as possible and aim for precision in the descriptions. The aim is not to evoke an emotional response in readers.

1) **Nouns and verbs do the hard work in the writing**. Put the effort into choosing accurate, specific nouns and verbs that these words deserve.
2) **Well-chosen adjectives and adverbs**. Enhance the effects of the nouns and verbs by appealing to readers' sense.
    - Personal subjective descriptions need descriptive adjectives and phrases to bring

your subject to life. Choose words that appeal to the senses, to people's common experiences; for example, "neatly folded layers of soft, pale-yellow wool."
- Accurate, objective descriptions need precise words that capture and identify aspects of the subject so that readers will see them as clearly as possible. Choose nouns, verbs, adjectives, and adverbs based on their accuracy rather than on the reaction they will provoke from readers. For example, "The deep magenta compound, when heated to 125 degrees, boiled explosively and burst the containing glass beaker."

3) **Use figurative language when appropriate**. Figures of speech, similes and metaphors, can be ready-made verbal pictures to show the audience.

3. Function of Descriptive Essays

1) **Express your ideas**. For example, you can write an essay for your classmates describing a childhood toy that you had that still evokes fond memories.
2) **Inform your reader**. For example, you can write an essay describing destruction or devastation you have observed as a result of a natural disaster (hurricane, flood), or an accident.
3) **Persuade your reader**. For example, in a letter to persuade your parents to permit you to rent a better apartment, you can include a description of your current apartment.

6.2 Integrating Description into an Essay

Sometimes description alone fulfills the purpose of an essay. In most cases, however, you will use description in essays that mainly rely on a different mode. For instance, in a narrative essay, description helps readers experience events, reconstruct scenes, and visualize action. Although most of the college essays will not be primarily descriptive, you can use description in essays that explain the causes or effects of a phenomenon, compare or contrast animal species, or illustrate defensive behavior in children, for example. Here are a few suggestions for combining description effectively with other patterns of development.

1) **Include only relevant details**. Whether you describe an event, a person, or a scene, the sensory details you choose should enhance the reader's understanding of the subject.
2) **Keep the description focused**. Select enough details to make the essential points and dominant impression clear. Readers may become impatient if you include too many descriptive details.

Part Two Strategies of Essay Development

3) **Make sure the description fits the essay's tone and point of view**. A personal description, for example, is not appropriate in an essay explaining a technical process.

Sample Essay

In her descriptive essay, Marie Wadsworth describes the Acadia National Park to make a point about its natural beauty. Notice how Wadsworth uses figurative language to help readers understand her point of view.

Acadia National Park

Acadia National Park lies off the rugged coast of Maine. It's mainly one large island—Mount Desert Island—plus some smaller islands and a nearby peninsula. According to the National Park Service brochure, Acadia was the first national park east of the Mississippi River. Though it's relatively small, Acadia stands out for the variety of its natural beauty—including mountains, lakes, and coastline.	Introduction: Location of the park Thesis
One way Acadia is beautiful is its small mountain range. Cadillac Mountain—which dominates the view as you approach the park from the mainland—is the highest in the park. According to the park brochure, it is 1,530 feet high. That may not seem like much, but it rises quickly from sea level, so it seems bigger than it is. Visitors to the park love driving to the top or biking there or climbing a steep trail. The view from the top, as you may imagine, is one of the most spectacular in the United States—lovely green, rugged islands dotting the bay and extending out into the Atlantic Ocean.	Topic sentence
Another way Acadia is beautiful is the small lakes nestled among the hills and mountains. Perhaps the most popular is Jordan Pond. Visitors love sitting at an outdoor restaurant at one end of the pond and eating the famed popovers served there—while viewing the nearby blueberry bushes, the grassy margin of the pond, and the hills and mountains beyond. With its excellent restaurant and placid scenery, it's probably the most civilized place in the park.	Topic sentence
Yet another way Acadia is beautiful is its coastline. The rugged coast is marked by large boulders at the edge of the water. One of the visitors' favorite places on the coast is Thunder Hole. At Thunder Hole, the rocks stand narrowly so that the incoming waves make a loud noise—like thunder—and splash high up. Every now and then a really big wave makes a really loud noise and splashes especially high up. These big waves can catch visitors by surprise. The last time I visited Thunder Hole,	Topic sentence

95

the visitors had been lured by several minutes of small waves and crept very close to Thunder Hole. Then—you guessed it!—a huge wave came in and completely drenched about 50 visitors, at the same time scaring them with the loud, thunderous noise. I guess you could call Thunder Hole the least civilized place in the park! 　　So despite its small size, Acadia stands out for its beautiful mountains, lakes, and coast. And whether visitors receive a civilized greeting (at Jordan Pond) or a surprise drenching, they all marvel at the spectacular and unforgettable sights there.	Conclusion: Summary of Acadia's beautiful scenery

Practice

　　Write an essay about a particular place that you can observe carefully or that you already know well. For example, choose a store you know well, a room you have lived in for some time, or a room in the college or university you attend.

Practice

　　Imagining you are working in a travel agency and you are to write a letter to prospective clients advertising a wonderful vacation destination. It might be a large city, a seaside town, an archeological site, a theme park that caters to families, a resort for honeymooners, a dude ranch, a lake, or a mountain hideaway. Your purpose is to get clients to sign up for the vacation.

Chapter 7

Exemplification: Explaining with Examples

In our daily conversations, we often provide examples—details, particulars, and specific instances—to explain statements that we make. Exemplification helps us see for ourselves the truth of the statement that has been made. In essays, too, explanatory examples help the audience fully understand the point. Lively, specific examples also add interest to the paper.

An essay that illustrates its point with examples moves readers from the general position of the thesis to clear examples that demonstrate specific aspects of its meaning. When you illustrate ideas with clear examples, you increase the audience's chance to see the truth of the statement. This is especially useful for persuading doubtful readers of the point.

7.1 Developing an Essay That Illustrates by Examples

Illustration with examples is an all-purpose writing technique that you will use throughout college or university. If you need to explain film noir lighting, you will provide examples from films showing that style of lighting. In an essay about changes in socializing habits, you may provide statistical examples of students' use of social media. Illustrating a particular poet's use of meter for an English essay would mean supplying examples from the poet's works. In an essay that emphasizes exemplification, you support it by illustrating it with examples. These examples may range from facts that you have researched to personal accounts. If, for instance, you decide to write an essay that claims capital punishment is immoral, you might cite several cases in which an innocent person was executed. Keep in mind that the examples should connect clearly to the main point so that readers will see the truth of the claim.

In most cases, the first paragraph will present the thesis; each body paragraph will contain a topic sentence and as many effectively arranged examples as necessary to explain or support each major point; the last paragraph will conclude the essay in some appropriate way. A body paragraph that uses one type of support—examples, maybe—is often convincing, but many good paragraphs contain several types of support: a couple of examples and some statistics, or a statement by an authority and an example, and so on. Meanwhile, interesting factual content can be as compelling as examples. Use enough examples to make the point clearly and persuasively. Put yourself in the reader's place: Would you be convinced with three brief examples? Five? One extended example? Two? Use your own judgment, but be careful to support or explain the major points adequately.

1. Writing a Thesis Statement for an Illustration Essay

Development by example is the most widely used of all the expository strategies and by far the most important. There should be a clear and logical relationship between the thesis and examples. Do the examples add up to the thesis? If not, revise the thesis statement. A thesis for an essay that illustrates its point by examples could be something like this:

- The HMCS Scotian recruitment ceremony, with its marching bands, spectacular stage lighting, and lines of highly decorated officers, seemed more like a show than a military procedure.

2. Tips for Essays That Illustrate by Examples

1) **Each specific example should support, clarify, or explain the general statement it illustrates**. Each example should provide readers with additional insight into the subject under discussion. Keep the purpose of the paragraphs in mind: don't wander off into an analysis of the causes of theft on your campus if you are only supposed to show various examples of it.

2) **Examples may be derived from your own thinking, observations, or experience**. They may be anecdotes, explanations, or descriptions of places or objects. You may use such examples for character analyses, explanations of procedures or viewpoints, or any number of essay types. There is no one type of "perfect example". The effectiveness of examples depends on the writer's purpose and audience, and the type of essay or report. Each has pros and cons.

Personal Examples. Drawn from personal experience, these can be effective in personal, creative, and some narrative writing, where the reader's bond with the writer is essential.

Pros: Such examples are new to readers and have some force, if well written, because they feel authentic.

Cons: These are "limited" because of their narrow, subjective nature. Not all audiences can relate to writers' personal experiences. Importantly, personal examples are not effective or acceptable in academic, business, technical, or professional writing.

Typical Examples. May be a fact or statistic supporting the writer's point in a general way. These may be effective as first-level support, but writers need to explain and focus such examples so they relate closely to supporting points.

Pros: Facts and statistics, correctly cited and from reliable sources, are easily accepted by readers and are solid, necessary components of college and university essays and reports.

Cons. Facts and statistics must be precisely related to the supporting points and/or details to which they are attached. If typical examples are too general or too loosely related to support material, they do not provide effective support. For instance, statistics about home accidents in general would be too general to work as specific evidence in an essay about fires in the home.

Hypothetical Examples are invented scenarios that illustrate a point. If well written and suitable for an essay's topic, purpose, and audience, these can bring vividness and life to supporting material.

Pros: Invented scenarios can generate energy and interest. They are useful if strongly related to a given supporting point: for instance, a brief hypothetical scenario about a student's difficulties facing credit-card bills in an essay about student financial concerns.

Cons: Because hypotheticals are not grounded in fact, they serve as a dramatic illustration of a supporting point. They are best used in combination with factual forms of support.

3) **Examples must be relevant, representative, accurate, and striking**.
   - **Relevant examples** have a direct and clear relationship to the thesis. If the essay advocates publicly funded preschool programs, support the case with examples of successful publicly funded programs, not privately operated programs.
   - **Representative examples** show a typical or real-life situation, not a rare or unusual one. In an essay arguing that preschool programs advance children's reading skills, one example of an all-day, year-round preschool would not be representative of all or most other programs.
   - **Accurate and specific examples** provide readers with enough information to evaluate their reliability. Notice how the second example below provides better (more specific) detail for the reader.

For example:
- Overly general most students in preschool programs have better language skills than children who don't attend such programs.
- Specific, detailed according to an independent evaluator, 73 percent of children who attended the Head Start program in Clearwater had better language skills after one year of attendance than students who did not attend the program.

3. Function of Illustration Essays

1) **Express your ideas**. You can explain what you consider to be the three most important qualities of a college instructor, supporting your opinion with vivid examples from your experience.
2) **Inform your readers**. You can describe to an audience of college students the qualities or achievements you think should be emphasized during job interviews and give examples that show why the qualities or achievements you choose are important to potential employers.
3) **Persuade your readers**. You can argue for or against an increased emphasis on physical education in public schools.

7.2 Integrating Illustration into an Essay

Examples are an effective way to support a thesis that relies on one or more other patterns of development. For instance, you might use examples in the following ways:
- to define a particular advertising ploy;
- to compare two types of small businesses;
- to classify types of movies;
- to show the effects of aerobic exercise, and;
- to argue that junk food is unhealthy because of its high fat and salt content.

Every method of development makes use of examples: they clarify arguments, explain steps in a procedure, elaborate on components of a category, and strengthen an argument. A division and classification essay on food intolerance requires relevant examples for each category; a descriptive process report explaining procedures in correcting computer-network problems needs examples of various problems and solutions. Many different types of examples function as agents of clarification in all forms of writing. When using examples in an essay where illustration is not the main technique of development, keep the following tips in mind:

1) **Choose effective examples**. They should be relevant, representative, accurate, specific, and striking.
2) **Use transitions** such as "for instance" or "for example". They make it obvious that an example follows.
3) **Provide enough details** to help readers understand how an example supports your point. Meanwhile, do not overwhelm readers with too many details.

Sample Essay

Study the use of specific examples in the brief essay that follows. If the writer were to revise this essay, where might he add more examples or details? How might he strengthen the introduction or conclusion to the essay?

If You Want to Get to Know a New Place, Go for a Run

Imagine this scene: I'm in a new town, on a new campus, and I don't know anyone. Everything feels strange and foreign—the food seems weird, I've gotten lost twice already, and I miss home. All I want to do is curl up on the bed and not leave the dorm room where I've been staying for orientation. But instead, a little voice pipes in, and somehow I find myself back out on those unknown campus streets. I lace up my running shoes and hit the pavement, and gradually, my mood lifts. I notice shop fronts and food stands I make a mental note to revisit; the runner's high kicks in, and by the end, I don't feel quite as lost. The benefits of jogging in a new place provide a closer look at new surroundings, a positive feeling associated with exercise, and even an adventure of self-finding.	Introduction: An anecdote that serves as a catchy lead-in Thesis
One of the important benefits of running through a new place is the closer look you get from the ground. Tourists often ride buses or take taxis in new cities, hopping from one crowded attraction to the next. But there's more to a new city than the popular sites. When I was visiting my friend, who had just moved into her first off-campus apartment, we went out on a run, and we had time to see the neighborhoods more directly, and feel the streets beneath our feet. We noticed things off the beaten track we normally wouldn't have caught—like the abandoned factory on the side of the road, for example, because we needed to have landmarks so we could remember our way back. In addition, we could people-watch while we jogged: strollers, dog-walkers, other runners all passed by. My friend acclimated to her	Topic sentence One example: Going for a run with a friend in new neighborhood

new part of town, and I got a closer glimpse of how it feels to actually live there, not just visit.

A bonus of taking in new scenery while running is the physical exercise you get. Research has shown cardio activity releases positive hormones and overall feelings of well-being. But a gym workout means you're stuck inside. When I started my new summer job, I was exhausted at the end of every work day. But I forced myself, when work was finished, to head into the park across the street with my coworker for a run, where we bonded while burning calories. Running provided us with the energy that I sorely needed after a long day at work, and it made us happy to discover the ins and outs of our office's surrounding environs.

Unlike in my regular route, where I always do the same course over and over, in a new location, getting lost can be a surprising adventure. For example, on a trip to visit my grandparents, who were staying at a lake house, I found myself on a run lost in the woods, with darkness approaching. I hadn't seen another human in over an hour. I was filled with fear, but also deeply struck by the beautiful landscape around me—the thicket of trees and the silver lake somewhere beyond my sight range. I was forced to try and retrace my steps, and eventually stumbled back to the road and found my way back. The "lost" part of my run ended up being my favorite part — the quiet forest, the untouched trails — it felt like my secret garden.

In conclusion, going running in a new place offers multiple benefits for better understanding the surroundings, and, even more importantly, better understanding ourselves.

	Topic sentence
	Example: Going for a run after work with a coworker
	Topic sentence
	Example: A trail run at the grandparents' lake house
	Conclusion: Summary of the benefits

Practice

Write an exemplification essay on the outstanding qualities (good or bad) of a person you know well. This person might be a member of your family, a friend, a roommate, a classmate, an instructor, a neighbor, a boss, or someone else. You may choose to write about three related qualities of the person.

Practice

Write an exemplification essay with a specific purpose and for a specific audience. Imagine that you have completed a year of college and have agreed to take part in the *college's summer orientation program for incoming students. You will be meeting with a small group of new students to help them get ready for college life. Prepare a presentation to the new students in which you make the point that college is more demanding than high school.*

Chapter 8

Process Analysis: Explaining How Something Works or Is Done

Every day you follow a series of steps in a definite order. With familiar, automatic processes such as making coffee, you are not really aware of following a specific sequence of steps. But if someone asks you for directions to a particular place, or you are trying to read and follow directions for a new electronic gadget that someone has given you, you are very aware that many steps are involved in giving information or learning something new. Your process essay teaches readers something. Process writing is a unique pattern and remarkable for its general usefulness. No other pattern of development supports its thesis with steps, and no other pattern succeeds or fails based on whether or not its readers can follow or perform its process.

8.1 Developing a Process Essay

In general, the purpose of a process essay is to explain the steps involved in an action, process, or event. Some process essays give readers instructions, others provide information, and still others focus on persuading readers. The type of essay you write depends on the purpose and topic. Most process analysis essays fall into two categories:

- A how-to essay explains how to do something to readers who want or need to perform the process. It may explain how to teach a child the alphabet, for instance. Your primary purpose in writing a how-to essay is to present the steps in the process clearly and completely so that readers can perform the task you describe.

- A how-it-works essay explains how something works to readers who want to understand the process but not actually perform it. For example, you might explain how a popular radio talk show screens its callers. Your primary purpose in writing a how-it-works essay is to present the steps in the process clearly enough so that readers can fully understand it.

Some essays contain elements of both types of process analysis. In writing about how a car alarm system works, for example, you might find it necessary to explain how to activate and deactivate the system as well as how it works.

1. Writing Your Thesis Statement for a Process Essay

A process analysis usually contains a clear thesis that identifies the process to be discussed and suggests why the process is important or useful to the reader. Writing a process-essay thesis statement could be a response to the following questions: *What*? (topic), *To* or *for whom*? (audience), and *Why*? (importance or value). The thesis for a how-to process essay could be something like this:

- Tired of takeout? Following these fairly easy steps will make the most helpless student a decent "survival cook".
- Anyone can plant a small container garden, and just about everyone will enjoy watching their flowers and plants grow day by day.

The thesis for a "how-it-works" process essay might be similar to the following:

- Learning how plant fertilizers work can make even a beginner's thumb "green" and increase the eco-friendliness of a home.
- Volunteering at a local community centre or hospital brings unexpected benefits for students.

2. Tips for Process Essays

A process analysis essay should include everything the reader needs to know to understand or perform the process. This usually means:

1) **To provide an explicit thesis statement**. In a process paper, the thesis might explain your purpose—why it is important to learn how to change the oil in your car or why learning to prepare a room for painting is worth knowing. On the other hand, it might explain something definitive about the process. For example, you might begin a paper on the digestive process by stating that, "the human body is a truly marvelous machine". Then, of course, you would have to show just how marvelous it is as you explain how it digests food.

2) **Process writing guides readers**. So consistent use of transitional words and phrases is essential. Some key types of transitions include the following:

- For a how-to process where time order is the main concern: *first, then, next, second, now, after that, finally;*
- For a how-it-works process where one step results in or causes another, or a descriptive process essay where time order shows one thing causing another: *so that, resulting in, leading to, in turn, because, with the result (or effect) that;*
- For either type of process, when an alternative or different approach or result is included: *but, however, instead, rather.*

3) **Explain each step in a separate paragraph**. If two steps are done or occur simultaneously, connect separate paragraphs with phrases such as "at the same time."
4) **Use the right verb tense**. If you are explaining something that happened only once, use the past tense: "After Mount Vesuvius erupted, it covered the city of Pompeii with pumice and ash." However, if you are discussing something that recurs, use the present tense: "During the next phase of digestion, food passes down the esophagus to the stomach."
5) **Write in the second person, directly addressing the audience as "you"**. However, if you are presenting information, as in the examples about Pompeii and digestion above, you should write in the more formal third person.

3. Function of Process Essays

1) **Express your ideas**. You can write an essay exploring how to relax after a period of hard work.
2) **Inform your reader**. You can write an essay telling them how to remain calm while giving a speech.
3) **Persuade your reader**. You can write an essay convincing them how it is important to exercise every day.

8.2 Integrating Process Analysis into an Essay

You may find it helpful to incorporate a process analysis into a discussion that relies on a different method of development. For instance, in a how-it-works essay about an alcohol abuse program for high school students, you might decide to include a brief process analysis of how alcohol impairs mental functioning. Here are a few suggestions for incorporating process analysis effectively into essays based on other methods of development.

1) **Explain only the major steps in the process** rather than every step in detail to avoid diverting readers from the primary focus of the essay.

2) **Introduce the process analysis with a transitional sentence**. Alert readers that a process analysis will follow. For example, here is how you might introduce a brief summary of the process by which AIDS spreads through HIV (human immunodeficiency virus).

For example:
- Before you explain to teenagers how to avoid contracting HIV, you need to let them know what they are avoiding. Teenagers need to know that HIV is transmitted by...

3) **Use the word *process* or *procedure***. So readers know that a process analysis is to follow. In the preceding example, the final sentence might be revised to read as follows:

For example:
- Teenagers need to know that HIV is transmitted by the following process.

4) **Once you have completed the process analysis, alert readers that you are about to return to the main topic**. You might conclude the process with a summary statement.

For example:
- Over all, teenagers need to know that HIV is transmitted through an exchange of bodily fluids.

Sample Essay

As you read this essay, notice how Lamott leads you through the steps in the writing process while at the same time revealing her attitude toward the task of writing.

Shitty First Drafts	
Very few writers really know what they are doing until they've done it. Nor do they go about their business feeling dewy and thrilled. They do not type a few stiff warm-up sentences and then find themselves bounding along like huskies across the snow. One writer I know tells me that he sits down every morning and says to himself nicely, "It's not like you don't have a choice, because you do—you can either type, or kill yourself." We all often feel like we are pulling teeth, even those writers whose prose ends up being the most natural and fluid. The right words and sentences just do not come pouring out like ticker tape most of the time. Now, Muriel Spark is said to have felt that she was taking dictation from God every morning—sitting there, one supposes, plugged into a dictaphone, typing away, humming. But this is a very hostile and aggressive position. One might hope for bad things to rain down on a person like this.	Introduction: The author presents information about her professional writing experience and the experiences of other writers.

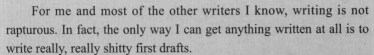

For me and most of the other writers I know, writing is not rapturous. In fact, the only way I can get anything written at all is to write really, really shitty first drafts.

The first draft is the child's draft, where you let it all pour out and then let it romp all over the place, knowing that no one is going to see it and that you can shape it later. You just let this childlike part of you channel whatever voices and visions come through and onto the page. If one of the characters wants to say, "Well, so what, Mr. Poopy Pants?" you let her. No one is going to see it. If the kid wants to get into really sentimental, weepy, emotional territory, you let him. Just get it all down on paper because there may be something great in those six crazy pages that you would never have gotten to by more rational, grown-up means. There may be something in the very last line of the very last paragraph on page six that you just love, that is so beautiful or wild that you now know what you're supposed to be writing about, more or less, or in what direction you might go — but there was no way to get to this without first getting through the first five and a half pages.

I used to write food reviews for California magazine before it folded. (My writing food reviews had nothing to do with the magazine folding, although every single review did cause a couple of canceled subscriptions. Some readers took umbrage at my comparing mounds of vegetable puree with various ex-presidents' brains.) These reviews always took two days to write. First I'd go to a restaurant several times with a few opinionated, articulate friends in tow. I'd sit there writing down everything anyone said that was at all interesting or funny. Then on the following Monday I'd sit down at my desk with my notes and try to write the review. Even after I'd been doing this for years, panic would set in. I'd try to write a lead, but instead I'd write a couple of dreadful sentences, XX them out, try again, XX everything out, and then feel despair and worry settle on my chest like an x-ray apron. It's over, I'd think calmly. I'm not going to be able to get the magic to work this time. I'm ruined. I'm through. I'm toast. Maybe, I'd think, I can get my old job back as a clerk-typist. But probably not. I'd get up and study my teeth in the mirror for a while. Then I'd stop, remember to breathe, make a few phone calls, hit the kitchen and chow down. Eventually I'd go back and sit down at my desk, and sigh for the next ten minutes. Finally I would pick up my one-inch picture frame, stare into it as if for the answer, and every time the answer would come: all I had to do was to write a really shitty first draft of, say, the opening paragraph. And no one was going to see it.

So I'd start writing without reining myself in. It was almost just typing, just making my fingers move. And the writing would be terrible. I'd write a lead paragraph that was a whole page, even though the entire review could only be three pages long, and then I'd start writing up descriptions of the food, one dish at a time, bird by bird, and the critics would be sitting on my shoulders, commenting like cartoon characters. They'd be pretending to snore, or rolling their eyes at my overwrought descriptions, no matter how hard I tried to tone those descriptions down, no matter how conscious I was of what a friend said to me gently in my early days of restaurant reviewing. "Annie," she said, "it is just a piece of chicken. It is just a bit of cake."

But because by then I had been writing for so long, I would eventually let myself trust the process—sort of, more or less. I'd write a first draft that was maybe twice as long as it should be, with a self-indulgent and boring beginning, stupefying descriptions of the meal, lots of quotes from my black-humored friends that made them sound more like the Manson girls than food lovers, and no ending to speak of. The whole thing would be so long and incoherent and hideous that for the rest of the day I'd obsess about getting creamed by a car before I could write a decent second draft. I'd worry that people would read what I'd written and believe that the accident had really been a suicide, that I had panicked because my talent was waning and my mind was shot.

The next day, I'd sit down, go through it all with a colored pen, take out everything I possibly could, find a new lead somewhere on the second page, figure out a kicky place to end it, and then write a second draft. It always turned out fine, sometimes even funny and weird and helpful. I'd go over it one more time and mail it in. Then, a month later, when it was time for another review, the whole process would start again, complete with the fears that people would find my first draft before I could rewrite it.

Almost all good writing begins with terrible first efforts. You need to start somewhere. Start by getting something—anything—down on paper. A friend of mine says that the first draft is the down draft—you just get it down. The second draft is the up draft—you fix it up. You try to say what you have to say more accurately. And the third draft is the dental draft, where you check every tooth, to see if it's loose or cramped or decayed, or even, God help us, healthy.

Revise

Proofread and write third draft if needed

Conclusion

Part Two　Strategies of Essay Development

 Practice

Choose a topic below as the basis to write a prescriptive (or how-to) process essay.
(1) How to shop for groceries in a minimum amount of time.
(2) How to do household cleaning efficiently.
(3) How to gain or lose weight.
(4) How to get over a broken heart.
(5) How to plan an event (party, wedding, garage sale, etc.).
(6) How to change daily habits to be kinder to the environment.
(7) How to find an internship (co-op position, summer job).
(8) How to manage your money while in college or university.
(9) How to deal with exam stress.

Chapter 9

Cause and Effect: Using Reasons and Results to Explain

Now, why did that happen? We ask this question every day at home, in college, and on the job in order to understand and cope with things that happen in our lives. For example, knowing why a computer crashed will help us avoid that problem, and knowing the causes and effects of a disease such as diabetes can help us control the condition. In other words, cause and effect reasoning helps us deal with everyday issues, whether large or small. Seeking to understand the reasons or causes for things as well as their consequences or effects is simply human nature. Therefore, the cause and effect method of development is one that readers will instinctively relate to.

9.1 Developing a Cause-and-Effect Essay

The type of essay you write depends on the topic and main point. If you want to tell readers the impact a person had on your life, the essay would focus on effects. If you want to explain why you moved out of your family home, it would focus on causes. Cause-and-effect essays are like process essays. However, while process papers explain how something happens, cause-and-effect papers discuss the reasons for or results of an event or situation. Cause-and-effect essays involve analysis as you examine either the causes or effects of some situation or event. Consequently, more time and attention are required at the planning stage as you work on the logical relationships of the causes or effects to the point you make in the thesis. You will work to avoid the logical errors; faulty lines of reasoning irritate the same readers who may be initially drawn to the essay.

Limit the essay to a discussion of recent, major causes or effects. In a short paper you generally don't have space to discuss minor or remote causes or effects. If, for example, you analyzed your car wreck, you might decide that the three major causes were defective brakes, a hidden yield sign, and bad weather. A minor, or remote, cause might include being slightly tired because of less-than-usual sleep, less sleep because of staying out late the night before, staying out late because of an out-of-town visitor, and so on. In some cases, you may want to mention a few of the indirect causes or effects, but do be reasonable. Concentrate on the most immediate, most important factors. Often, a writer of a 500- to 800-word essay will discuss no more than two, three, or four major causes or effects of something; trying to cover more of either frequently results in an underdeveloped essay that is not convincing.

1. Writing Your Thesis Statement for a Cause-and-Effect Essay

In a cause-and-effect essay, you develop the thesis through cause-and-effect reasoning. Essays that deal with causes set out the reasons why some debatable or interesting situation exists. When you write a "cause" thesis statement, you will usually give a brief description of the effect, then provide an argument for the correctness of the causes you offer. To be sure that such a thesis truly involves causes, test it by writing the topic and viewpoint, followed by *because*. For example: Students from Japan would find Canadian students lazy (the effect) because... (the causes). Essays that discuss effects set out the results of a similarly debatable situation or circumstance. The thesis statements will reverse the procedure for writing a thesis for a cause essay by briefly describing or discussing the causes, then presenting an argument for the rightness of effects you offer. To be sure that such a thesis truly supplies effects, test it by writing it this way: Lower standards in high school caused these results (the effects)... In both cases, remember to suggest or state directly whether the essay will deal with causes or effects.

For example:

Causes: The root causes of unsportsmanlike behavior lie in how society elevates athletes to positions of fame and heroism, making them unaccountable for their behavior.

Effects: Unsportsmanlike behavior produces negative effects on fans, other players, and the institutions they represent.

Causes and Effects: Unsportsmanlike behavior has deep roots in society's inflated regard for athletes, producing negative effects on fans, other players, and the institutions they represent.

If the thesis makes dogmatic, unsupportable claims ("This national health care plan will lead to a complete collapse of quality medical treatment") or overly broad assertions ("Peer pressure causes alcoholism among students"), you won't convince the reader. Limit or qualify the thesis whenever necessary by using such phrases as "may be" "a contributing factor" "one of the main reasons" "two important factors" and so on (e.g. "Peer pressure is *one of the major causes of* alcoholism among students").

2. Tips for Cause-and-Effect Essays

1) **Cause-and-effect essays begin with topics that are usually situations, events, or problems**. Working out logically correct causes or effects for the topic means you need to analyze before you write. You break apart the topic, and you examine its causes or effects:

   - A cause is an action or situation that provokes some result or effect—it is a stimulus. Useful synonyms for cause include *reason (why), root, factor, source, origin,* and *basis*.
   - An effect is the result of some cause, stimulus, or event—it is an outcome. Useful synonyms for effect include *consequence, result, upshot,* and *conclusion*.

   Therefore, performing a logic check on supporting points for a cause or effect thesis is necessary before drafting. List the cause and its effects in the outline, or list the effect and its causes, then make sure that the causes and effects are truly and logically related.

2) **A single cause usually involves multiple effects, and one effect is usually the result of multiple causes**. Take special care in your planning to avoid oversimplifying a cause–effect situation. For example, to blame gun violence in schools on videogames oversimplifies the case and ignores an important range of other possible causes. Similarly, generalizing from one instance to an assertion that something is always the case ignores all other possible contributing causes or effects—it bases its conclusion on insufficient evidence. Readers would likely be irritated by an essay arguing that all students are addicted to social media if it is based on a description of one student who Tweets all the time.

3) **Causes and/or effects may be nearer, or more closely related—these may be called immediate causes (or effects), or may be distant and not easy to discern—these are often called remote causes (or effects)**. In a brief essay, try to confine yourself to immediate causes or effects; while remote causes or effects may be true and logically connected, without sufficient explanation of how their connections come about, readers may have difficulty following the logic. For example: immediate causes for the sinking of the Titanic would be its collision with the iceberg and the failure of nearby ships' radio signals. More remote causes could be weather conditions and the types of

rivets used in its construction. Typically, remote causes are more speculative and less provable, another reason to avoid them.

4) **Readers of cause-and-effect essays benefit from the reinforcement that consistent use of transitions will provide.** Your attention to effective transitions will help readers see the connections you present between causes and effects as correct and logical, making the essay clearer and more persuasive.
   - Transitions for causes essays: *first, another, because (of), among (the causes), factoring (into), causing, creating;*
   - Transitions for effects essays: *consequently, then, as a consequence, so, resulting (from), as a result, thus, therefore.*

Remember, if you choose chronological (sequential) order or order of importance for causes or effects, you have additional transitions at your disposal:
   - Chronological order: *first, second, next, then, after, in addition, another;*
   - Order of importance: *more than, even more, better (worse), particularly, significantly.*

3. Function of Cause-and-Effect Essays

1) **Express your ideas**. You can write an essay about the effects of winning a large cash prize in a national contest.
2) **Inform your reader**. You can write a memo to your supervisor at work analyzing the reasons of preventing employees from working overtime.
3) **Persuade your reader**. You can write a letter to the dean of academic affairs about a problem at the school, discussing causes, effects, or both and proposing a solution to the problem.

9.2 Integrating Cause and Effect into an Essay

Although some of the essays will focus solely on causal analysis, other essays will combine cause and effect with other patterns. For example, in an essay comparing two popular magazines that have different journalistic styles, you might explain the effects of each style on the reading experience. Use the following tips to integrate causal analyses into essays that rely on other patterns of development.

1) **Introduce the causal analysis.** Use transitional words and expressions to prepare readers for a causal explanation. For example, in writing about the college president's decision to expand the Career Planning Center, you might introduce the discussion of causes by writing, "Three primary factors were responsible for her decision."

2) **Keep the causal explanation direct and simple.** Since the overall purpose is not to explore causal relationships, an in-depth analysis of causes and effects will distract readers from the main point. So focus on only the most important causes and effects.
3) **Use causal analysis to emphasize why particular points or ideas are important.** For example, if you are writing an explanation of how to hold a successful yard sale, readers are more likely to follow your advice to keep the house locked and valuables concealed if you include anecdotes and statistics that demonstrate the effects of not doing so (such as thefts and break-ins during such sales).

Sample Essay

In the following essay, the writer explains why working in a local motel damaged her self-esteem, despite her attempts to do a good job. Note that the writer uses many vivid examples and specific details to show the reader how she was treated and, consequently, how such treatment made her feel.

It's Simply Not Worth It

It's hard to find a job these days, and with our county's unemployment rate reaching as high as seven percent, most people feel obligated to "take what they can get". But after working as a maid at a local motel for almost a year and a half, I decided no job is worth keeping if it causes a person to doubt his or her worth. My hard work rarely received recognition or appreciation, I was underpaid, and I was required to perform some of the most disgusting cleaning tasks imaginable. These factors caused me to devalue myself as a person and ultimately motivated me to return to school in hope of regaining my self-respect.	Introduction: Her job as a motel maid Thesis: No appreciation, low pay, disgusting tasks (causes) produce damaged self-esteem and action (effects)
It may be obvious to say, but I believe that when a maid's hours of meticulous cleaning are met only with harsh words and complaints, she begins to lose her sense of self-esteem. I recall the care I took in making the motel's beds, imagining them as globs of clay and molding them into impeccable pieces of art. I would teeter from one side of a bed to the other, over and over again, until I smoothed out every intruding wrinkle or tuck. And the mirrors—I would vigorously massage the glass, erasing any toothpaste splotches or oil smudges that might draw my customer's disapproval. I would scrutinize the mirror first from the left side, then I'd move to the right side, once more to the	Cause one: Lack of appreciation

left until every possible angle ensured an unclouded reflection. And so my efforts went, room after room. But, without fail, each day more than one customer would approach me, not with praise for my tidy beds or spotless mirrors, but with nitpicking complaints that undermined my efforts: "Young lady, I just checked into Room 143 and it only has one ashtray. Surely for $69.95 a night you people can afford more ashtrays in the rooms."

If it wasn't a guest complaining about ashtrays, it was an impatient customer demanding extra towels or a fussy stay-over insisting his room be cleaned by the time he returned from breakfast at 8:00 am "Can't you come to work early to do it?" he would urge thoughtlessly. Day after day, my spotless rooms went unnoticed, with no spoken rewards for my efforts from either guests or management. Eventually, the ruthless complaints and thankless work began wearing me down. In my mind, I became a servant undeserving of gratitude.

The lack of spoken rewards was compounded by the lack of financial rewards. The $7.30/hour appraisal of my worth was simply not enough to support my financial needs or my self-esteem. The measly $3.65 I earned for cleaning one room took a lot of rooms to add up, and by the end of the month I was barely able to pay my bills and buy some food. (My mainstay became ninety-two cent, generic macaroni and cheese dinners.) Because the flow of travelers kept the motel full for only a few months of the year, during some weeks I could only work half time, making a mere $584.00 a month. As a result, one month I was forced to request an extension on my rent payment. Unsympathetically, my landlord threatened to evict me if I didn't pay. Embarrassed, yet desperate, I went to a friend and borrowed money. I felt uneasy and awkward and regretted having to beg a friend for money. I felt like a mooch and a bum; I felt degraded. And the constant reminder from management that there were hundreds of people standing in unemployment lines who would be more than willing to work for minimum wage only aided in demeaning me further.

In addition to the thankless work and the inadequate salary, I was required to clean some of the most sickening messes. Frequently, conventions for high school clubs booked the motel. Once I opened the door of a conventioneer's room one morning and almost gagged at the odor. I immediately beheld a trail of vomit that began at the bedside and ended just short of the bathroom door. At that moment I cursed the

Cause two: Low pay

Cause three: Repulsive duties

inventor of shag carpet, for I knew it would take hours to comb this mess out of the fibers. On another day I spent thirty minutes dislodging the bed linen from the toilet where it had been stuffed. And I spent what seemed like hours removing from one of my spotless mirrors the lipstick-drawn message that read, "Yorktown Tigers are number one." But these inconsiderate acts were relaying another message, a message I took personally: "Lady, you're not worth the consideration—you're a maid and you're not worth respecting."

I've never been afraid to work hard or do jobs that weren't particularly "fun". But the line must be drawn when a person's view of herself becomes clouded with feelings of worthlessness. The thankless efforts, the inadequate wage, and the disgusting work were just parts of a total message that degraded my character and caused me to question my worth. Therefore, I felt compelled to leave this demeaning job in search of a way to rebuild my self-confidence. Returning to school has done just that for me. As my teachers and fellow students take time to listen to my ideas and compliment my responses, I feel once again like a vital, valued, and worthwhile person. I feel human once more.

Conclusion: Review of the problem and a brief explanation of the solution she chose

Practice

Provide brief causes or effects for at least two of the eight statements below. Make sure that you have three separate and distinct items for the statement. Don't provide two rewordings that essentially the same thing.

(1) Many youngsters are terrified of school.
(2) Young people tend to get married later in life than their parents used to.
(3) Society would benefit if nonviolent criminals were punished in ways other than jail time.
(4) My relationship with (name a relative or friend) has changed over time.
(5) Growing up in my family has influenced my life in significant ways.
(6) A bad (or good) teacher can have long-lasting impact on a student.
(7) The average workweek should be no more than forty hours.
(8) It is easy to fall into an unhealthy diet living under too much stress.

Chapter 10

Comparison or Contrast: Showing Similarities or Differences

Comparison and contrast aren't new to you; they are extremely common ways of thinking. Actually, you analyze similarities and differences when you make everyday decisions (when you shop for a pair of jeans or select a sandwich in the cafeteria) as well as when you make important decisions (deciding which college to attend or which person to date). The purpose of comparing or contrasting is to understand each of the two things more clearly and, at times, to make judgments about them. Sometimes you use comparison and contrast to describe something new: by telling readers how a thing is similar to or different from something they know, you can help them understand the new thing. For instance, to explain a rotary automobile engine, you'd probably compare and contrast it to the conventional automobile engine. However, besides explaining something new, comparison and contrast also appear frequently in decision making: Because A and B share some characteristics but differ in others, one is better and the other worse. When you chose the college you're attending, you probably compared and contrasted available schools, and most likely you'll use comparison and contrast again when you choose your major.

Using comparison and contrast involves looking at similarities (comparison), differences (contrast), or both. Comparison or contrast writing begins with the way you ordinarily think about things. Writing about two sides of an issue or about two related topics, however, is more demanding than discussing them. In this respect, examples in advertisements or magazine articles are misleading: comparisons between Toyota and Honda models, for example, could be set out as bulleted points opposite each other. You read both lists and compare a bulleted item in one column with the bulleted point in the other column. Writing essays, though, does not set out bulleted points but rather topics and supporting details for each point so that readers can compare or contrast along with you.

10.1 Methods of Development

A comparison or contrast essay calls for one of two types of development. Details can be presented one side at a time or point by point. Each format is illustrated below.

1. Block Pattern (One-Side-at-a-Time)

The one-side-at-a-time structure may be used either for the supporting paragraphs or for the entire essay. In both cases, the one-side-at-a-time method presents all the points for one side followed by all the points for the other side. Look at the following supporting paragraph of an essay "A Vote for McDonald's":

For one thing, going to the Chalet is more difficult than going to McDonald's. The Chalet has a jacket-and-tie rule, which means I have to dig a sport coat and tie out of the back of my closet, make sure they're semiclean, and try to steam out the wrinkles somehow. The Chalet also requires reservations. Since it is downtown, I have to leave an hour early to give myself time to find a parking space within six blocks of the restaurant. The Chalet cancels reservations if a party is more than ten minutes late. Going to McDonald's, on the other hand, is easy. I can feel comfortable wearing my jeans or warm-up suit. I don't have to do any advance planning. I can leave my house whenever I'm ready and pull into a doorside parking space within fifteen minutes.

The first half of this paragraph fully explains one side of the contrast (the difficulty of going to the Chalet). The second half of the paragraph deals entirely with the other side (the ease of going to McDonald's). When you use this method, be sure to follow the same order of points of contrast (or comparison) for each side. An outline of the paragraph shows how the points for each side are developed in a consistent sequence.

Outline

One Side at a Time
Thesis: Going to the Chalet is more difficult than going to McDonald's.
  I. Chalet
     1. Dress code
     2. Advance reservations

3. Leave an hour early

   4. Find parking space

II. McDonald's

   1. Casual dress

   2. No reservations

   3. Leave only fifteen minutes ahead of time

   4. Plenty of free parking

2. Point-by-Point Pattern

Now look at the supporting paragraph below, which is taken from an essay "Studying: Then and Now":

Ordinary studying during the term is another area where I've made changes. In high school, I let reading assignments go. I told myself that I'd have no trouble catching up on two hundred pages during a fifteen-minute ride to school. College courses have taught me to keep pace with the work. Otherwise, I feel as though I'm sinking into a quicksand of unread material. When I finally read the high school assignment, my eyes would run over the words but my brain would be plotting how to get the car for Saturday night. Now, I use several techniques that force me to really concentrate on my reading.

The paragraph contrasts two styles of studying point by point. The following outline illustrates the point-by-point method.

Outline

Point-by-Point

Thesis: Studying is something I do differently in college than in high school.

I. Keeping up with reading assignments

   1. High school

   2. College

II. Concentration while reading

   1. High school

   2. College

3. Which Pattern Should You Use

As you prepare to compose the first draft, you might ask yourself, "Which pattern of organization should I choose—Point-by-Point or Block?" Indeed, this is not your simple "paper or plastic" supermarket choice. It's an important question—to which there is no single, easy answer. For most writers, choosing the appropriate pattern of organization involves thinking time in the prewriting stage, before beginning a draft. Many times, the essay's subject matter itself will suggest the most effective method of development. The Block Pattern might be the better choice when a complete, overall picture of each subject is desirable. For example, you might decide that the "then-and-now" essay (the disastrous first day at a new job contrasted with your success at that job today) would be easier for readers to understand if the description of "then" (the first day) was presented in its entirety, followed by the contrasting discussion of "now" (current success). On the other hand, the essay topic might best be discussed by presenting a number of distinct points for the reader to consider one by one. Essays that evaluate, that argue the superiority or advantage of one thing over another ("A cat is a better pet for students than a dog because..."), often lend themselves to the Point-by-Point Pattern because each of the writer's claims may be clearly supported by the side-by-side details.

However, none of the preceding advice always holds true. There are no hard-and-fast rules governing this rhetorical choice. Each writer must decide which method of organization works best in any particular comparison/contrast essay. Before drafting begins, therefore, writers are wise to sketch out an informal outline or rough plan using one method and then the other to see which is more effective. By spending time in the prewriting stage "auditioning" each method of development, you may spare yourself the frustration of writing an entire draft whose organization doesn't work well for your topic. Therefore, remember that an outline is an essential step in planning and writing a clearly organized paper.

4. Using Analogy to Compare

If you point out similarities between (compare) things that are otherwise quite different (for example, Forrest Gump's statement, "Life is like a box of chocolates.") you are creating an analogy. An analogy is a special form of comparison in which one part of the comparison is used simply to explain the other, as in the following example:

In like manner, geologists will sometimes use **the calendar year** as a unit to represent the time scale, and in such terms the Precambrian runs from New Year's Day until well after Halloween. Dinosaurs appear in the middle of December and are gone the day after Christmas. The last ice sheet melts on December 31st at one minute before midnight, and the Roman Empire lasts five seconds. With **your arms spread wide**... to represent all time on earth, look at one hand with its line of life. The Cambrian begins in the wrist, and the Permian Extinction is at the outer end of the palm. All of the Cenozoic is in a fingerprint, and in a single stroke with a medium-grained nail file you could eradicate human history. Geologists live with the geologic scale. Individually, they may or may not be alarmed by the rate of exploitation of the things they discover, but, like the environmentalists, they use these repetitive analogies to place the human record in perspective—to see the Age of Reflection, the last few thousand years, as a small bright sparkle at the end of time.

This passage uses two analogies—the twelve-month calendar and the distance along two widespread arms—to explain the duration of geologic time. For another example, in the passage below, an analogy is made to explain a complex or unfamiliar phenomenon (how the immune system works) in terms of a familiar one (how mall security works).

For example:

The human body is like a mall, and the immune system is like mall security. Because the mall has hundreds of employees and thousands of customers, security guards must rely on photo IDs, name tags, and uniforms to decide who should be allowed to open cash registers and who should have access to the vault. In the same way, white blood cells and antibodies need to use DNA cues to recognize which cells belong in a body and which do not. Occasionally security guards make mistakes, wrestling Kookie the Klown to the ground while DVD players "walk" out of the service entrance, but these problems amount only to allergic reactions or little infections. If security guards become hypervigilant, detaining every customer and employee, the situation is akin to leukemia, in which white blood cells attack healthy cells. If security guards become corrupt, letting thieves take a "five-finger discount," the situation is akin to AIDS. Both systems—mall security and human immunity—work by correctly differentiating friend from foe.

Analogies are not limited to abstract, scientific concepts. Writers often use analogies to make nontechnical descriptions and explanations more vivid or to make an imaginative point of comparison that serves a larger argument. Consider the following examples:

- But now that government has largely withdrawn its "handouts" (to the welfare poor), now that the overwhelming majority of the poor are out there toiling in Wal-Mart or Wendy's—well, what are we to think of them? Disapproval and condescension no longer apply, so what outlook makes sense?
- The "working poor", as they are approvingly termed, are in fact the **major philanthropists** of our society. They neglect their own children so that the children of others will be cared for; they live in substandard housing so that other homes will be shiny and perfect; they endure privation so that inflation will be low and stock prices high. To be a member of the working poor is to be an anonymous donor, a nameless benefactor, to everyone else. As Gail, one of my restaurant coworkers put it, "you give and you give."

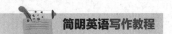

This passage suggests that the working poor in the United States are among society's "major philanthropists". Analogies are tricky. They can be useful, but they are rarely consistently accurate at all major points of comparison. For example, in the preceding analogy, the working poor can be seen as philanthropists in the sense that they have "made a great sacrifice" but not in the sense that they are selflessly sharing their wealth. Analogies can powerfully bring home a point, but skilled writers use them with caution. Nevertheless, you will run across analogies regularly; indeed, it would be hard to find a book without at least one. Analogies come in a variety of lengths, from several sentences to an entire essay, depending upon the writer's purpose. For abstract information and in certain writing situations, analogy is often the writing strategy of choice. As you practice the writing, you may find that incorporating an analogy into one of the essays is an effective way to explain, emphasize, or help support an idea.

10.2 Developing a Comparison or Contrast Essay

Writers of comparison and contrast essays often wish to convince readers that something—a restaurant, a movie, a product—is better (or worse) than something else: "Mom's Haven is a better place to eat than McPhony's." But not all comparison or contrast essays assert the absolute superiority or inferiority of the subjects. Sometimes writers simply want to point out the similarities or differences in two or more people, places, or objects, and that's fine, too—as long as the writer avoids the "so-what" thesis problem.

The purpose of a comparison or contrast essay is to make a point by showing readers that two distinct items are either similar or different. Whether you choose to compare or contrast two items depends on the specific point you want to convey to readers. Suppose, for instance, the main point of the essay is that home-cooked hamburgers are superior to fast-food burgers. To convince the audience of your claim, you might contrast the two items, pointing out those differences—price, taste, and nutrition—that make the homemade dish better. If, however, the main point is that tap water is just as good as store-bought bottled water, you could compare the two, pointing out the similarities that support the main point. Tap water and bottled water, for example, might be equally clean, fresh, and mineral-rich. In both examples above, comparing or contrasting is used to convince readers of a larger main point.

In other words, tell readers your point and then use comparison or contrast to support that idea; don't just compare or contrast items in a vacuum. Ask yourself, "What is the significant point I want readers to learn or understand from reading this comparison/contrast essay? Why do they need to know this?"

1. Writing Your Thesis Statement for a Comparison or Contrast Essay

In academic writing, comparison and contrast are valuable because they offer readers a new way to see familiar concepts or things. Writing an effective thesis for such an essay requires you to have a purpose for examining and interpreting the results of setting up likenesses and/or differences. That purpose is crucial; it becomes your point, your thesis.

That purpose will usually emerge during prewriting stage. As you work on the comparison/contrast essay, ask yourself, *What did I learn from this? Why did I compare or contrast these?* or *What important or significant ideas emerged from putting these two ideas together?* The thesis communicates what you learned. A comparison or contrast thesis does not announce "A and B are very different", or "A and B have important similarities". Neither of these offers a point derived from comparing or contrasting. Instead, an effective thesis offers readers what the writer discovered from setting one thing up against another—that "something new" is the writer's purpose. For example, "A and B's similarities are so pronounced that buyers could easily be fooled..." Therefore, a formula for a comparison/contrast thesis might be:

> Topic + intention to compare or contrast + suggestion or statement of outcome/ discovery gained from comparing and/or contrasting

In some cases, it might also be appropriate to mention the basis of comparison and/or contrast. Examples of a comparison essay's thesis would be:

- The coverage of the student walk-out in the *Vancouver Sun* and the *Vancouver Province* was so similar that the reporters might have plagiarized each other.
- Similar appeals in commercials for three popular breakfast cereals reveal America's obsession with fitness and health.
- Although the mechanical structure of the rotary automobile engine is obviously different from that of the conventional automobile engine, the rotary engine offers little worthwhile improvement.

Examples of a contrast essay's thesis would be:

- The contrasts between the cooking styles of the two chefs are so pronounced that diners often do not recognize a dish they ordered previously.
- The contrast between the two cities Niagara Falls, Ontario, and Niagara Falls, New York, demonstrates two different approaches to appreciating nature and preserving the environment.

Although they both depend on internal combustion, the rotary automobile engine is a significant improvement over the conventional automobile engine.

2. Tips for Comparison and Contrast Essays

1) **Develop a viewpoint about what you are comparing or contrasting.** For a successful essay, you must decide what point you wish to make and what you have learned as you focus on similarities or differences. For example, if you are listing points to compare a year you spent in high school with the year you are now spending in university, you may find that there are good points about both experiences. Gradually, you may emerge with a thesis stating that both forms of education have value but in different ways.

2) **Comparison or contrast essays present two items or ideas that have a common basis for consideration.** You analyze those items or ideas for appropriate points of comparison or contrast. Presenting three or more items or ideas involves the Division and Classification method of development.

3) **As for other methods of development involving analysis, prepare for a comparison or contrast essay by creating a two-column outline.** Clarify the basis for comparing or contrasting so that you can express it in a few words. Now, set up two columns, place the basis-for-comparison phrase at the top of the page or screen, then note the points of comparison or contrast as numbered items opposite each other in the columns. Finally, add point-form notes of the supporting details under each point of comparison for each side. With this type of outline, you will see clearly whether or not both sides or both items are accurately compared or contrasted.

4) **To keep readers with you as you show similarities (comparisons) and differences (contrasts).** Use transitions appropriately at the sentence-to-sentence level.
   - To emphasize similarity, use *similarly, just as... so, like, just like, likewise, in the same way, in addition,* and *also;*
   - To emphasize difference, use *in contrast (to), unlike, but, in opposition to, on the other hand, however, conversely,* and *on the contrary.*

5) **Analogies interest readers just because of the apparent unlikeliness of the comparison.** On the other hand, if you contrast two items that seem quite similar, you may also intrigue readers by surprising them with the differences you discover.

3. Function of Comparison or Contrast Essays

1) **Express your ideas**. You can compare the lifestyle today with the lifestyle you intend to follow after you graduate from college.

2) **Inform your reader**. You can compare resources available through the college library

with those available on the open Web.

3) **Persuade your reader**. You can compare two views on a controversial issue, arguing in favor of one of them, or compare two methods of doing something (such as disciplining a child or training a pet), arguing that one method is more effective than the other.

10.3 Integrating Comparison or Contrast into an Essay

Although you will write some essays using comparison and contrast as the primary pattern of development, in most cases you will integrate comparison or contrast into essays that rely on other patterns, such as description, process analysis, or argument. Comparison or contrast can be particularly effective in persuasive essays. Use the following tips to incorporate comparison or contrast into essays based on other patterns of development.

1) **Determine the purpose of the comparison or contrast**. What will it contribute to the essay?
2) **Introduce the comparison or contrast clearly**. Use transitional words and expressions to guide readers into the comparison or contrast and then back to the essay's primary pattern of development, and tell readers how the comparison or contrast supports the main point. Do not leave it to the audience to figure out why you have included the comparison.
3) **Keep the comparison or contrast short and to the point**. Avoid distracting readers from the main message.
4) **Organize the points of the comparison or contrast appropriately**. Use point-by-point or subject-by-subject organization, even though the comparison or contrast is part of a larger essay.

Sample Essay

Because there are two popular ways to develop comparison/contrast essays, this section offers two essays so that each pattern is illustrated.

Block Pattern

The essay compares kinds of school classes. Note how the writer deals first with one kind of class and its elements (teacher, students, results), then another. The essay is short enough that readers don't get lost in all the differences.

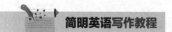

Learning or Not: Active and Passive Classes

Everyone who has gone to school knows that some classes are better, more interesting, livelier than others. We have all sat through classes where we learned little except the facts and to be quiet. We also have been part of classes where we actively learned by being challenged by teachers and the subject to learn for ourselves. Although classes often seem outwardly alike in having a teacher, in having some students, and in producing some results, the differences between passive and active classes are enormous.

Passive Classes

The passive kind of class usually has a teacher who lectures, puts outlines and terms on the chalkboard, and dispenses information to the students. Like my sophomore biology teacher, Mrs. Noguida, who rarely looked up from the orange notebook in which she had carefully typed all her lectures, teachers in a passive classroom simply dictate information and answers. They tell the students how to think and what to think. They pour facts into the students like water into a sieve. The students are forced, usually by the teacher's authority, to sit, listen, take notes, and regurgitate only what the teacher has said.

The only kinds of questions are about form: "What is the work in subpoint (1)?" or "How do you spell minuscule?" The results in such a class are measured by multiple-choice or true-false questions, or questions that require memorized answers: "What is Newton's First Law?" "What are the three causes of the American Civil War?" The results in such classes are also measured by how quickly the students forget the facts they had poured into them.

Active Classes

The other kind of class, the active kind, usually has a teacher who stimulates the students to learn for themselves by asking students questions, by posing problems, and most of all by being a student, too. Such a teacher might plan the outline of a course, but doesn't force the class in only one direction. Instead, like Ms. Cerrillo, my junior history teacher, a teacher in an active class uses the discussion to lead to learning. Instead of lecturing on the causes of the Civil War, Ms. Cerrillo gave us a list of books and articles and said, "Find out what caused the Civil War." We had to search for ourselves, find some answers, then discuss what we found in class. From the discussions, we all learned more than just the facts; we also learned how complex the causes were.

Students in active classes like that become more involved in their learning; they ask questions about why and how. The results in the active

	Introduction
	Thesis
	Teaching methods of teachers
	Learning methods of students
	Teaching methods of teachers
	Learning methods of students

130

Part Two Strategies of Essay Development

class are usually measured by essay answers, individual projects, and a change in attitude on the students' part. Learning becomes fun; although students may forget the facts just as quickly, their attitudes toward learning and their excitement in developing answers for themselves don't end with the last class. We all remember having to learn that "4 x 9=36" and having to memorize dates such as 1914—1918. And those kinds of classes are important for laying some groundwork, but not much true learning takes place there. There is a difference between knowing a fact and understanding it. Despite their outward similarities, the passive kind of class is clearly inferior to the active one for helping students understand the world around them.	Conclusion: The passive kind of class is clearly inferior to the active one for helping students understand the world around them

Point-by Point-Pattern

As you read, note the author's use of concrete details and examples to support the comparative analysis. How successfully does the author communicate her point? Did the essay cause you to reconsider your own study habits?

When It's Time to Study, Get Out of Your Pajamas	
On the surface, home seems like the best place to get work done: you don't have to get out of your pajamas, and everything you need is right there, from textbooks to snacks to a bathroom you don't have to wait in line for. You don't have to worry about traveling to a good study spot or finding a good seat when you get there. But when you compare working at home with working in a public place, the increased organization and focus that you need to work in public makes up for the inconvenience of taking your work with you.	Introduction Thesis
The first advantage of working in public is going from hanging out at home mode to working and studying mode. Putting effort into getting ready to go—getting dressed, organizing your materials, the travel time to where you're going—is like getting your study game face on. Though many people are most comfortable studying in cozy clothes, pajamas get you ready for sleeping and eating pancakes. Showering, putting on fresh clothes and a pair of shoes gets you ready for facing your to-do list. A better-organized study session is also a more effective one. At home, if you need something, such as a book or highlighter, you can always stop what you're doing and get it, no matter what room	Point 1: Mindset: Working and studying mode vs. hanging out at home mode

it's in. But interrupting your work flow to find something that should already be close by is both a waste of time and an easy way to get distracted. It's better to consider exactly which supplies and materials you need to get the work done before you begin and to put everything in one bag to take with you. There is also the advantage of not being surrounded by lots of other things you might like to do—dishes, other work that's due later, the marble collection you've been meaning to organize—and being in a place where you can only interact with what you need to get done.

Of course, once you've made your way to the destination—maybe it's a favorite coffee shop, or a quiet floor of the library—you are going to be surrounded by lots of other people, more than you're likely to have around you at home. Luckily, strangers will be much more respectful of the boundaries than a roommate or family member who might only see the unfinished chores or the conversation they've been meaning to have with you once you're both home. It's much harder to say no to people you know than to strangers. No one in the coffee shop will ask you to do anything other than maybe move your books off a chair or watch their laptop while they use the bathroom. Second of all, there's a good chance all these other people share the same goal of working quietly and making the most of their time. Your roommates, on the other hand, might have plans to binge—watch a TV series you haven't caught up on or get ready for a night out. Besides being distracted by the noise, it can be frustrating to be around others who can focus on fun when you need to get work done. Even if you live alone, studying in public, surrounding yourself with others who have the same goals of getting work done can make you feel less lonely than you might if you study at home alone. It might even be motivating.

Point 2: Surrounding people: respectful quiet strangers vs. talkative friends and family

Wherever you work, you will need to take breaks, and a public place is more likely to provide you with shorter ones. At a coffee shop, you can reward yourself for getting through a chapter by buying yourself a treat. If you need a longer break, you can walk from one end of the library to the other or find a friend studying nearby to have lunch with before you both return to work. At home, a break is more likely to involve a household chore, which might lead to another household chore, like the way watching one episode of that half-hour show will lead you to watch the next four of them. Even though it might cost you a little bit of money, the study breaks you take in public are less likely to be as distracting as the ones you would take at home.

Point 3: Duration of breaks: short breaks vs. time-consuming breaks

Part Two Strategies of Essay Development

There's a big advantage to learning to study anywhere, of course. But the focus and organization required to work in public encourages you to be a more efficient and attentive worker. Even if you factor in commuting time, working at home can be a bigger waste of time in the end. The efforts you put into leaving your house and committing to getting work accomplished will show in the work itself. So, the next time you're up against an important school project, consider leaving your home to best focus on your work.	Conclusion: Summary of the advantages of working or studying in a public place

Practice

Write an essay of comparison or contrast on one of these following topics.

(1) Two teachers you've had.
(2) Two stages of education you've received.
(3) Two restaurants you've eaten in.
(4) Two parenting styles you've observed.
(5) Two friends you've had.
(6) Two pets you've had or seen.
(7) Two sports you're acquainted with.
(8) Two singers or bands you've heard.
(9) Two forms of communication.
(10) Two ways of spending.
(11) Two places you've lived.

Chapter 11

Definition: Explaining What You Mean

In talking with other people, we sometimes offer informal definitions to explain just what we mean by a particular term. Suppose, for example, we say to a friend, "Larry is really an inconsiderate person." We might then explain what we mean by "inconsiderate" by saying, "He borrowed my accounting book 'overnight' but didn't return it for a week. And when I got it back, it was covered with coffee stains." Definitions clarify what you mean when you use a word in a specific situation. The meanings of words can be elastic, changing with your intention and the context. You live in a world of newly coined words and terminologies as well as constant redefinitions of terms—consider awesome, for example. Frequently, however, you will find it necessary to provide an extended definition—that is, a longer, more detailed explanation that thoroughly defines the subject. For example, if you wanted to define the term happiness, you would probably have trouble coming up with a brief definition because the emotion is experienced in a wide variety of situations, and the term may mean different things to different people. Hence, you could explore the term in an essay and explain what it means to you.

11.1 Developing a Definition Essay

Most forms of academic writing—from essays and reports to proposals and literature reviews—include brief (one- or two-sentence) definitions of terms. Meanwhile, some essays are developed through the extended definitions to clarify, and deepen readers' understanding of a term—whether the term refers to something concrete or abstract. The main purpose of a definition essay is to explain your understanding of a term or concept.

You might define a complex, abstract concept such as *heroism* by giving concrete examples of it, helping readers see what the term connotes to you. Or you might give a new twist to a familiar term such as *homemade* by presenting a series of narratives—anecdotes about homemade things and their qualities. As with many methods of development, your purpose is to persuade the audience that the definition is a legitimate one. Definition essays extend and formalize the process of explaining and clarifying, expanding on the understanding and use of a term in a more complete and structured way. In a written definition, you make clear in a more complete and formal way your own personal understanding of a term. Such a definition typically starts with one meaning of a term. The meaning is then illustrated with a series of details. Keep in mind that a definition essay does not simply repeat a word's dictionary meaning. Instead, it conveys what a particular term means to you. For example, if you were to write about the term *patriotism*, you might begin by presenting the definition of the word. You might say patriotism means displaying the flag, or supporting the government. Or perhaps you think patriotism is about becoming politically active and questioning government policy. Whatever definition you choose, be sure to provide specific instances so that readers can fully understand your meaning of the term. For example, in writing an essay on patriotism, you might describe three people whom you see as truly patriotic. Writing about each person will help ensure that readers see and understand the term as you do.

1. Writing Your Thesis Statement for a Definition Essay

The thesis statement for a definition essay identifies the subject (term being defined) and provides a brief, general statement of the writer's understanding of that term's meaning. Effective thesis statements, depending on the subject:

- place a term within a larger category of like things,

or
- specify a term's meaning by stating what it is and what it is not,

or
- explain the origin of the term.

This is an example of a definition thesis statement that places its subject (or term) within a larger category of like things:

- Anger is an intense emotion.

This is an example of a definition thesis statement that states what the subject is and what it is not:

- A good friend is honest and caring, never harsh or smothering.

This is an example of a definition thesis statement that explains the origin of the term/subject:

- Being consistently virtuous requires strength of character; in fact, *virtus*, the Latin root of the word virtue, means strength.

Definition essay thesis statements may also suggest the writer's point of view by suggesting his or her reason for presenting a more detailed definition, e.g., "… baseball fans seem to define insanity because they are insanely loyal."

2. Tips for Definition Essays

1) **Use the definition method and every other method of development.** You could narrate a brief anecdote to explain what you mean by "courage", or you might describe, in an essay about environmental management, the appearance of a deforested area. You will naturally use various types of examples to explain any term you define, and you may contrast what the word *discipline* means with its opposite for a psychology paper based on definition.

2) **Definition essays aim to precisely clarify a writer's ideas about the meaning of some term, concept, or process.** Therefore, it is more appropriate for writers to place their emphasis on the topic being defined, on clarifying their ideas, rather than on their connection to the topic. Writing in the third person voice is preferable. Although the definition or interpretation of something may derive from your own experiences, you need not assert your presence as *I* in the definition or support.

3) **Use a number of techniques, such as differentiation, determining boundaries, use of synonyms, and exploring connotations or shades of meanings.** This broad menu allows you to select a way of managing the meanings of the topic that will suit the purpose and audience.

4) **Dictionary definitions are useful, but not as part of opening sentences ("According to Oxford… ").** Because they often display two techniques you may wish to incorporate in writing your own definition. As we know, dictionary definitions usually show a word in its category or a larger group of similar things, then show how it differs from those similar items. Differentiating means saying what something is not so as to clarify what it is, e.g., a food sensitivity is not a true food allergy.

5) **Create a definition by setting out a limited or specific meaning for some term.** Set your own boundaries around what that term or concept will mean for the essay; this is sometimes called a stipulative definition because it sets out meanings on which the content of a paper will depend.

6) **Work through a variety of synonyms for the topic.** When you do so, you are imitating a typical conversational or teaching pattern: the speaker uses a new word, then gives a number of synonyms so that listeners can home in on words familiar to

them. For instance, a professor might use a somewhat unfamiliar word like *mendacity*, then offer a list of such words as *deceit, dishonesty, fraudulence,* and *untruthfulness* so that students will connect one or more of those words to the new term.

7) **The key to successful definition is specificity of supporting detail.** Definitions make ideas specific by setting boundaries around them, and are as precise as possible in capturing the essence of a term's meaning.

3. Function of Definition Essays

1) **Express your ideas.** You can choose a specific audience and write an essay defining and expressing your views on *parenting*.
2) **Inform your reader.** You can write an essay defining a term from a sport, hobby, or form of entertainment for a classmate who is unfamiliar with the term.
3) **Persuade your reader.** You can write an essay for readers of the local newspaper in which you define *age discrimination* and demonstrate that the problem is either increasing or decreasing in your community.

11.2 Integrating Definition into an Essay

Because of the importance of establishing clear definitions to communicate effectively, nearly any method of development will make use of definition. Including standard or extended definitions in writing that is based on other patterns of development is common. For example, you may need to include a definition in a response to an essay exam question. Definitions should also be included when terms are likely to be unfamiliar to the reader or when terms may be understood differently than intended. The following kinds of terms usually require definition.

- **Judgmental or controversial terms**. Define terms that imply a judgment or that may be controversial. If you describe a policy as "fiscally unsound", for example, make clear whether you mean "spending more money than we earn" "paying an interest rate that is too high", or something else.
- **Technical terms**. When writing for a general audience, define specialized terms that readers may find unfamiliar. In law, for example, you may need to define terms like *writ, deposition, hearing,* and *plea* for a general audience.
- **Abstract terms**. Terms that refer to ideas or concepts, such as *loyalty, heroism,* and *conformity,* may need to be defined because they can seem vague or mean different things to different people.

Part Two Strategies of Essay Development

In general, if you are not sure whether a term needs a definition, include one. You may choose to provide the definition in a separate sentence or section, or you can incorporate a brief definition or synonym into a sentence, using commas, dashes, or parentheses to set off the definition.

For example:

- Implicit memory, or the nonconscious retention of information about prior experiences, is important in eyewitness accounts of crimes.
- Empathy—a shared feeling of joy for people who are happy or distress for people who are in pain—explains the success of many popular films.

Sample Essay

A writer with an interest in running wrote the following essay defining "runner's high". Note that he uses several methods to define his subject, one that is difficult to explain to those who have not experienced it firsthand.

Blind Paces

After running the Mile-Hi ten-kilometer race in my hometown, I spoke with several of the leading runners about their experiences in the race. While most of them agreed that the course, which passed through a beautifully wooded yet overly hilly country area, was difficult, they also agreed that it was one of the best races of their running careers. They could not, however, explain why it was such a wonderful race but could rather only mumble something about the tall trees, cool air, and sandy path. When pressed, most of them didn't even remember specific details about the course, except the start and finish, and ended their descriptions with a blank—but contented—stare. This self-satisfied, yet almost indescribable, feeling is often the result of an experienced runner running, a feeling often called, because of its similarities to other euphoric experiences, "runner's high".	Introduction: An example and a general definition of the term
Because this experience is seemingly impossible to define, perhaps a description of what runner's high is not might, by contrast, lead to a better understanding of what it is. I clearly remember—about five years ago—when I first took up running. My first day, I donned my tennis shorts, ragged T-shirt, and white discount-store tennis shoes somewhat ashamedly, knowing that they were symbolic of my novice status. I plodded around my block—just over a half mile—in a little more than four minutes, feeling and regretting every painful step. My shins and thighs revolted at every jarring move, and my lungs wheezed	Definition by negation, contrast

139

uncontrollably, gasping for air, yet denied that basic necessity. Worst of all, I was conscious of every aspect of my existence—from the swinging of my arms to the slap of my feet on the road, and from the sweat dripping into my eyes and ears and mouth, to the frantic inhaling and exhaling of my lungs. I kept my eyes carefully peeled on the horizon or the next turn in the road, judging how far away it was, how long it would take me to get there, and how much torture was left before I reached home. These first few runs were, of course, the worst—as far from any euphoria or "high" as possible. They did, however, slowly become easier as my body became accustomed to running.

After a few months, in fact, I felt serious enough about this new pursuit to invest in a pair of real running shoes and shorts. Admittedly, these changes added to the comfort of my endeavor, but it wasn't until two full years later that the biggest change occurred—and I experienced my first real "high". It was a fall day. The air was a cool sixty-five degrees, the sun was shining intently, the sky was a clear, crisp blue, and a few dead leaves were scattered across the browning lawn. I stepped out onto the road and headed north towards a nearby park for my routine jog. The next thing I remember, however, was not my run through the park, but rather my return, some fortytwo minutes and six miles later, to my house. I woke, as if out of a dream, just as I slowed to a walk, cooling down from my run. The only memory I had of my run was a feeling of floating on air—as if my real self were somewhere above and detached from my body, looking down on my physical self as it went through its blind paces. At first, I felt scared—what if I had run out in front of a car? Would I have even known it? I felt as if I had been asleep or out of control, that my brain had, in some real sense, been turned off.

Now, after five years of running and hundreds of such mystical experiences, I realize that I had never lost control while in this euphoric state—and that my brain hadn't been turned off, or, at least, not completely. But what does happen is hard to prove. George Sheehan, in a column for Runner's World, suggests that "altered states", such as runner's high, result from the loss of conscious control, from the temporary cessation of left-brain messages and the dominance of right-brain activity (the left hemisphere being the seat of reason and rationality; the right, of emotions and inherited archetypal feelings). Another explanation comes from Dr. Jerry Lynch, who argues, in his book

Personal example	
Effects of the "high"	
Possible causes of the feeling: Two authorities	

Part Two   Strategies of Essay Development

The Total Runner, that the "high" results from the secretion of natural opiates, called beta endorphins, in the brain (213). My own explanation draws on both these medical explanations and is perhaps slightly more mystical. It's just possible that indeed natural opiates do go to work and consequently our brains lose track of the ins and outs of everyday activities—of jobs and classes and responsibilities. And because of this relaxed, drugged state, we are able to reach down into something more fundamental, something that ties us not only to each other but to all creation, here and gone. We rejoin nature, rediscovering the thread that links us to the universe.	The writer's explanation
My explanation is, of course, unscientific and therefore suspect. But I found myself, that day of the Mile-Hi Ten K run, eagerly trying to discuss my experience with the other runners: I wanted desperately to discover where I had been and what I had been doing during the race for which I received my first trophy. I didn't discover the answer from my fellow runners that day, but it didn't matter. I'm still running and still feeling the glow—whatever it is.	Conclusion: An incomplete understanding doesn't hamper enjoyment
Works Cited Lynch, J. 1987. *The Total Runner: A Complete Mind-Body Guide to Optimal Performance*. New Jersey: Prentice Hall. Sheehan, G. 1988. Altered States. *Runner's World, 23*(8), 14. 1988, p14.	In a formal research paper, the "Works Cited" list appears on a separate page.

 Practice

Below are an introduction and supporting points for an essay that defines the word "maturity". Plan out and write the supporting paragraphs and a conclusion for the essay.

The Meaning of Maturity

Being a mature student does not mean being an old-timer. Maturity is not measured by the number of years a person has lived. Instead, the yardstick of maturity is marked by the qualities of self-denial, determination, and dependability.

Self-denial is an important quality in the mature student…

Determination is another characteristic of a mature student…

Although self-denial and determination are both vital, probably the most important measure of maturity is dependability…

In conclusion…

Practice

Choose one of the terms below as the subject to write a definition essay. Each term refers to a certain kind of person.

Slob; Cheapskate; Loser; Good neighbor; Busybody; Whiner; Con artist; Optimist; Pessimist; Team player; Bully; Scapegoat; Hypocrite; Snob; Tease; Practical joker; Procrastinator; Loner.

Chapter 12

Division or Classification: Explaining Categories or Parts

You divide and classify every day. When you return home from the weekly trip to the supermarket with five bags packed with the purchases, how do you sort them out? You might separate food items from nonfood items. Or you might divide and classify the items into groups intended for the freezer compartment, the refrigerator, and the kitchen cupboards. Sorting supermarket items in such ways is just one simple example of how we spend a great deal of our time organizing our environment in one manner or another. Classification and division are ways of organizing information: various items may be classified according to their similarities, or a single topic may be divided into parts. We might classify different kinds of flowers as annuals or perennials, for example, and classify the perennials further as dahlias, daisies, roses, and peonies. We might also divide a flower garden into distinct areas: for herbs, flowers, and vegetables. Many of your college textbooks use division or classification to organize information. For example, a biology text might divide animals into birds, mammals, fish, and reptiles; a biology text might classify animals from the most to least endangered as well. A first-aid manual could divide burns into those caused by fire, chemicals, and electrical shock; a first-aid manual could also classify burns as first, second, or third degree depending on how serious they are.

12.1 Developing a Division or Classification Essay

Classification or division is another strategy of expository writing, whereby a writer creates a prose text to convey information to an audience. A classification or division essay is generally easy to develop. Each part or category is identified and described in a major part of the body of the essay. Frequently, one body paragraph will be devoted to each category. Division is the act of separating something into its component parts so that it may be better understood or used by the reader. When you think of division, think of dividing, separating, or breaking down one subject (often a large or complex or unfamiliar one) into its parts to help people understand it more easily. Classification systematically groups a number of things into categories to make the information easier to grasp. Classification differs from division in that it sorts and organizes many things into appropriate groups, types, kinds, or categories. Division separates subjects into parts, types, or regions, much like cutting a pie into slices.

For example:
- Our employees include students, homemakers, and recent immigrants.
- My neigbourhood is made up of ranch houses, two-story colonials, and split-levels.

Classification ranks things on a scale, much like a teacher grading quizzes from A to F:
For example:
- Our employees are paid hourly, daily, or monthly.
- My neigbourhood is made up of houses with two, three, and four bedrooms.

In division or classification essays you choose a classifying principle that suits the audience and purpose. Writing about contemporary music might involve the classifying principle of *tastes* in music and the categories of *R&B, New Folk,* and *Rap.* To write about new computer animation software, you must find a classifying principle and categories within software relevant to your subject and reader.

The main focus of the essays for readers is the way they present valid and interesting divisions of a topic. You can write an essay that uses division to discuss different type of students at the college—students can be categorized by their major, their ethnic background, their residence, or the way they study. You can also write an essay that uses classification to rank types of students at the college—students can be classified from youngest to oldest, best to worst, those who work full-time, part-time, or not at all, or poorest to richest.

1. Writing Your Thesis Statement for a Division or Classification Essay

The division or classification essay is built upon the classifying principle you choose and the particular divisions or categories you present for the topic. The thesis statement should, then, present: (1) the topic, (2) the intention to divide or classify, (3) the purpose for dividing the topic or classifying principle, and (4) the categories, if appropriate.

The "trick" with division-and-classification thesis statements is that with this method of development, the classifying principle and categories you apply to the topic actually represent the viewpoint. This type of thesis statement is another variation of the "topic + viewpoint" formula. Here is an example of a division or classification thesis statement following this formula:

- There are many different brands and models of cell phones: (1) but, based on users' preferences (2) they all fall into three categories (3) the functional, the decorative, and (4) the fully loaded.

Here, the writer's viewpoint is expressed by the phrase "users' preferences". It indicates that personal preference is a meaningful and potentially interesting classifying principle for cell phones. In most cases the thesis also should suggest why the classification or division is relevant or important. Here are more examples of effective thesis statements.

- Most people consider videos a form of entertainment; however, videos can also serve educational, commercial, and political functions.
- The Grand Canyon is divided into two distinct geographical areas—the North Rim and the South Rim—each offering different views, activities, and climatic conditions.
- By recognizing the three kinds of poisonous snakes in this area, campers and backpackers may be able to take the proper medical steps if they are bitten.

2. Tips for Division or Classification Essays

1) **Select one principle of classification or division and stick to it.** If you are classifying students by major, for instance, don't suddenly switch to classification by college: French, economics, psychology, arts and sciences, math and chemistry. Decide on what basis of division you will classify or divide the subject and then be consistent throughout the essay.

2) **Account for all the parts in the division or classification.** Don't, for instance, claim to classify all the evergreen trees native to your hometown and then leave out one or more species. For a short essay, narrow the ruling principle rather than omit categories. You couldn't, for instance, classify all the architectural styles in China in a short paper, but you might discuss the major styles on your campus. In the same manner, the enormous task of classifying all types of mental illness might be narrowed to the most common forms of childhood schizophrenia. However you narrow the topic, remember that in a formal classification, all the parts must be accounted for.

3) **One concept or item can be fruitfully divided into interesting and appropriate**

groups or classifications. The basic concept behind classifying is taking an assortment of things or ideas and showing how that assortment can be classified into groups that reveal something new. Dividing or classifying allows you to present a new or different idea as a result of performing the activities—this is fundamental to the idea of writing a good thesis statement. Dividing up a subject like insects by size does not present a new view of insects; dividing up insects by how they interact with people would offer something new to readers.

4) **One important fact about support for division or classification essays is that simply supplying examples does not constitute classifying.** When you classify, you first decide on categories, then provide supporting details of various types.

5) **Description is essential to effective support in division or classification essays.** At the very least, you must describe the characteristics that members of the classifications possess. To give the essay flavour and accuracy as well as appeal to readers, you will want to use sharp, skillful descriptions.

6) **Definition, process, and cause and effect analysis can all play effective parts in a division or classification essay.** You could use process to outline the steps by which something came to be included in one of the classifications; you could even include an anecdote to illustrate one of the classifications.

7) **Transitions are essential to help readers follow the method of development and purpose.** Use appropriate transitions to open paragraphs: For example, if you use climactic order, then transitions such as "... an even more important... " or " ... more significant (than)... " can be used; if you choose a different order, such as order of location or geographic order, then locate readers in the topic sentences so they follow the way they are being shown the material. Within paragraphs, use sentence-level transitions to connect supporting details so that each member of a group or category seems appropriately connected.

3. Function of Classification or Division Essays

1) **Express your ideas**. To explain whether you are proud of, or frustrated with the ability to budget money, you might classify budget categories that are easy to master versus those that cause problems.

2) **To inform your reader**. You can write an essay for the readers of the college newspaper classifying college instructors' teaching styles.

3) **To persuade your reader**. You can categorize types of television violence to develop the argument that violence on television is either harmful to children or not harmful to children.

12.2 Integrating Classification or Division into an Essay

Classification or division are often used along with one or more other patterns of development.

- An essay that argues for stricter gun control may categorize guns in terms of their firepower, purpose, or availability.
- A narrative about a writer's frustrating experiences in a crowded international airport terminal may describe the different parts or areas of the airport.

When incorporating classification or division into an essay based on another pattern of development, keep the following tips in mind.

1) **Avoid focusing on why the classification or division is meaningful**. When used as a secondary pattern, the significance of the classification or division should be clear from the context in which it is presented.
2) **State the principle of classification briefly and clearly**.
3) **Name the categories or parts**. In the sentence that introduces the classification or division, name the categories or parts to focus the readers' attention on the explanation that follows.

Sample Essay

In the following essay, the writer divided the books into three types. Note the writer's use of description and examples to help the reader distinguish one type from another.

My Favorite Escape: Books	
When I was in the Navy, I was stationed in southern Spain for four years on a Spanish base. There were a few American luxuries I had to do without, such as McDonald's Big Macs, fresh milk, and American television. The one I got along without best was the television. Since I'm an avid reader, I had no problem entertaining myself when I was off duty. Books are actually more entertaining than television because I can use my imagination when I read. I especially enjoy books that provide a sort of sacred haven or "never, never land" for my mind—a place where I can go when I want to relax or forget my problems. The books I enjoy the most are fiction novels because I can escape into the exciting action they provide. My favorite "escape" novels are classical literature, adventurous spy stories, and horror/fantasy stories.	Lead-in sentences Thesis

Classical literature is enjoyable because I have to actually think about what I'm reading rather than just skimming the book. Novels like *The Great Gatsby* by F. Scott Fitzgerald and *The Agony and the Ecstasy* by Irving Stone are examples of one type of literature I enjoy. Fitzgerald's novel not only portrays the era in which he lived, but also contains symbolism that adds depth and meaning to the story. Stone's novel is very similar to Fitzgerald's in that it contains symbolism and reflects an era of history; however, Stone writes about actual historical figures and the time in which they lived rather than about his own. *The Agony and the Ecstasy* is the story of Michelangelo's life. Because Stone is so descriptive in his interesting novel, the story almost comes to life. I can easily visualize Michelangelo chipping away at a block of marble that is later to become the marvelous statue of David. Long after I read novels like these, I still think about their themes or hidden meanings. These novels not only enrich my mind with history, but they also test my reasoning.	Type one: Classical literature
I also enjoy adventurous spy stories because they are intriguing, although they are not as believable as classical literature. The situations in this type of novel are realistic enough and some could possibly happen, but when all of the situations revolve around one man, I know it's highly unlikely that it really could happen. This is the appeal these books hold for me, though. Because they depict reality carried to the extreme, they are exciting. Novels written by Robert Ludlum are excellent examples of spy novels. Most of his protagonists are antiheroes who have an almost superhuman will to live. Although stabbed, shot, blown up, and beaten up, his antiheroes always crawl to their victory over the villain. In addition, his plots always involve the salvation of the American government by eliminating the corrupt antagonists. Packed with action, Ludlum's exciting novels are easy to read and to escape into.	Type two: Adventurous spy stories
Classical literature and spy novels are two types of "escape" books I enjoy. A third type, the one I enjoy the most, is the horror/fantasy novel. Because most of the stories could not possibly happen, I find this type the most interesting. Novels written by Stephen King or Peter Straub are always exciting. Although their novels start out with normal characters and situations, the stories end up with weird creatures and circumstances involved. For instance, Stephen King's *Salem's Lot* opens with a middle-aged widower who returns to his	Type three: Horror/fantasy novel

hometown after his wife's tragic death. The town is eventually taken over by vampires. The bizarre elements are so carefully and subtly woven into the normal events, I can't determine exactly where the deviation between normal and weird begins. Plots that involve seemingly typical American small towns with creepy undercurrents, nightmare-like creatures with human traits, and bizarre events as well as the normal human antiheroes make excellent "escape" reading. It's this type of novel that I find difficult to put down. My creative imagination is unleashed to fully appreciate the horror/fantasy novels. I feel relaxed when I let my mind flow with the unusual events as they happen.

Unlike television, reading novels is more satisfying because I have to use my imagination in order to visualize the story. Because of this, I become so involved in the story that I feel as if I'm one of the novel's characters. I enjoy this involvement; it can make me forget everyday conflicts that dampen my spirit. After escaping into my favorite fiction novels, such as classical literature, spy novels, and horror/fantasy novels, I feel refreshed and relaxed.

Conclusion: Summary of benefits of reading the three types of books

  Practice

Below is an introduction, a thesis, and supporting details for a classification essay on stress in college. Finish writing the supporting paragraphs and a conclusion for the essay.

College Stress

Jack's heart pounds as he casts panicky looks around the classroom. He doesn't recognize the professor, he doesn't know any of the students, and he can't even figure out what the subject is. In front of him is a test. At the last minute his roommate awakens him. It's only another anxiety dream. The very fact that dreams like Jack's are common suggests that college is a stressful situation for young people. The causes of this stress can be academic, financial, and personal.

Academic stress is common…

In addition to academic stress, the student often feels financial pressure…

Along with academic and financial worries, the student faces personal pressures…

In conclusion …

Practice

Use classification to develop an essay about one of the following topics. You'll need to limit the topic before you attempt to classify it.

Music; Food; Pet owners; Advertisements; Electronic devices; Insects; Restaurants; Television shows; Kinds of students on the campus; Bosses or co-workers to avoid or cultivate; Diets, exercise, or stress-reduction programs (or the participants); Different types of "good" teachers or "bad" teachers; Excuses for skipping classes.

Part Three
Special Assignments

The third section of this book addresses several kinds of assignments frequently included in composition classes and in many other college courses. If you have worked through Parts One and Part Two of this book, you have already practiced many of the skills demanded by these special assignments. Information in the next several chapters will build on what you already know about good writing.

Chapter 13

Writing a Summary

In many of the college courses, you'll likely be asked to summarize what someone else has said. Boiling down a text to its basic ideas helps you focus on the text, figure out what the writer has said, and understand (and remember) what you're reading. In fact, summarizing is an essential academic skill, a way to incorporate the ideas of others into your own writing.

13.1 What Is a Summary

Summaries are among the most often-used writing formats. A summary delivers a condensed version of the content of some original work, so it is an efficient way to present information in a time when the quantity of information available is expanding quickly. A summary is an objective, condensed version of the original material, presenting the main ideas in your own words. It reproduces, in reduced form and in third person voice, the viewpoint and support of the original text.

Although summaries are always more concise than the original texts, the length of a particular summary often depends on the length and complexity of the original text and the purpose of the summary. A summary is not an outline. It is written in sentences and paragraphs so readers understand the general ideas of the original text, and their relationships, in an easy-to-follow form. A summary is a reduced, reworded version of some original text. Paraphrasing is a necessary step in writing a summary, which is a concentrated version of the original.

1. Summarizing: A Skill

Writing a summary brings together a number of important reading, study and writing skills. To condense the original assigned material, you must preview, read, evaluate, organize, and perhaps outline it. Summarizing, then, can be a real aid to understanding; you must "get inside" the material and realize fully what is being said before you can reduce its meaning to a few words. Summarizing is an acquired skill, but if you learn (1) to read the original carefully, (2) to analyze and outline its main ideas, and (3) to express those main ideas in your own words, you will be prepared to face most summarizing challenges.

2. How to Summarize an Article

Step 1: Preview and Review the Source Material

If you are summarizing an article or a shorter printed piece on any subject, begin by printing or photocopying it so that you can highlight important points, strike through repetitive material, and note the main ideas right on the original. Take a few minutes to preview an article by taking a quick look at the following:

1) **Title.** The title often summarizes what the article is about. Sometimes, however, a title may be attention-grabbing but not very helpful. "The New, Old Jamaica", a title of the *Saturday Night* article, could refer to many ideas related to Jamaica.

2) **Subtitle.** A subtitle, a caption, or any words in large print often provide quick insight into the meaning of an article. For example, in a *Newsweek* article titled "Growing Old, Feeling Young", the following caption appeared: "Not only are Americans living longer, they are staying active longer—and their worst enemy is not nature, but the myths and prejudices about growing old." In short, the subtitle, the caption, or any other words in large print under or next to the title often provide a quick insight into the meaning of an article.

3) **First and last paragraphs.** In the first paragraph the author may state the subject and purpose of the article. The last paragraph may present conclusions or a summary. Opening and closing paragraphs are points of maximum attention for readers seeking information. Journalists and website creators know this and structure their content accordingly.

4) **Headings, subheadings, special typography and graphics.** Headings or subheadings provide clues to an article's main points and indicate what each section is about. Note carefully any pictures, charts, or diagrams. Page space in a magazine or journal is limited, and such visual aids are used to illustrate important points. Note words or phrases set off in *italic type* or boldface; note also bulleted lists or boxed material. These ideas have been emphasized because they are important.

Read the article for all you can understand the first time through. Do not slow down or turn back. Check or otherwise mark main points and key supporting details. Pay special attention to all the items noted in the preview. Also, look for definitions, examples, and enumerations (lists of items), which often indicate key ideas. You can also identify important points by turning any headings into questions and reading to find the answers to the questions. Go back and reread more carefully the areas you have identified as most important. Also, focus on other key points you may have missed in the first reading. Take notes on the material. Concentrate on getting down the main ideas and the key supporting points.

Step 2: List the Main Ideas, Write a First Draft, and Revise the Summary

Before you begin the summary, list all the main ideas in the source material. Number these ideas, and leave space after each to fill in the supporting details. Leave some time, if possible, before reviewing and editing the list. Check the list of ideas and support against the original material. Look for omissions, for repetition in either the original or in the list, and for duplications of ideas in examples, quotations, or explanations. With the edited list, prepare the first draft of the summary, keeping these points in mind:

1) **Identify, at the start of the summary, the title and author of the work.** For example, "In 'AI is changing the way people relate to other beings' (*The Economist*, May 24, 2022), James Bridle states…"
2) **Write the draft in the third person.** Never use *I* or *we*; when you summarize, you are invisible as a writer. The summary contains no commentary or views of your own. Do not change a single idea that appears in the original.
3) **Express the main points and key supporting details in your own words.** Your task is to put the original entirely into your own words, then reduce it. Do not imitate the style of the original.
4) **Limit the use of quotations.** You should quote from the material only to illustrate key points. A one-paragraph summary should not contain more than one quoted sentence.
5) **Preserve the balance and proportion of the original work.** If the original text devoted 70% of its space to one idea and only 30% to another, the summary should reflect that.

Step 3: Prepare for Your Second Draft

Ideally, first draft are a bit long. It is better to include a few too many details than to omit necessary information. Prepare the second draft by following these tips:

1) **Check the required word count or length.** Use the word counter on the wordprocessing software or simply count each word, including *a* and *the*.
2) **Review the summary to reduce wordy phrases,** such as "because of the fact that…" (just use "because"), "in order to…" (just use "to").
3) **Note each major idea and its support as it appears on the revised list, and note each in the draft.** Can each idea be rephrased more concisely?
4) **Write a final draft of the summary.**

3. Tips for Writing a Summary

1) **Read the text carefully.** To write a good summary, you need to read the original text carefully to capture the writer's intended meaning as clearly and evenhandedly as you can.

2) **State the main points concisely and accurately.** Summaries of a complete text are generally between 100 and 250 words in length, so you need to choose words carefully and to focus only on the text's main ideas. Leave out supporting evidence, anecdotes, and counterarguments unless they're crucial to understanding the text.

3) **Describe the text accurately and fairly—and using neutral language.** Present the author's ideas evenhandedly and fairly; a summary isn't the place to share the opinion of what the text says. Use neutral verbs such as *states, asserts,* or *concludes,* not verbs that imply praise or criticism like *proves* or *complains.*

4) **Use signal phrases. Distinguish what the author says.** Introducing a statement with phrases such as "he says" or "the essay concludes" indicates explicitly that you're summarizing what the author said. When first introducing an author, you may need to say something about their credentials.

For example:

- Political philosopher Danielle Allen analyzes the language of the *Declaration of Independence*. Later in the text, you may need to refer to the author again as you summarize specific parts of the text. These signal phrases are typically briefer: *Allen then argues…*

5) **Use quotations sparingly.** You may need to quote keywords or memorable phrases, but most or all of a summary should be written in your own words, using your own sentence structures.

4. How to Summarize a Book

To write a summary of a book, first preview the book by briefly looking at the following:

1) **Title.** A title is often the shortest possible summary of what a book is about. Think about the title and how it may summarize the whole book.

2) **Table of contents.** The contents will tell you the number of chapters in the book and the subject of each chapter. Use the contents to get a general sense of how the book is organized. You should also note the number of pages in each chapter. If thirty pages are devoted to one episode or idea and an average of fifteen pages to other episodes or ideas, you should probably give more space in the summary to the contents of the longer chapter.

3) **Preface.** You will probably find out why the author wrote the book. Also, the preface may summarize the main idea developed in the book and may describe briefly how the book is organized.
4) **First and last chapters.** In these chapters, the author may preview or review important ideas and themes developed in the book.
5) **Other items.** Note how the author has used headings and subheadings to organize information in the book. Check the opening and closing paragraphs of each chapter to see if these paragraphs contain introductions or summaries. Look quickly at charts, diagrams, and pictures in the book, since they are probably there to illustrate key points. Note any special features (index, glossary, appendixes) that may appear at the end of the book. Next, adapt the steps for summarizing an article.

Sample Summary

To illustrate the preceding guidelines, here is an essay and a brief summary of the essay. Note that the writer did not offer his opinion of Stevens' proposal, but, instead, objectively presented the essay's main idea.

College for Grown-Ups

A cruel paradox of higher education in America is that its most coveted seats are reserved for young people. Four-year residential colleges with selective admissions are a privileged elite in the academic world, but their undergraduate programs effectively discriminate on the basis of age. Admissions officers typically prefer that the best and brightest be children.

Yet leaving home at a young age to live on a campus full-time is not without serious financial, psychological and even physical risk. People make major investment decisions when they are choosing colleges, but with minimal information about quality and fit. Meanwhile flagship public universities, which rely on tuition to offset diminished public subsidies, condone Greek systems that appeal to many affluent families but also incubate cultures of dangerous play. The so-called party pathway through college is an all-encompassing lifestyle characterized by virtually nonstop socializing, often on the male-controlled turf of fraternity houses. Substance abuse and sexual assault are common consequences.

Even at the schools where the party pathway is carefully policed, life on a residential campus can be a psychological strain. A substantial body of research demonstrates that first-generation college students, those from low-income families and racial minorities are particularly at risk for feelings of exclusion, loneliness and academic alienation. The costs of leaving college can be large for everyone: lost tuition, loan debt and a subtle but consequential diminishment of self-esteem.

The source of these problems is baked into the current organization of residential higher education. Virtually all selective schools arrange their undergraduate programs on the presumption that teenagers are the primary clients. Administrators plan dormitory architecture, academic calendars and marketing campaigns to appeal to high school juniors and seniors. Again the cruel paradox: In the ever-growing number of administrators and service people catering to those who pay tuition, there are grown-ups all over campus, but they are largely peripheral to undergraduate culture.

If we were starting from zero, we probably wouldn't design colleges as age-segregated playgrounds in which teenagers and very young adults are given free rein to spend their time more or less as they choose. Yet this is the reality.

It doesn't have to be that way. Rethinking the expectation that applicants to selective colleges be fresh out of high school would go far in reducing risk for young people while better protecting everyone's college investment. Some of this rethinking is already underway. Temporarily delaying college for a year or two after high school is now becoming respectable among the admissions gatekeepers at top schools. Massive Online Open Courses (MOOCs) and other forms of online learning make it possible to experience fragments of an elite education at little or no cost.

In the Bay Area, where I live, people are tinkering further with conventional campus models. The Minerva Project, a San Francisco start-up with offices two blocks from Twitter, offers classic seminar-style college courses via a sophisticated interactive online learning platform and accompanies them with residencies in cities all over the world. Nearby in the SoMa district, Dev Bootcamp, a 19-week immersive curriculum that trains people of all ages for jobs in the tech industry, is a popular alternative. Some successfully employed graduates brag of bypassing college altogether.

At Stanford, where I teach, an idea still in the concept phase developed by a student-led team in the university's Hasso Plattner Institute of Design calls for the replacement of four consecutive college years in young adulthood with multiple residencies distributed over a lifetime. What the designers call Open Loop University would grant students admitted to Stanford multiple years to spend on campus, along with advisers to help them time those years strategically in light of their personal development and career ambitions. Today's arbitrarily segregated world of teenagers and young adults would become an ever-replenished intergenerational community of purposeful learners.

This utopian ideal is admittedly quite a distance from the institutional arrangements we have inherited, which encourage the nation's most privileged young people to enter and finish college by the ripe old age of 22. But the status quo is not sustainable. Unrelenting demand for better-educated workers, rapidly developing technological capacity to support learning digitally and the soaring costs of conventional campus life are driving us toward substantial change.

While innovators continue to imagine more flexible forms of college, traditionalists might champion two proven models: community colleges, which were designed to educate people of all ages and walks of life together, and the G.I. Bill, which sent more than two million grown-ups to college, made campus culture much more serious and helped American higher education become the envy of the world.

A Summary of "College for Grown-Ups"

In the *New York Times*, Mitchell L. Stevens contends that college is a privilege wasted on the young. Stevens, a professor at Stanford University, argues that sending new high school graduates off to college places these students at great financial, psychological, and even physical risk. The source of these risks is "baked" into the existing setup in place at most traditional colleges and universities. Stevens suggests a number of alternatives, including a mandatory delay in enrollment after high school, MOOCs, immersive curricula, and lifelong education. He concludes that the "status quo is not sustainable".

Practice

Write a summary of an essay that interests you in a recent issue of the 21st Century.

Practice

Write an essay-length summary of a book you have read.
Make sure that:
(1) Keep the basic proportion of ideas of your original.
(2) Include all main ideas.
(3) Include only essential supporting points. Eliminate repetitive support.
(4) Maintain the same order presented in the original document.
(5) Add nothing to the original document.
(6) Use appropriate cue phrases, if needed.
(7) Use only your own words (paraphrases), except where a quotation might be unavoidable.
(8) Display the word count required by your assignment.

Chapter 14

Writing a Book Report

Each semester, you will probably be asked by at least one instructor to read a book or an article and write a paper recording your response to the material. In these reports or reaction papers, your instructor will most likely expect you to do two things: summarize the material and detail your reaction to it. This chapter will explain and illustrate how to write a book report, which includes two parts: a summary of the work and your reaction to the work.

1. A Summary of the Work

To develop the first part of a report, do the following:
1) **Identify the author and title of the work, and include in parentheses the publisher and publication date.** With magazines, give the date of publication.
2) **Write an informative summary of the material.** Condense the content of the work by highlighting its main points and key supporting points. (Refer to Chapter One for a complete discussion of summarizing techniques.) Use direct quotations from the work to illustrate important ideas.

Do not discuss in great detail any single aspect of the work while neglecting to mention other equally important points. Summarize the material so that the reader gets a general sense of all key aspects of the original work. Also, keep the summary objective and factual. Do not include in the first part of the paper your personal reaction to the work; your subjective impression will form the basis of the second part of the paper.

2. Your Reaction to the Work

In the second part, you are expected to write your response. You can respond in various ways, for instance, by taking a position on the text's argument, by analyzing the text in some way, or by reflecting on what it says. You can also evaluate the work, that is, you state and defend the judgments you've made about its quality and its significance. To develop the second part of a report, do the following:

1) **Read closely and critically to understand what the text says.** Try to get a sense of how—and how well—it does so, and to think about your own reaction to it. Only then can you decide how to respond.

2) **Respond to what the text says (its ideas), to how it says it (the way it's written), or to where it leads your personal reaction.** Or you might write a response that mixes those ways of responding. You might, for example, combine a personal reaction with an examination of how the writing caused that reaction.

3) **Agree or disagree with the author's argument, supporting with good reasons and evidence.** You might agree with parts of the argument and disagree with others. You might find that the author has ignored or downplayed some important aspect of the topic that needs to be discussed or at least acknowledged. Here are some questions to consider that can help you think about what a text says:

- What does the writer claim?
- What reasons and evidence does the writer provide to support that claim?
- What parts of the text do you agree with? Is there anything you disagree with—and if so, why?
- Does the writer represent any views other than their own? If not, what other perspectives should be considered?
- Are there any aspects of the topic that the writer overlooks or ignores?
- If you're responding to a visual text, how do the design and any images contribute to your understanding of what the text "says"?

4) **Consider what elements the writer uses to convey their message—facts, stories, images, and so on.** You'll likely pay attention to the writer's word choices and look for any patterns that lead you to understand the text in a particular way. To think about the way a text is written, you might find some of these questions helpful:

- What is the writer's message? Is there an explicit statement of that message?
- How well has the writer communicated the message?
- How does the writer support what he says: By citing facts or statistics? By quoting experts? By noting personal experiences? Are you persuaded?
- Are there any words, phrases, or sentences that you find notable and that contribute to the text's overall effect?

5) **Focus on how your personal experiences or beliefs influenced the way you understood the text or on how it reinforced or prompted you to reassess some of those beliefs.** You could also focus on how to see the topic in new ways—or note questions that it's led you to wonder about. Some questions that may help you reflect on your own reaction to a text include:

- How did the text affect you personally?
- Is there anything in the text that really got your attention? If so, what?
- Do any parts of the text provoke an emotional reaction—make you laugh or cry, or make you uneasy? What prompted that response?
- Does the text remind you of any other texts?
- Does the text support (or challenge) any of your beliefs? How?
- Has reading this text given you any new ideas or insight?
- How is the work related to your life, experiences, feelings, and ideas? For instance, what emotions did it arouse in you? Did it increase your understanding of an issue or change your perspective?

6) **Check with your instructor to see whether you should emphasize any specific point.** For example, focus on any of the questions below:
   - How is the assigned work related to ideas and concerns discussed in the course? What points made in the course textbook, class discussions, or lectures are treated more fully in the work?
   - How is the work related to problems in our present-day world?

7) **Evaluate the merit of the work:** the importance of its points; its accuracy, completeness, and organization; its overall quality and significance, and so on. You should also indicate here whether you would recommend the work to others, and why.

Here are some important matters to consider as you prepare a report:

1) **Apply the four basic standards of effective writing (unity, support, coherence, and clear, error-free sentences).**
   - Make sure each major paragraph presents and then develops a single main point. For example, in the model report that follows, a paragraph summarizes the book, and the three paragraphs that follow detail three separate reactions that the student writer had. The student then closes the report with a short concluding paragraph.
   - Support with specific reasons and details any general points or attitudes you express. Statements such as "I agreed with many ideas in this article" and "I found the book very interesting" are meaningless without specific evidence that shows why you feel as you do. Look at the model report to see how the main point or topic sentence of each paragraph is developed by specific supporting evidence.
   - Organize the material in the paper. Follow the basic plan of organization already described: an introduction, a summary consisting of one or more paragraphs, a reaction consisting of two or more paragraphs, and a conclusion. Use transitions to connect the parts of the paper.
   - Proofread the paper for grammar, mechanics, punctuation, and word use.

2) **Support your response. Whatever your response, you need to offer reasons and evidence to support what you say.**
   - If you're responding to what the text says, you may offer facts, statistics, anecdotal evidence, and textual evidence. You'll also need to consider—and acknowledge—any possible counterarguments, positions other than yours.
   - If you're responding to the way the text is written, you may identify certain patterns in the text that you think mean something, and you'll need to cite evidence from the text itself.
   - If you're reflecting on your own reaction to the text, you may connect its ideas with your own experiences or beliefs or explore how the text reinforced, challenged, or altered your beliefs.

3) **Document quotations from all works by giving the page number in parentheses after the quoted material.** You may use quotations in the summary and reaction parts of the paper, but do not rely too much on them. Use them only to emphasize key ideas.

Sample Report

Here is a report written by a student in an introductory sociology course. Look at the paper closely to see how it follows the guidelines for report writing described in this chapter.

A Report on *I Know Why the Caged Bird Sings*	
In *I Know Why the Caged Bird Sings*, Maya Angelou tells the story of her earliest years. Angelou, a dancer, poet, and television producer as well as a writer, has continued her life story in three more volumes of autobiography. I Know Why the Caged Bird Sings is the start of Maya Angelou's story; in this book, she writes with crystal clarity about the pains and joys of being black in America.	Introductory paragraph
I Know Why the Caged Bird Sings covers Maya Angelou's life from age three to age sixteen. We first meet her as a gawky little girl in a white woman's cut-down lavender silk dress. She has forgotten the poem she had memorized for the Easter service, and all she can do is rush out of the church. At this point, Angelou is living in Stamps, Arkansas, with her grandmother and uncle. The town is rigidly segregated: "People in Stamps used to say that the whites in our town were so prejudiced that a Negro couldn't buy vanilla ice cream." Yet	Part 1: Summary Topic sentence for summary paragraph

Part Three | Special Assignments

Angelou has some good things in her life: her adored older brother Bailey, her success in school, and her pride in her grandmother's quiet strength and importance in the black community. There is laughter, too, as when a preacher is interrupted in midsermon by an overly enthusiastic woman shouting, "Preach it, I say preach it!" The woman, in a frenzied rush of excitement, hits the preacher with her purse; his false teeth fly out of his mouth and land at Angelou's feet. Shortly after this incident, Angelou and her brother are taken by her father to live in California with their mother. Here, at age eight, she is raped by her mother's boyfriend, who is mysteriously murdered after receiving only a suspended sentence for his crime. She returns, silent and withdrawn, to Stamps, where the gloom is broken when a friend of her mother introduces her to the magic of great books. Later, at age thirteen, Angelou returns to California. She learns how to dance. She runs away after a violent family fight and lives for a month in a junkyard. She becomes the first black female to get a job on the San Francisco streetcars. She graduates from high school eight months pregnant. And she survives.

I am impressed with the vividness of Maya Angelou's writing style. For example, she describes the lazy dullness of her life in Stamps: "Weekdays revolved in a sameness wheel. They turned into themselves so steadily and inevitably that each seemed to be the original of yesterday's rough draft." She also knows how to bring a scene to life, as when she describes her eighth-grade graduation. For months, she has been looking forward to this event, knowing she will be honored for her academic successes. She is even happy with her appearance: her hair has become pretty, and her yellow dress is a miracle of hand-sewing. But the ceremony is spoiled when the speaker—a white man—implies that the only success available to blacks is in athletics. Angelou remembers: "The man's dead words fell like bricks around the auditorium and too many settled in my belly... The proud graduating class of 1940 had dropped their heads." Later, Angelou uses a crystal-clear image to describe her father's mistress sewing: "She worked the thread through the flowered cloth as if she were sewing the torn ends of her life together." With such vivid details and figures of speech, Maya Angelou recreates her life for her readers.

I also react strongly to the descriptions of injustices suffered by blacks two generations ago. I am as horrified as the seven-year-old Maya when some "powhitetrash" girls torment her dignified

Part 2: Reaction
Topic sentence for first reaction paragraph

Topic sentence for second reaction paragraph

165

grandmother, calling her "Annie" and mimicking her mannerisms. In another incident, Mrs. Cullinan, Angelou's white employer, decides that Marguerite (Angelou's given name) is too difficult to pronounce and so renames her Mary. This loss of her name—a "hellish horror"—is another humiliation suffered at white hands, and Angelou leaves Mrs. Cullinan's employ soon afterward. Later, Angelou encounters overt discrimination when a white dentist tells her grandmother, "Annie, my policy is I'd rather stick my hand in a dog's mouth than in a nigger's"—and only slightly less obvious prejudice when the streetcar company refuses to accept her application for a conductor's job. We see Angelou over and over as the victim of a white society.

    Although I am saddened to read about the injustices, I rejoice in Angelou's triumphs. Angelou is thrilled when she hears the radio broadcast of Joe Louis's victory over Primo Carnera: "A Black boy. Some Black mother's son. He was the strongest man in the world." She weeps with pride when the class valedictorian leads her and her fellow eighth-graders in singing the Negro National Anthem. And there are personal victories, too. One of these comes after her father has gotten drunk in a small Mexican town. Though she has never driven before, she manages to get her father into the car and drives fifty miles through the night as he lies intoxicated in the backseat. Finally, she rejoices in the birth of her son: "He was beautiful and mine, totally mine. No one had bought him for me." Angelou shows us, through these examples, that she is proud of her race—and of herself. *(Topic sentence for third reaction paragraph)*

    I Know Why the Caged Bird Sings is a remarkable book. Angelou could have been just another casualty of race prejudice. Yet by using her intelligence, sensitivity, and determination, she succeeds in spite of the odds against her. And by writing with such power, she lets us share her defeats and joys. She also teaches us a vital lesson: With strength and persistence, we can all escape our cages—and sing our songs. *(Concluding paragraph)*

 Practice

Write a book report on one of your interested books. Include an introduction, a one-paragraph summary, a reaction consisting of one or more paragraphs, and a brief conclusion. Make sure that each major paragraph in your report develops a single main point.

Chapter 15

Preparing a Multimedia Presentation

At some point in your academic career, you will probably be asked to give a presentation. In fact, you may give many presentations before you graduate, and you almost certainly will give presentations on the job. This chapter contains practical suggestions for preparing and giving effective presentations with a multimedia component.

15.1 Planning Your Presentation

The more carefully you plan your presentation, the more comfortable you will be in delivering it. Here are the steps to follow in planning a presentation.

1) **Select your topic.** First, make sure you understand the assignment and the type of presentation you are to give. Then consider the audience: What topics are important to the listeners and will sustain their interest? Here are a few suggestions for choosing a topic:
   - Choose a topic that you find interesting or know something about. You will find it easier to exude and generate enthusiasm if you speak about a topic that is familiar and that you enjoy.
   - Choose a topic that is appropriate and of value to the audience. Learning how to choose a day care center may be of value to young parents, but you may have difficulty sustaining the interest of average college students with such a topic. Trivial topics such as how to create a particular hairstyle or a report about characters on a soap opera are unlikely to have sufficient merit for college instructors.

2) **Choose a topic you can explain fully in the time allotted.** If the topic is too broad, your presentation will go over time, or you may resort to generalities that lack supporting evidence.
3) **Identify your purpose.** Determine whether the purpose is to express, inform, or persuade. Then define the purpose more specifically. For a persuasive presentation, for example, do you want to convince the audience that a change in policy is needed or simply to encourage them to consider the issue with an open mind?
4) **Research your topic.** Unless your presentation is to be based on your personal knowledge or experience, you will need to research the topic.

15.2 Drafting Your Presentation

Once you have made a plan, begin drafting your presentation, develop a thesis and generate supporting ideas. Based on your research, create a working thesis. Use idea-generating strategies to develop a variety of supporting reasons, and consider which will be most effective, given your purpose and audience.

1) **Organize the presentation.** Using the patterns of organization that will make your presentation easier for the audience to follow and for you to remember the order of the main points. For example, you could use classification to organize a presentation on types of procrastinators, providing four main categories of procrastinators with descriptive details to explain each. When organizing, consider saving the most convincing evidence or examples for last, as audience members are likely to recall the end of your presentation more clearly than the beginning.
2) **Draft the body of the presentation.** When you write an essay, readers can reread if they miss a point. When you give a presentation, listeners do not have that option, so reiterate the thesis frequently to make your presentation easier to follow, and use plenty of transitions to ensure that listeners don't get lost. Select evidence that the audience would find convincing. Including different types of evidence that reinforce one another, such as statistics to support the examples you include, will help listeners recall the main points. Emotional appeals can be more memorable for an audience than statistics, but reinforce any emotional appeals you make with concrete evidence. Including meaningful evidence adds credibility to your presentation.
3) **Work references to the sources into the presentation.** Use signal phrases to incorporate references to authors or works (or both), and include background information about the author or work, to provide context. If you use quotations, avoid

tedious expressions such as "I quote here" or "I want to quote an example". Instead, integrate your quotations into your speech as you would integrate quotations into an essay.

4) **Draft the introduction and conclusion.** Your introduction should grab the audience's attention, introduce the topic, and establish a relationship between you and the audience. To build a relationship with the audience, try to make connections with them. You might mention others who are present; refer to a shared situation (a previous class or another student's presentation), or establish common ground by referring to a well-known event, personality, or campus issue. The conclusion is a crucial part of your presentation because it is the last opportunity to leave a strong impression on the audience. You should summarize the speech and let the audience know your presentation is ending. The conclusion should also remind listeners of the importance of the topic. Consider closing with a powerful quotation or anecdote that reinforces the main point.

15.3 Using Presentation Software

Presentation software, like PowerPoint and keynote, allows you to list or summarize your main points and to embed multimedia evidence—audio, video, and image files—in support of your claims.

1) **Use presentation software to aid understanding.** Project key words or concepts you want to emphasize or provide an outline so the audience can follow the main points.
2) **Use a design template that suits the audience and purpose.** A simple color scheme with a sharp contrast between text and background will be easiest to read. Avoid using reds and greens if differences between the two colors are significant, because color-blind members of the audience will not be able to differentiate between them. Use subdued color schemes and easily readable fonts (such as Arial or Verdana) for business or academic presentations. For PowerPoint slides, use just a few animation schemes (how text enters and leaves a slide) consistently.
3) **Format the slides so they are easily readable.** Use a large point size (usually 24 points or greater) so everyone in the audience can read the text easily. Keep the number of words per slide low: slides crammed with text are difficult to read, and if audience members are busy reading lengthy slides, they are not listening to what you are saying. A good rule of thumb is to use no more than six bullet points per slide, with no more than six words per bullet point. (If you can do so clearly, use just words and phrases rather than complete sentences.)

4) **Use presentation software to display visuals and graphics.** Photos, cartoons, graphics, and embedded videos can convey the message in a memorable way. They also keep the audience interested and alert. But keep graphics simple, so the audience can take them in at a glance, and use visuals and graphics only when they are relevant to your point, not just as decoration.

5) **Edit your slides carefully.** Check for errors in spelling, grammar, and formatting as well as other kinds of typos. Run the entire slide show for yourself several times before presenting it to correct any errors you find.

15.4 Delivering an Effective Presentation

Try to think of your talk as less of a formal production than a conversation with interested peers. You are not an actor hired to perform but rather someone knowledgeable and at ease who sincerely wants to share information and stimulate thought. To communicate the ideas well, here are some suggestions for a pleasing delivery.

1) **Monitor your voice.** You need to speak loud enough to reach the back row in the room, and you need to speak slowly enough to be understood, pronouncing each word clearly. Avoid a monotone; practice pausing to give emphasis to key words or concepts (if it helps, write the word "pause" in red ink in various places in your note cards).

2) **Make eye contact.** Sweep the different parts of the room with your glance so that everyone feels included in the comments. You should know the work well enough that you do not have to read the notes; instead, use the notes or outline as prompts or reminders of what you want to say next.

3) **Avoid distractions.** Practicing your talk so that the words flow smoothly will help rid yourself of annoying expression such as "ummm" and "you know". Gestures can effectively emphasize points but don't overdo them, and if you are standing, try to find a balance between remaining rigid (no hiding behind the lectern) and moving or shifting around too much. You want listeners to focus on what you are saying, so on the day of your presentation dress neatly. Bring a watch or have a clock somewhere in your line of sight so you can discreetly check that your talk is moving along with time to finish as scheduled.

4) **Use instructional aids properly.** Visual aids that present a few key words or lines can be effective in some cases, though tiny print, complex graphs, crowded screens, and overly flashy images can be more distracting than helpful. Remember that you want your audience's close attention on your ideas, not on your props.

Part Three Special Assignments

5) **Adjust and adapt.** Watch the audience's reactions—their facial expressions and body language. If they seem confused or restless, you might need to slow down, speed up, simplify, or restate a point in a slightly different way.

6) **End well.** Sometimes the concluding restatement of the main point can best be followed with a humorous comment or a serious thought or a call for action, depending on the subject matter and purpose. Some assignments include a brief question-and-answer period after your presentation; if so, as you plan the talk, try to anticipate what some of the questions might be so that you are ready to succinctly address them. Plan a comment that announces the end of the Q & A session ("If anyone has additional questions, I can answer them after class."), and do thank your audience for listening.

As you prepare to give your presentation, try to relax. Breathe deeply and evenly if you are nervous; as yoga students know, controlling the breath helps focus the mind and body. Visualize success—and unless a somber subject matter dictates otherwise, approach the listeners with a warm, friendly smile.

Chapter 16

Writing a Personal Statement

For some applications, you may be asked to submit an essay, a personal statement, or a response paper. For example, you might be applying for admission to an academic program (social work, engineering, optometry school) or for an internship, a scholarship, or a research grant. Whatever the situation, what you write and how well you write it will be important factors in the success of the application. This chapter takes a personal statement as an example to illustrate how to write a successful application essay. The personal statement, the opportunity to sell yourself in the application process, generally falls into one of two categories:

1) **The general, comprehensive personal statement.** This allows you maximum freedom in terms of what you write and is the type of statement often prepared for standard medical or law school application forms.
2) **The response to very specific questions.** Often, business and graduate school applications ask specific questions, and the statement should respond specifically to the question being asked. Some business school applications favor multiple essays, typically asking for responses to three or more questions.

Tips for a Personal Statement

1) **Understand what you are being asked to write and why.** How does the essay fit into the entire application?
2) **Think about your purpose and audience:**
   - What do you want to gain (internship, scholarship, job interview), and how could the writing help you gain it?
   - Who are the readers? What do they know about you? What should they know? What will they look for?

3) **Focus on the instructions for writing the essay.** What type of question is it? What topics are you asked to write about? What hints do the directions give about possible organization, emphasis, style, length, and method of submitting the essay?

4) **Answer the questions that are asked.** Don't be tempted to use the same statement for all applications. It is important to answer each question being asked, and if slightly different answers are needed, you should write separate statements. In every case, be sure your answer fits the question being asked.

5) **Do some research, if needed.** If a school wants to know why you're applying to it rather than another school, do some research to find out what sets your choice apart from other universities or programs. If the school setting would provide an important geographical or cultural change for you, this might be a factor to mention.

6) **Tell what you know.** The middle section of the essay might detail your interest and experience in the particular field, as well as some of the knowledge of the field. Too many people graduate with little or no knowledge of the profession or field they hope to enter. Be as specific as you can in relating what you know about the field and use the language professionals use in conveying this information. Refer to experiences (work, research, etc.), classes, conversations with people in the field, books you've read, seminars you've attended, or any other source of specific information about the career you want and why you're suited to it. Since you will have to select what you include in the statement, the choices you make are often an indication of the judgment.

- Write in a style that is personal but professional. Use words that fit the subject and the readers. Avoid clichés, and balance generalizations with concrete examples and details.

- Refine the first draft into a polished piece. First, get feedback from another student or, if appropriate, a professor, and revise the essay. Second, edit the final version thoroughly: You don't want typos, incorrect names, and grammar errors to derail your application.

The essay is not the application form, and it is not a resume. In other words, the essay is the best opportunity that you'll have to either delve into something you wrote in the application form or to expound on something new that doesn't really fit on the application form. It doesn't help you to regurgitate what's already on the application form. While you don't want to repeat information from the application form verbatim in the essay, it's usually a good idea to have some continuity between the form and the essay. If you write an essay about how your greatest passion in life is playing the piano and how you spend ten hours a week practicing, this hobby should be mentioned in the application form along with any performances you've given or awards you've won. It doesn't make sense to write about how you love an activity in the essay and then to have no mention of it in the application form. Remember that the admissions officers are looking at your application in its entirety, and they should have a complete and cohesive image of you through all the pieces, which include the application form, essay, transcript, recommendations, and interview.

The secret of writing a successful personal statement is that any topic can be a winner but it all depends on your approach. If you spend the time to analyze the subject and can convey that quality of thought that is unique to you through words, you'll have a powerful essay. It doesn't have to be beautifully written or crafted as the next great novel. At its core the essay is not a "writing test." It's a "thinking test". So you do need to spend the time to make sure that your thoughts are conveyed correctly on paper. It may not be pretty writing but it has to be clear.

Sample Application Essay

Ariela fits a great deal of information about herself and her family into her response to the essay prompt, which asks for a description of "the world you come from" and an explanation of how "that world shaped your dreams and aspirations". These challenging questions require writing about outside influences as well as one's personal goals. Ariela does a wonderful job of focusing the essay by presenting us her family life—mostly in the first three paragraphs—and explaining how this nurtured a "thirst for scientific knowledge"—described in the last three paragraphs. While she also mentions her school (AP science classes), clubs (Science Bowl Team), and summer opportunities (an internship at Stanford), these all fit within the context of Ariela's family life, particularly her parents who encouraged the "scientific spark" they saw in their daughter. This central thesis holds the short essay together.

February 28, 2020
Ariela Koehler

Personal Statement

Growing up with separated parents has not been the easiest life, but it has been my life. When I was younger, I'd hate going out to eat with my dad and seeing a family of four happily enjoying a meal. If my mother and father ever went out together to a restaurant, it was with me, once a year for my birthday, and was usually interspersed with various disagreements.

It was when I was in first grade that I began to realize that, although my parents had their differences and no longer loved each other, I was the one thing that united them. I had no basis to be envious of what I thought of as "complete" families.

Both my mother and father, wanting the best for me, recognized early on my love and fascination with all things scientific. They worked to create opportunities for me to pursue my interest. My mother would read at bedtime, at my request, nature field guides instead of nursery rhymes. The two of us often made long journeys at 3:00 am to witness meteor showers in the clear skies of the mountains. She encouraged me to set up experiments around the house, which I happily did—measuring the growth of palm tree saplings and dissecting owl pellets to extract the mouse bones inside. An environmental scientist, my father could not wait to transfer all of his scientific knowledge into my young head. Needless to say, many of his spontaneous lectures were far above my grasp—I still vaguely remember a quantum physics talk he gave me when I was eight—but they inspired me to learn more on my own.

My thirst for scientific knowledge grew over the years, without limits in any one specific area. Then, in January four years ago, my Aunt Diane died after a five-year battle with breast cancer. It was during my aunt's illness that I realized I could use my natural love of science to benefit others facing similar challenges.

I have continually pushed myself closer to this goal by excelling in my AP science classes, studying biotechnology at UC Davis through the COSMOS program, and competing as a member of my school's Science Bowl Team. This past summer, I had the opportunity to intern at the Reijo Pera Lab at Stanford University through the Stanford Institutes of Medicine Summer Research Program. During this two-month internship, I worked with human embryonic stem cells to explore the function of PRDM1, a potentially-useful gene in the creation of regenerative medicines.

The scientific spark my parents recognized years ago has shaped my life, and with it, I wish to shape the lives of others. I aspire to become a biomedical researcher, a career that harnesses my long-time fascination of science and my commitment to improve the quality of life for those facing medical challenges. It would be a privilege to work alongside scientists, exploring new treatments and technologies to create exciting new options for patients and their families.

Chapter 17

Writing a Business Letter

Business letters are written to do many things—for example, share ideas, promote products, ask for help, introduce other documents (such as a proposal) that accompany the letter, or to apply for a job. Putting a message in writing gives you time to think about, organize, and edit what you want to say. In addition, a written message serves as a record of important details for both the sender and the recipient. The writer should state the purpose of the letter in the first few lines, provide supporting information in the paragraphs that follow, and maintain a courteous and professional tone throughout. Include enough information to identify clearly any documents you refer to in the letter.

17.1 Parts of the Business Letter

1) **Heading**. The heading gives the writer's complete address, either in the letterhead (company stationery) or typed out, followed by the date.
2) **Inside address**. Include the name, title, and street address of the recipient, with words like Street or Avenue spelled out.
3) **Salutation**. The convention is to address recipients of business letters as *Dear*, even if you've never met the person before. Use the recipient's title (abbreviated), such as Gen., Rev., Mr., or Ms., and address your letter to a specific person, even if you have to telephone the company to find out the name to use.
4) **Body**. The body should consist of single-spaced paragraphs with double-spacing between paragraphs. If the body goes to a second page, put the reader's name at the top left, the number 2 in the center, and the date at the right margin.
5) **Complimentary Closing**. For the complimentary closing, use *Sincerely*, *Yours sincerely*, or *Yours truly* followed by a comma; use *Best wishes* if you know the person well.

6) **Signature**. The signature includes the writer's name both handwritten and typed.

7) **Initials**. When someone types the letter for the writer, that person's initials appear (in lowercase) after the writer's initials (in capitals) and a colon.

8) **Enclosure**. If a document (brochure, form, copy, or other form) is enclosed with the letter, the word *Enclosure* or *Encl.* appears below the initials.

9) **Copies**. If a copy of the letter is sent elsewhere, type *cc:* beneath the enclosure line, followed by the person's or department's name.

Sample Letter

Box 143
Balliole College
Eugene, OR 974-405-125
August 29, 2020

Ms. Ada Overlie
Ogg Hall, Room 222
Balliole College
Eugene, OR 97440-0222

Dear Ms. Overlie,

    As the president of the Earth Care Club, I welcome you to Balliole Community College. I hope the year will be a great learning experience both inside and outside the classroom.

    That learning experience is the reason I'm writing—to encourage you to join the Earth Care Club. As a member, you could participate in the educational and action-oriented mission of the club. The club has most recently been involved in the following:

- Organizing a reduce, reuse, recycle program on campus;
- Promoting cloth rather than plastic bag use among students;
- Giving input to the college administration on landscaping, renovating, and building for energy efficiency;
- Putting together the annual Earth Day celebration.

    Which environmental concerns and activities would you like to focus on? Bring them with you to the Earth Care Club. Simply complete the enclosed form and return it by September 9. Then watch the campus news for details on our first meeting.

Yours sincerely,
Dave Wetland
President

DW:kr
Encl. membership form
Cc: Esther du Toit, membership committee

Part Three | Special Assignments

17.2 E-Mail

Electronic mail, or e-mail, is fast, easy, and efficient, as you can compose or forward a message to one person or many people, across the building or across the world, from a variety of sites. Many students and instructors rely on e-mail to exchange information about assignments and schedules as well as to follow up on class discussions. E-mail messages are also increasingly being used in place of business letters, and e-mail is a broader medium of communication than the business letter. E-mail allows you to do the following:

- Send, forward, and receive many messages quickly and efficiently, making it ideal for group projects and other forms of collaboration;
- Set up mailing lists (specific groups of e-mail addresses) so that you can easily send the same message to several people at the same time;
- Organize messages in "folders" for later reference, and reply to messages.

1. Tips for Writing an E-mail

1) **Use a helpful subject line**. To ensure that the message will be opened and read, always use specific words in the subject line to clearly delineate the central focus or key words of your correspondence. Using a specific subject line will also be helpful if the reader wants to reread the message later and needs to find it quickly in a long list of e-mails.

2) **Begin appropriately**. Unlike a traditional business letter, e-mail normally needs no heading or inside address, but a new communication should begin with an appropriate greeting, depending on the formality of the occasion. For example, if you are writing an officer of another company to ask for information, you might begin with a traditional salutation (*Dear Mr. Hall*). An informal memo to a coworker might have a more casual greeting, depending on your relationship to that person (*Hello, Bill; Good morning, Ms. Merrill*).

3) **Keep your message brief**. Long messages are difficult to read on screens; all that scrolling up and down to check information can be tiresome. If the message is long, consider use of an attachment. Try to clearly state the purpose, explain in a concise manner, and conclude gracefully.

4) **Make it easy to read.** To avoid contributing to the reader's eyestrain, write messages that are visually pleasant. Keep the paragraphs short, and skip a line between each paragraph. If the message is long, break it up with headings, numbered lists, or "bullets". Use a readable, plain font.

5) **Check your tone.** Your e-mail messages should sound professional and cordial. Unlike personal e-mail, business e-mails should be written in standard English and be straight to the point. Be especially careful about the use of irony or humor. It is easy for readers to misinterpret your words and meaning in an e-mail message and react in a manner opposite the one you intended. Strive for a polite, friendly tone, using the clearest, most precise words you can muster.

6) **Sign off.** If the e-mail is performing a task similar to that of a business letter, you may wish to close in a traditional way.

   For example:

   Yours truly,

   Scott Muranjan

   You may also want to create a standard sign-off that not only includes your name but also your title, telephone and fax numbers, and postal and e-mail addresses. Such information is helpful for readers who wish to contact you later. However, if your e-mail is more akin to an informal memo between coworkers, you may find it appropriate to end with a friendly thought or word of thanks and your first name:

   For example:

   I'm looking forward to working with you on the Blue file. See you at Tuesday's meeting.

   Scott

   Allow your sense of occasion and audience to dictate the kind of closing each e-mail requires.

7) **Revise, proofread, copy, send.** The very ease of e-mail makes it tempting to send messages that may not be truly ready to go. All your correspondence should look just that: professional. Take some time to revise for clarity and tone; always proofread. Double-check figures and dates, and run the spell-checker if you have one. If time permits, print out important messages to look over before you hit the "Send" button. If you need to keep track of the correspondence, make a computer file or a print copy for your office.

Sample Business E-mail

A business e-mail lacks some parts of a paper letter: the return-address heading, handwritten signature, and envelope. Your mailing address falls at the end of the letter rather than the top. Otherwise, it has the same parts listed above: salutation, body, close, and typed signature.

To: Ryan Thompson@yahoo.com
Cc: Larry Mendes; James MacGregor
Subject: Klenk File
Attached: Klenk Billing Corrected.doc (24KB)

Dear Mr. Thompson,

Attached please find the corrected billing for this client. My research indicated that we overbilled the project for lumber. I have included the correct numbers.

Let me know if you need anything else on this matter.

Kaitlyn Botano, Office Assistant
Thompson Builders
345 West End Avenue
Pittsburgh, PA 12231
Phone: 555-212-2121
Fax: 555-212-2122

Chapter 18

Writing a Résumé and a Cover Letter

Résumés summarize your education, work experience, and other accomplishments for prospective employers. Application letters introduce you to those employers. When you send a letter (also called cover letter) and résumé applying for a job, you are making an argument for why that employer should want to meet you and perhaps hire you. In a way, the two texts together serve as an advertisement selling your talents and abilities to someone who likely has to sift through many applications to decide whom to invite for an interview. That's why résumés and application letters require a level of care that few other documents do. Résumés and application letters are obviously very different genres—yet they share one common purpose, to help you find a job. Thus, they are presented together in this chapter. Most employers invite applicants to upload résumés and job application letters to their Websites or to send the application letter as an e-mail message with the résumé attached. If you are sending a hard copy résumé and job application letter, print both documents on good-quality white paper.

18.1 Résumés

A résumé is one of a job seeker's most important tools. If done well, a résumé not only tells potential employers about your education and work background, it says a lot about your attention to detail, writing skills, and professionalism. The purpose of a résumé (along with your cover letter) is to get an interview. Research has shown that it takes an average of ten interviews to receive one job offer, so the résumé needs to be persuasive and perfect. Given this, the résumé must be user-centered and persuasive. A résumé should provide information in table format that allows a potential employer to evaluate your qualifications. It should include your name and address, the position you seek, the qualifications and education, the working experiences, any special skills or awards, and how to obtain your references. All the information should fit on one uncrowded page unless your education and experience are extensive. Here's an example, a résumé written by a college student applying for an internship before her senior year.

Emily W. Williams

28 Murphy Lane
Springfield, Ohio 45399
Phone: 937-555-2640
Email: ewilliams22@gmail.com
LinkedIn: www.linkedin.com/EmilyWWilliams

Skills
- Communicating in writing and verbally, face-to-face and in various media
- Organizing and analyzing data
- Collaborating with other people on a team to achieve goals within deadlines
- Fluent in French
- Software: Microsoft Word, Microsoft Excel, SPSS, ATLAS.ti, Avid Pro Tools

Education
Wittenberg University, Springfield, Ohio
- BA in Marketing expected in May 2020
- Minor in Psychology
- Current GPA: 3.67
- Recipient, Community Service Scholarship

Clark State Community College, Springfield, Ohio
- AA in Business Administration, 2018
- GPA: 3.88
- Honors: Alpha Lambda Delta National Honor Society

Experience
August 2018—Present: Department of Psychology, Wittenberg University, Springfield, Ohio
Research Assistant
- Collect and analyze data
- Interview research study participants

Summer 2018: Landis and Landis Public Relations, Springfield, OH
Events Coordinator
- Organized local charity campaigns
- Coordinated database of potential donors
- Produced two radio spots for event promotion

Summers 2016—2017: Springfield Aquatic Club, Springfield, OH
Assistant Swim Coach
- Instructed children aged 5–18 in competitive swimming

1. Key Features of Résumés

1) **A structure that suits your goals and experience.** There are conventional ways of organizing a résumé but no one right way. You can organize a résumé chronologically or functionally, and it can be targeted (customized for a particular job application) or not. A chronological résumé is the most general, listing pretty much all your academic and work experience from the most recent to the earliest. A targeted résumé will generally announce the specific goal up top, just beneath your name, and will offer information selectively, showing only the experience and skills relevant to your goal. A functional résumé is organized around various kinds of experience and is not chronological. You might write a functional résumé if you wish to demonstrate a lot of experience in more than one area and perhaps if you wish to downplay dates. Combination résumés, like Emily Williams's, allow you to combine features from various types of résumés to present yourself in the best light; Emily's initial emphasis on skills is functional, while her education and experience are listed chronologically.

2) **Succinct.** A résumé should almost always be short—one page if at all possible. Entries should be parallel but do not need to be written in complete sentences— "Produced two radio spots", for instance, rather than "I produced two radio spots". Use action verbs ("instructed" "produced") to emphasize what you accomplished.

3) **A design that highlights key information.** It's important for a résumé to look good and to be easy to skim; typography, white space, and alignment matter. Your name should be bold at the top, and the information you want the readers to see first should be near the top of the page. Major sections should be labeled with headings, all of which should be in one slightly larger or bolder font. And you need to surround each section and the text as a whole with adequate white space to make the parts easy to read—and to make the entire document look professional.

2. Tips for Writing a Résumé

1) **Define your objective.** Defining your objective as specifically as possible helps you decide on the form the résumé will take and the information it will include.

2) **Consider how you want to present yourself.** Begin by gathering the information you will need to include. As you work through the steps of putting your résumé together, think about the method of organization that works best for your purpose— chronological, targeted, functional, or combination.

3) **Contact information.** At the top of your résumé, list your full name, a permanent address (rather than your school address), and a permanent telephone number with area code.

4) **Your e-mail address.** Your e-mail address should sound professional; addresses like

hotbabe334@gmail.com do not make a good first impression on potential employers. If possible, get an address that uses your name and a common provider, such as Gmail, iCloud mail, or Outlook.

5) **Your skills**. What have you learned to do, both in school and in jobs or volunteer work that you've done? Make a list, and phrase each one in terms of what you can do, as Williams does. Avoid such phrases as "hard worker" "detail-oriented" and "self-starter". As you revise your résumé to fit different job postings, choose skills from the list that match the job's requirements. As you list your education, experience, and other activities, think in terms of the skills you acquired and add them to the list.

6) **Your education**. Start with the most recent: degree, major, college attended, and minor (if any). You may want to list your GPA (if it's over 3.0) and any academic honors you've received. If you don't have much work experience, list education first.

7) **Your work experience**. As with education, list your most recent job first and work backward. Include job title, organization name, start and end dates, and responsibilities. Describe them in terms of your duties and accomplishments. If you have extensive work experience in the area in which you're applying, list that first.

8) **Community service**, **volunteer, and charitable activities**. Many high school students are required to perform community service, and many students participate in various volunteer activities that benefit others. List the skills and aptitudes that participation helped you develop or demonstrate.

9) **Other activities**, **interests**, **and abilities**. What do you do for fun? What skills do your leisure activities require? (For example, if you play a sport, you probably have a good grasp of the value of teamwork and the drive to practice something until you've mastered it. You should describe your skills in a way that an employer might find attractive.)

10) **Choose references**. This is usually done by stating, "References are available on request", but before you start applying for jobs, ask people to serve as references, so they will be ready. It's a good idea to provide each reference with a one-page summary of relevant information about you (for example, give professors a list of courses you took with them, including the grades you earned and the titles of papers you wrote).

11) **Choose your words carefully**. Remember, your résumé is a sales document—you're trying to present yourself as someone worth a second look. Focus on your achievements, using action verbs that say what you've done. Be honest—employers expect truthfulness, and embellishing the truth can cause you to lose a job later.

12) **Consider key design elements**. Make sure your résumé is centered on the page and

Part Three | Special Assignments

that it looks clean and clear. It's usually best to use a single, simple font (Times New Roman, Calibri, Arial, and Cambria are good ones) throughout and to print on white paper. Use bold type and bullets to make the résumé easy to read, and limit it to no more—and no less—than one full page.

13) **Edit and proofread carefully**. Your résumé must be perfect. Show it to others, and proofread again. You don't want even one typo or other error.
14) **Send the résumé as a PDF if it's sent by e-mail**. PDFs look the same on all devices, whereas Word or other formats may not. Make sure potential employers see your résumé as you intended.

18.2 Cover Letters

Almost every job application needs a cover letter. Even if a job notice only mentions sending a résumé, the chance of being successfully noticed in a deluge of applications is greatly improved if you "cover" (accompany) your résumé with a professional letter, one that is tailored to fit the employer and job you are seeking. A cover letter is the first document an employer sees, so it is often the first impression you will make. Take advantage of this important first impression and prepare the reader for your application, stating why you are writing, why you are a good match for the job and the organization, and when you will contact him or her. A cover letter can:
- Explain your experiences in a story-like format that works with the information provided in your resume;
- Allow you to go in-depth about important experiences/skills and relate them to job requirements;
- Show the employer that you are individualizing (tailoring) this job application;
- Provide a sample of your written communication skills.

In order to impress prospective employers when writing a cover letter, you must first know what they are looking for in candidates. Learning more about the company itself—and what they value—can help you do this. Here are some suggestions:
- Read the job advertisement carefully;
- Research the corporate website, read and try to understand their mission statement (sometimes an organization's mission may not be overtly stated);
- Call "insiders" (people that work with the company);
- Refer to your university's career center if you are at college.

To prepare each cover letter, follow the basic steps for writing the traditional business letter. In the first paragraph, clearly tell the reader why you are writing: the specific job you are applying for and why. Devote one or more paragraphs in the "body" of your letter to explaining why you (a successful product of your education, training, experiences, previous employment, etc.) are a good match for the advertised position and/or how you might benefit the organization. Your concluding paragraph should express thanks for the employer's consideration and briefly reemphasize your interest in the job; in this paragraph you may also mention contact information or explain access to your credentials. In some situations, you may indicate your availability for an interview. If the employer is interested, he or she will read your résumé for more details and possibly distribute copies to others involved in the hiring process.

Sample Cover Letter

Emily Williams wrote this letter to seek a position at the end of her junior year. Williams tailored her letter to one specific reader at a specific organization. The letter cites details, showing that it is not a generic application letter being sent to many possible employers. Rather, it identifies a particular position—the public relations internship—and stresses the fit between Williams's credentials and the position. Williams also states her availability.

---

28 Murphy Lane
Springfield, OH 45399
May 19, 2021

Barbara Jeremiah, President
Jeremiah Enterprises
44322 Commerce Way
Worthington, OH 45322

Re: Public Relations Internship Opening (Ref. ID: 27C)

Dear Ms. Jeremiah,

    I am writing to apply for the public relations internship advertised in the Sunday, May 15, *Columbus Dispatch*. The success of your company makes me eager to work with you and learn from you.

    My grasp of public relations goes beyond the theories I have learned in the classroom. I applied those theories last summer at Landis and Landis, the Springfield public relations firm, where I was responsible for organizing two charity events that drew over two hundred potential donors each. I also learned to use sound productions software to produce promotional radio spots. Since Jeremiah Enterprises focuses on nonprofit public relations, my experience, training, and initiative will allow me to contribute to your company's public relations team.

Part Three Special Assignments

I will be available to begin any time after May 23, when the spring term at Wittenberg ends. I have attached my résumé, which provides detailed information about my background. I will phone this week to see if I might arrange an interview.

Sincerely,

Emily W. Williams
Encl: Résumé

Part Four

Punctuation and Expression

If we want the world to take seriously what we think and say, we need to pay attention to the grammar and language. We need to edit the sentences so that they're clear, choose the language carefully, and use punctuation purposefully. This part provides guidelines to help you edit what you write.

Chapter 19

Punctuation

There's more to good writing than just getting commas and apostrophes in the right places—yet those commas and apostrophes are important, too. We don't try to cover everything about punctuation in this part of the book—just those rules we think will be especially helpful for you.

19.1 Comma

The followings are nine most important uses of the comma:
1) **To join independent clauses with coordinating conjunctions.** Put a comma before the coordinating conjunctions (*and, but, for, nor, or, so,* and *yet*) when they connect two independent clauses. The comma signals that one idea is ending and another is beginning.

   For example:
   - Most people think the avocado is a vegetable, yet it is actually a fruit.
   - The blue ribbon went to Susanna, and Sarah got the red ribbon.

   Although some writers omit the comma, especially with short independent clauses, you'll never be wrong to include it.

   For example:
   - I was smart, and I knew it.

   No comma is needed between the verbs when a single subject performs two actions.

   For example:
   - Many fast-food restaurants now give calorie counts on menus and offer a variety of

healthy meal options.

2) **To set off introductory words.** Use a comma after an introductory word, phrase, or clause to mark the end of the introduction and the start of the main part of the sentence.

For example:

- Typically, a girl has a best friend with whom she sits and talks, frequently telling secrets.
- In terms of wealth rather than income, the top 1 percent control 40 percent.
- When Miss Emily Grierson died, our whole town went to her funeral.

3) **To separate items in a series.** Use a comma to separate the items in a series. The items may be words, phrases, or clauses.

For example:

- The ethics of contemporary surgery are often a problem for the patient, the doctor, and the patient's family.
- I spend a great deal of time thinking about the power of language—the way it can evoke an emotion, a visual image, a complex idea, or a simple truth.

4) **To set off nonessential elements.** A nonessential (or nonrestrictive) element is one that could be deleted without changing the basic meaning of the sentence; it should be set off with commas. An essential (or restrictive) element is one that is needed to understand the sentence; therefore, it should not be set off with commas.

Nonessential

For example:

- Spanish, which is a Romance language, is one of six official languages at the United Nations.
- The detail about being a Romance language adds information, but it is not essential to the meaning of the sentence and so is set off with commas.

Essential

For example:

- Navajo is the Athabaskan language that is spoken in the Southwest by the Navajo people.
- The detail about where Navajo is spoken is essential: Navajo is not the only Athabaskan language; it is the Athabaskan language that is spoken in the Southwest.

Note that the meaning of a sentence can change depending on whether or not an element is set off with commas.

For example:
- My sister, Mary, just published her first novel.
- The writer has only one sister.
- My sister Mary just published her first novel.
- The writer has more than one sister; the one named Mary just published a novel.

Essential and nonessential elements can be clauses, phrases, or words.

Clauses

For example:
- He always drove Chryslers, which are made in America.
- He always drove cars that were made in America.

Phrases

For example:
- I fumble in the dark, trying to open the mosquito netting around my bed.
- I see my mother clutching my baby sister.

Words

For example:
- At 8:59, Flight 175 passenger Brian David Sweeney tried to call his wife, Julie.
- At 9:00, Lee Hanson received a second call from his son Peter.
- Sweeney had only one wife, so her name provides extra but nonessential information. Hanson presumably had more than one son, so it is essential to specify which son called.

5) **To set off transitional expressions.** Transitions such as *thus, nevertheless, for example,* and *in fact* help connect sentences or parts of sentences. They are usually set off with commas.

For example:
- The real world, however, is run by money.

When a transition connects two independent clauses in the same sentence, it is preceded by a semicolon and is followed by a comma.

For example:
- There are few among the poor who speak of themselves as lower class; instead, they refer to their race, ethnic group, or geographic location.

6) **To set off direct quotations.** Use commas to set off quoted words from the speaker or source.

For example:
- Pa shouts back, "I just want to know where the gunfire is coming from."
- "You put a slick and a con man together," she said, "and you have predatory lenders."
- "Death and life are in the power of the tongue," says the proverb.

7) **To set off direct address, *Yes or No*, interjections, and tag questions.**

   For example:
   - Direct Address: "Yes, Virginia, there really is a Santa Claus."
   - Yes or No: No, you cannot replace the battery on your iPhone.
   - Interjection: Oh, a PS4. How long did you have to wait to get it?
   - Tag Question: That wasn't so hard, was it?

8) **With addresses, place names, and dates.**

   For example:
   - Send contributions to Human Rights Campaign, 1640 Rhode Island Ave., Washington, DC 20036.
   - Athens, Georgia, is famous for its thriving music scene.
   - Amelia Earhart disappeared over the Pacific Ocean on July 2, 1937, while trying to make the first round-the-world flight at the equator.

   Omit the commas, however, if you invert the date (*on 2 July 1937*) or if you give only the month and year (*in July 1937*).

9) **Between coordinate adjectives unless they are joined by *and*.** Coordinate adjectives are sets of adjectives that independently modify a noun.

   For example:
   - The bulldog is noted for its wrinkled, flattened face.

Both wrinkled and flattened modify face independently. That is not the case with cumulative adjectives.

When an adjective's modification is cumulative, it modifies not only the noun but also the whole adjective-noun phrase it precedes.

   For example:
   - Alicia wore a red felt hat.

Here *red* modifies not just hat but the phrase felt hat. Notice that no comma is used with cumulative adjectives. Coordinate adjectives are reversible, whereas cumulative adjectives aren't. That is, *flattened, wrinkled face* works as well as *wrinkled, flattened face*. On the other hand, *felt red hat* just sounds foolish. And *And* fits naturally between coordinate adjectives, but not between cumulative adjectives. Thus, you could write *wrinkled and flattened face* but not *red and felt hat*.

19.2 Semicolon

The semicolon is stronger than a comma but weaker than a period. This chapter presents the two most important uses of the semicolon.

1) **Between independent clauses.** Closely related independent clauses are most often joined with a comma plus *and* or another coordinating conjunction. If the two clauses are closely related and don't need a conjunction to signal the relationship, they may be linked with a semicolon.

   For example:
   - The silence deepened; the room chilled.

   A period would work in the above example, but the semicolon suggests a stronger connection between the two independent clauses. Another option is to use a semicolon with a transition that clarifies the relationship between the two independent clauses. Put a comma after the transition.

   For example:
   - There are no secret economies that nourish the poor; on the contrary, there are a host of special costs.

2) **In a series with commas.** Use semicolons to separate items in a series when one or more of the items contain commas.

   For example:
   - There are images of a few students: Erwin Petschaur, a muscular German boy with a strong accent; Dave Sanchez, who was good at math; and Sheila Wilkes, everyone's curly-haired heartthrob.
   - Key European air routes include stops in Lisbon, Portugal; Rome, Italy; Frankfurt, Germany; and Istanbul, Turkey.

19.3 Colon

Colons are used to direct attention to words that follow the colon: an explanation or elaboration, a list, a quotation, and so on.

For example:
- What I remember best, strangely enough, are the two things I couldn't understand and over the years grew to hate: grammar lessons and mathematics.
- I sized him up as fast as possible: tight black velvet pants pulled over his boots, black jacket, a red-green-yellow scarf slashed around his neck.
- She also voices some common concerns: "The product should be safe, it should be easily accessible, and it should be low-priced."
- Fifteen years after the release of the Carnegie report, College Board surveys reveal data are no different: test scores still correlate strongly with family income.

Colons are also used after the salutation in a business letter, in ratios, between titles and subtitles, between city and publisher in bibliographies, between chapter and verse in biblical references, and between numbers that indicate hours, minutes, and seconds.

For example:
- Dear President Michaels: ...
- For best results, add water to the powder in a 3:1 ratio.
- The Last Campaign: How Harry Truman Won the 1948 Election.
- New York: Norton, 2014.
- "Death and life are in the power of the tongue" (Proverbs 18:21).
- The morning shuttle departs at 6:52 am.

Note that put the colon only after a whole subject-verb-object structure:

For example:
- Genetic counseling requires the following: a knowledge of statistical genetics, an awareness of choices open to parents, and the psychological competence to deal with emotional trauma.

19.4 Dashes

Dashes are used to set off material you want to emphasize. Unlike colons, dashes can appear not only after an independent clause but also at other points in a sentence. To set off material at the end of a sentence, place a dash before it, to set off material in the middle of the sentence, place a dash before and after the words you want to emphasize.

For example:
- After that, the roller coaster rises and falls, slowing down and speeding up—all on its own.

- It did not occur to me—possibly because I am an American—that there could be people anywhere who had never seen a Negro.

Dashes are often used to signal a shift in tone or thought.

For example:

- The best way to keep children home is to make the home atmosphere pleasant—and let the air out of the tires.

Keep in mind that dashes are most effective if they are used only when material needs particular emphasis. Too many dashes can interfere with the flow and clarity of your writing.

19.5 Quotation Marks

This section presents the important uses of quotation marks (" "and ' ') and rules for using other punctuation in relation to quotation marks.

1) **Use quotation marks to enclose someone's spoken or written words.**

   For example:
   - "That's exactly how I feel," my mother said, and then my parents watched the news, and whatever came on after the news.
   - Upon the opening of the world's first underground passenger train in 1863, the editor of the *London Times* wrote that it was "an insult to common sense to think that people would choose to travel in darkness across London".

2) **Use quotation marks around the titles of essays, articles, chapter headings, short stories, short poems, and songs.**

   For example:
   - "Two Friends" (short story)
   - "New Car Designs" (newspaper article)
   - "Sparks" (song)
   - "Multiculturalism and the Language Battle" (lecture title)
   - "The New Admissions Game" (magazine article)
   - "Reflections on Advertising" (chapter in a book)
   - "Blink" (television episode from *Doctor Who*)
   - "Annabel Lee" (short poem)

3) **Use quotation marks around special words to: (1) show that a word is being discussed as a word, (2) indicate that a word or phrase is directly quoted, (3) indicate that a word is slang, or (4) point out that a word is being used in a humorous or ironic way.**

　　For example:
- A commentary on the times is that the word "honesty" is now preceded by "oldfashioned".
- She said she was "incensed".
- I drank a Dixie and ate bar peanuts and asked the bartender where I could hear "chanky-chank", as Cajuns call their music.
- In an attempt to be popular, he works very hard at being "cute".

4) **Use single quotation marks to punctuate quoted material within a quotation.**

　　For example:
- In "Flight of the Anasazi", Stephen H. Lekson concludes that a combination of prolonged drought and erratic rainfall "might have 'pushed' Four Corners peoples from their ancestral homes".

5) **The period and the comma go inside quotation marks; the semicolon and the colon go outside.** If the quoted material is a question, the question mark goes inside; if the quoted material is a part of a whole sentence that is a question, the mark goes outside. The rules for exclamation points are the same as those for question marks.

　　For example:
- According to cartoonist Matt Groening, "Love is a snowmobile racing across the tundra; suddenly it flips over, pins you underneath, and at night the ice weasels come."
- "Love is a snowmobile racing across the tundra; suddenly it flips over, pins you underneath, and at night the ice weasels come," says cartoonist Matt Groening.
- According to cartoonist Matt Groening, "Love is a snowmobile... suddenly it flips over, pins you underneath, and at night the ice weasels come"; Groening also advises that bored friends are one of the first signs that you're in love.
- Did he really say, "At night the ice weasels come"?
- Lisa asked, "Do you think you're in love or just in a snowmobile?" As usual, Homer replied, "D'oh!"

6) **When you provide parenthetical documentation for a quotation, put it after the closing quotation mark, and put any end punctuation that's part of the sentence after the parentheses.**

For example:
- An avid baseball fan, Tallulah Bankhead once said, "There have been only two geniuses in the world: Willie Mays and Willie Shakespeare" (183).

19.6 Hyphen

This section provides tips for when to use hyphens(-) and when to omit them.

1) **Use a hyphen to make some compound words.**

    For example:
    - great-great-grandfather (noun)
    - starry-eyed (adjective)
    - mother-in-law (noun)
    - three-year-old (adjective)

Writers sometimes combine words in new and unexpected ways. Such combinations are usually hyphenated.

For example:
- She prefers novels with they-lived-wretchedly-ever-after endings.
- And they pried pieces of baked-too-fast sunshine cake from the roofs of their mouths and looked once more into the boy's eyes.

Note: Consult a dictionary to find how it lists a particular compound word. Some compound words (*living room*) do not use a hyphen and are written separately. Some are written solid (*bedroom*). Some do not use a hyphen when the word is a noun (*ice cream*) but do use a hyphen when it is a verb or an adjective (*ice-cream sundae*).

2) **Some words with prefixes use a hyphen; check the dictionary if necessary.** (Hint: If the second word begins with a capital letter, a hyphen is almost always used.)

    For example:
    - ex-wife
    - self-esteem
    - non-English
    - mid-May

3) **In a series of compound adjectives, place a space (or a comma and a space, when appropriate) following the hyphen in every item except the last one.**

    For example:

- We have cedar posts in four-, six-, and eight-inch widths.
- She found herself on both the best- and the worst-dressed lists.

4) **Use a hyphen to mark the separation of syllables when you divide a word at the end of a line.** Do not divide one-syllable words; do not leave one or two letters at the end or the beginning of a line. (In most dictionaries, dots are used to indicate the division of syllables: va • ca • tion.)

In the essays you should avoid using fragment sentences.

Chapter 20

Expression

The writing style is how you express yourself. Basic to that style are principles of punctuation (such as those you studied in the preceding chapter) and of grammar—both part of the way we communicate with each other in writing. This chapter presents some grammar "dos" and "don'ts" to help you deal with expression problems common in the writing. It also demonstrates techniques that will help you advance the style beyond the basics so you express yourself skillfully.

20.1 Subordination

Subordination and coordination are ways of showing the exact relationship of ideas within a sentence. Through subordination, we show that one idea is less important than another. When we subordinate, we use dependent words such as *when, although, while, because,* and *after*. Through coordination, we show that ideas are of equal importance. When we coordinate, we use the words *and, but, for, or, nor, so,* and *yet*. Keep in mind that, very often, the relationship among ideas in a sentence will be clearer when subordination rather than coordination is used. The challenge is to combine related ideas into one sentence, giving them just the right emphasis. To succeed, you must learn subordination—making less important ideas part of more important ideas. We all know that a subordinate is someone who ranks lower than someone else. Parts of a sentence have a rank structure, too.

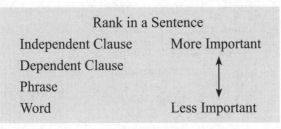

```
                    Rank in a Sentence
        Independent Clause      More Important
        Dependent Clause              ↑
        Phrase                        ↓
        Word                    Less Important
```

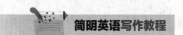

Ideas expressed in an independent clause naturally seem more important than ideas expressed with only a word. Subordination, then, reduces the emphasis of an idea by lowering its position on the rank structure. To subordinate an idea originally in an independent clause, we might place it in a dependent clause, a phrase, or, sometimes, even a word. For example:

Original: Art flew to Gila Bend. He arrived on time.

Subordination (dependent clause): Because he flew to Gila Bend, Art arrived on time.

Subordination (phrase): By flying to Gila Bend, Art arrived on time.

Subordination here has two effects:

- It shows what the writer considers the important idea: Art's arriving on time (expressed in the independent clause).
- It shows the relationship between the two ideas: The words *because* in the first revision and *by* in the second revision serve as road signs. They tell readers to be ready for a cause-effect relationship. (Because something happened, something else resulted: "Because he flew to Gila Bend, Art arrived on time.") These road signs make the reader's task much easier.

We could have subordinated the second independent clause if we had decided that Art's flying to Gila Bend was more important than the idea that he arrived on time.

Original: Art flew to Gila Bend. He arrived on time.

Subordination (dependent clause): Art flew to Gila Bend, where he arrived on time.

Subordination (phrase): Art flew to Gila Bend, arriving on time.

When you write, therefore, you must decide which ideas you wish to emphasize and which you wish to subordinate.

"But," you might protest, "I use subordination all the time." Sure you do—though probably not enough. The following are some ideas in grade-school style, early college style, and a more sophisticated style.

For example:

Grade-school style: The girl is playing tennis. Her name is Sally. She is a beginner. She is taking lessons. Karen is teaching her. Karen is a professional. Karen teaches at the Andromeda Club. Karen teaches every Tuesday morning.

Early college style: Sally is playing tennis. She is taking beginning lessons from Karen. Karen is a professional, and she teaches at the Andromeda Club every Tuesday morning.

Improved style: Sally is taking beginning tennis lessons from Karen, a professional who teaches at the Andromeda Club every Tuesday morning.

The last revision certainly is easier to read than either of the other versions. Why? Subordination pushes the unimportant ideas to the side so the readers can easily see the most important idea, the independent clause. In the following examples you can see how a string of simple sentences can be revised into an effective piece of writing:

For example:

Monotonous: The moon is now drifting away from the earth. It moves away at the rate of about one inch a year. This movement is lengthening our days. They increase a thousandth of a second every century. Forty-seven of our present days will someday make up a month. We might eventually lose the moon altogether. Such great planetary movement rightly concerns astronomers, but it need not worry us. It will take 50 million years.

Revised: The moon is now drifting away from the earth <u>about one inch a year. At a thousandth of a second every century,</u> this movement is lengthening our days. Forty-seven of our present days will someday make up a month, <u>if we don't eventually lose the moon altogether.</u> Such great planetary movement rightly concerns astronomers, but it need not worry us. It will take 50 million years.

In the revision, underlining indicates subordinate structures that were simple sentences in the original. With five sentences instead of the original eight, the revision emphasizes the moon's movement, the lengthening days, and the enormous span of time involved.

Applying Subordination During Editing

Here's a final tip to help you with subordination. On a first draft, you're naturally too busy thinking of ideas and how they relate to each other to worry about subordination at the sentence level. When you edit the draft—during the rewriting phase—pay attention to how you piece ideas together within sentences. Depending on the time you have available, you may even want to make a trip through the paper, beginning to end, just working on the best way to combine ideas into better sentences. The results will be worth the effort. You can use the structures listed below to subordinate information:

1) Use a subordinate clause beginning with a subordinating conjunction: *although, because, if, whereas,* **etc.**

For example:
- Although some citizens had tried to rescue Independence Hall, they had not gained substantial public support.

2) **Use a subordinate clause beginning with a relative pronoun:** *who, whoever, which, that.*

For example:
- The first strong step was taken by the federal government, which made the building a national monument.

3) **Use a phrase.**

For example:
- Like most national monuments, Independence Hall is protected by the National Park Service. (Prepositional phrase.)
- Protecting many popular tourist sites, the service is a highly visible government agency. (Verbal phrase.)

4) **Use an appositive.**

For example:
- The National Park Service, a branch of the Department of Interior, also runs Yosemite and other wilderness parks.

5) **Use a short modifier.**

For example:
- At the red brick Independence Hall, park rangers give guided tours and protect the irreplaceable building from vandalism.

20.2 Sentence Variety

After studying the subordination, you are wrong if you think that "good" writing consists of one complicated sentence after another. In fact, good writing has a mixture of varied sentence lengths and varied sentence structures. Although experienced writers avoid varying sentences just for the sake of variety, good sentence variety is important for good coherence—the smooth flow from one idea to the next. If you find yourself writing many short sentences in a row, or beginning many sentences with the subject of the independent clause, ask yourself, "Do my sentence patterns help my ideas flow smoothly? Or do they make my ideas seem fragmented, choppy?" This section will give you some tips on how to vary the sentences to achieve better coherence.

1. Sentence Length

Actually, not very many beginning writers have poor sentence variety from writing

Part Four | Punctuation and Expression

only long sentences. The problem is usually a series of short sentences:

For example:
- The new governor was sworn in today. He is a Democrat. Ten thousand people attended the ceremony. The governor gave a brief inaugural address. The governor promised to end unemployment. He said he would reduce inflation. He also promised to improve the environment. The audience gave him a standing ovation.

Pretty dismal, right? The average sentence length is only 6.25 words, and all the sentences except the second are either 6 or 7 words long—not overwhelming variety. Let's use the technique of subordination to come up with something better:

For example:
- The new Democratic governor was sworn in today. At a ceremony 10,000 people attended, he gave a brief inaugural address, promising to end unemployment, reduce inflation, and improve the environment. The audience gave him a standing ovation.

This version is certainly much easier to read, mainly because we've eliminated choppiness and subordinated some unimportant ideas. The average sentence is now 12 words long, within the desirable goal of 12 to 20 words per sentence.

2. The Problem of Complex Sentences

Although beginning writers tend toward short, choppy sentences, writers in business, industry, and government sometimes tend the other way. Some even believe that writing long, complex sentences is a mark of their educational competence. They think their superiors expect them to write long sentences, and they aim to please. Here's a sample of the type of writing that results:

For example:
- Whether the terrorists style themselves as separatists, anarchists, dissidents, nationalists, or religious true believers, what marks them as terrorists is that they direct their violence against noncombatants with the goal of terrorizing a wider audience than the immediate victims, thereby attempting to gain political influence over the larger audience. In one variant of terrorism, organizational terrorism, represented by such groups as the Red Army Faction in Germany, the Red Brigades in Italy, Direct Action in France, and 17 November in Greece, small, tightly knit, politically homogeneous organizations that are incapable of developing popular support for their radical positions resort to terrorism to gain influence. In a second variant of terrorism, that conducted within the context of ethnic separatist or countrywide insurgencies, such as in the Philippines, El Salvador, and Colombia, groups conducting paramilitary or guerrilla operations against the established

government turn to attacks on the populace at large to undermine the government's credibility, legitimacy, and public support.

These three sentences, all roughly the same length, average 54 words each. You can understand what they say, of course—if you read very carefully. Yet, today, successful writers—and the people they work for—are insisting on something else. They're demanding simpler writing so that busy readers don't have to struggle with the material they need to understand. Sentence averages in the 12- to 20-word range simply communicate more effectively. If most of the sentences contain thirty-five words or more, the main ideas may not stand out from the details that support them. Break some of the long sentences into shorter, simpler ones. Sometimes a series of compound sentences will be as weak as a series of brief, simple sentences, especially if the clauses of the compound sentences are all about the same length:

For example:

Monotonous: Physical illness may involve more than the body, for the mind may also be affected. Disorientation is common among sick people, but they are often unaware of it. They may reason abnormally, or they may behave immaturely.

Revised: Physical illness may involve the mind <u>as well as the body</u>. <u>Though often unaware of it</u>, sick people are commonly disoriented. They may reason abnormally <u>or behave immaturely</u>.

The first passage creates a seesaw effect. The revision, with some main clauses shortened or changed into modifiers (underlined), is both clearer and more emphatic.

3. Sentence Structure

Let's look again at the bad example that began the discussion on sentence length. Notice how many sentences begin with the subject (and its modifiers) of an independent clause:

For example:
- The new governor was sworn in today. He is a Democrat. Ten thousand people attended the ceremony. The governor gave a brief inaugural address. The governor promised to end unemployment. He said he would reduce inflation. He also promised to improve the environment. The audience gave him a standing ovation.

Every sentence begins with the subject of an independent clause, which makes it hard for readers to move from idea to idea. To make this paragraph easier to read, some of the sentences should begin with dependent clauses, others with phrases, and still others with transitional words. For example, look again at the revision:

For example:
- The new Democratic governor was sworn in today. *At a ceremony 10,000 people attended*, he gave a brief inaugural address, promising to end unemployment, reduce inflation, and improve the environment. The audience gave him a standing ovation.

The introduction to the second sentence provides nice relief.

For example:
- I used to think doing exercise was too much trouble, but now I know differently. I once had a roommate who seemed like an exercise fanatic to me, but now that I have formed the habit of regular exercise, I can see how different my life is now that I exercise compared to when I did not exercise. I wish everyone knew how much better life is with regular exercise, but I know some people will never try it.

This example repeats a simple sentence structure that begins with a noun/verb phrase, "I know" or "I think" or "I have", too often. It also relies on a sentence pattern that includes coordinating conjunctions and repeating word choices. This repetitive style makes the paragraph seem overly simplistic. Vary the sentence style to improve it.

For example:
- I used to think that doing exercise was too much trouble. My roommate, who jogged regularly, seemed like an exercise fanatic to me. Now that I have formed the habit of working out regularly, I can see how it improves my life. Everyone should do something physically challenging every day.

A reader can easily get bored reading a paragraph that employs the same sentence structure over and over again. To keep the prose lively—and the reader interested—try to vary the sentence structure. Many sentences, of course, should begin with the subject of an independent clause; still, they should not all look alike. They could end with a dependent clause, they could contain a couple of independent clauses, or they could contain a series of parallel phrases or clauses. The sentences in the paragraph you are now reading, for example, all begin with the subject of an independent clause, but after that beginning, their structures vary considerably.

4. Applying Sentence Variety During Editing

You may think you would never begin a lot of sentences all the same way. And surely you'd never string together all short, choppy sentences or long, overly complex ones. Yet, in the first draft many of us write with just those patterns. We think of an idea and write it down: "subject—verb"; we think of another idea and write it down: "subject—verb"; and so on. Similarly, we become comfortable writing sentences with about the same lengths—short ones or long ones, whichever way we're used to writing. If we don't take the time to rewrite the draft, the sentences look much the same. Check the last few pages to see if you've fallen into this bad habit. Good writing is not an automatic process, a flow of uninterrupted inspiration flowing forth onto the page. Good writing results from a painstaking and very conscious process. Don't just hope sentence variety will happen in your writing. After you write a draft, ask yourself these questions:

- Are the sentences different lengths?
- Do the sentences begin in a variety of ways?
- Do the sentences that begin with the subject of an independent clause have a variety of structures?

If the answers are "no", edit the paper for sentence variety. Be careful, though, not to sacrifice clarity for the sake of variety. And don't create grotesque, unnatural sentences. Variety is a means to achieve good writing—not the goal itself.

5. An Editing Example

Because this section looks separately at sentence length and sentence variety, you may think good writers always look at each separately as they revise their work. Certainly you could revise that way if you find it helpful. In most cases, though, that's not how writers work through their revisions. Experienced writers usually revise for varied lengths and varied structures at the same time. Let's begin with a short paragraph with overly simple and repetitive sentence style.

For example:

- Scientists have known of sickle-cell anemia for a long time. It still remains a menace for African-Americans. The problem is that nobody has discovered a cure. Scientists have experimented with several drugs. They have experimented with other chemicals. Some of these reduce a few ill effects of the disease. The fight against sickle-cell anemia has been waged on a small scale. Serious research is just beginning.

These eight sentences average 8.6 words per sentence, and only the next-to-last sentence falls in the desired range of 12- to 20-words per sentence. In addition, each sentence begins with the subject of an independent clause. Now let's edit for both varied sentence lengths and structures. We do this by looking at what ideas can be combined and which ideas should be emphasized in those combinations through subordination.

1) The first two sentences share the idea of time ("for a long time" and "still remains"). Let's use subordination to combine them and focus on the continuing menace of the disease: *Although scientists have known of sickle-cell anemia for a long time, it*

remains a menace for African-Americans.

2) Sentences four and five both deal with scientific testing, while sentence six indicates only limited positive results have been achieved. Sentence three contains the bottom line—no cure. We can combine all four sentences into one effective one: *While scientists have tested several drugs and chemicals, and some reduce a few ill effects, nobody has discovered a cure.*

3) The seventh sentence can stand alone. We can strengthen it by adding "only"—a point the preceding sentences reinforce: *The fight against sickle-cell anemia has been waged on only a small scale.*

4) The eighth sentence stands on its own. Don't be concerned that it has only five words. With the other sentences in the paragraph now considerably longer, a short sentence adds to the variety: *Serious research is just beginning.*

Now let's put all our revised sentences together and evaluate the results:

- Although scientists have known of sickle-cell anemia for a long time, it remains a menace for African-Americans. While scientists have tested several drugs and chemicals, and some reduce a few ill effects, nobody has discovered a cure. The fight against sickle-cell anemia has been waged on only a small scale. Serious research is just beginning.

We now have four sentences averaging 14.5 words per sentence. The first two sentences begin with dependent clauses, while the third and fourth sentences begin with the subjects of independent clauses. We've achieved the desired range for sentence lengths, and the sentences present varied sentence patterns.

20.3 Parallelism

Now that you've studied sentence variety, you may be afraid of writing sentences that repeat simple patterns. Don't be. Some ideas work best in sentences that clearly show a pattern. When you analyze an idea, you take pains to discover similarities and differences among its parts. Whether you intend to compare or contrast those elements, you want readers to see how the parts are alike or different. Parallelism is the key. Parallel structure emphasizes the connection between the elements and can make your writing rhythmic and easy to read. *Been there, done that. Eat, drink, and be merry. For better or for worse. Out of sight, out of mind.* All of these common sayings are parallel in structure, putting related words in the same grammatical form. The grammatical similarity of the items in the pair or series strongly signals to the reader that they are equally important, similar in meaning, and related in the same way to the rest of the sentence. The principle of parallel construction is simple: be sure ideas that are similar in content and function look the same. Parallelism works because the similarity of the appearance of the items shows clearly the pattern of the thought. The principle of parallelism applies most often to the following:

- two or more items in a series (usually with a coordinating conjunction);
- a pair of items with correlative conjunctions—a special type of series and conjunctions we'll explain later in this section.

1. Items in a Series

The principle of parallelism requires that all items in a series must be grammatically alike. That is, all words in a series must be the same type of word, all phrases the same type of phrase, and all clauses the same type of clause. Grammatical likeness also applies to sentences in a series: each item in the series must be a complete sentence—not a fragment—and, therefore, the same "type" of sentence. However, the structures within these complete sentences can vary, so the patterns within the sentences may appear somewhat different. Here are sentences with parallel constructions:

Words in series: I saw John and Mary.
　　　　　　　　I saw John, Bill, and Mary.
Phrases in series: I see him going to work and coming home.
　　　　　　　　　I plan to eat in a restaurant and to see a movie.
Dependent clauses in series: The phone rang when I reached the motel but before I unpacked my suitcases.
Independent clauses in series: I liked the parrot, so I bought it for my mother.
Complete sentences in series: She sold the car for three good reasons: It had no tires. It had no brakes. It had no engine.

Notice that each item—word, phrase, clause, or sentence—in a series has the same form as the other items in the same series.

2. Words in a Series

The words in a series of words seldom present special problems. However, the articles that appear with the series can create a minor parallelism problem. Notice the placement of the articles in these sample sentences:

For example:
Wrong: I bought food for **the** dog, cat, and **the** horse.
Correct: I bought food for **the** dog, cat, and horse.
Correct: I bought food for **the** dog, **the** cat, and **the** horse.

The correct sentences have either an article before the entire series or an article before every item in the series.

3. Phrases in a Series

Unlike words in a series, phrases often cause problems. Many times students mix types of phrases. Be sure that *-ing* phrases fit with other *-ing* phrases, *to* phrases with *to* phrases, and so forth.

For example:

Wrong: I like swimming in the pond, cycling down the lane, and **to** ride horses in the pasture.

Correct: I like swimming in the pond, cycling down the lane, and riding horses in the pasture.

Correct: I like to swim in the pond, to cycle down the lane, and to ride horses in the pasture.

Wrong: I plan to study hard, **doing** well on my exams, and to graduate with honors.

Correct: I plan to study hard, to do well on my exams, and to graduate with honors.

Correct: I plan on studying hard, doing well on my exams, and graduating with honors.

4. Clauses in a Series

Clauses in a series seldom cause major problems. However, if the series contains dependent clauses, you can help readers by signaling the beginning of each dependent clause. Consider this sentence:

For example:
- I expect to be entertained if I'm going to pay nine dollars to get in a theater and I'm going to sit there for two hours.

What does the *and* join? Does it join the two independent clauses?

For example:
- <u>I expect to be entertained</u> if I'm going to pay nine dollars to get in a theater and <u>I'm going to sit there for two hours.</u>

Or does it join two dependent clauses?

For example:
- I expect to be entertained if <u>I'm going to pay nine dollars to get in a theater</u> and <u>I'm going to sit there for two hours.</u>

The intended meaning is probably the second one: the *and* joins two dependent clauses. Readers will see the separation of the items more easily if the writer repeats the word that signals the beginning of the clauses:

For example:
- I expect to be entertained *if I'm going to* pay nine dollars to get in a theater and *if I'm going to* sit there for two hours.

Now the meaning is clear. Here's another sample: *"I can see that you don't like the meal and that you'd rather not be here," she pouted.* Notice that the repetition of *that* (which signals the beginning of dependent clauses) makes the parallel construction clear.

In addition to having like words, like phrases, and like clauses in a series within a sentence, be sure that the items in the series are the same type of grammatical unit. Do not, for instance, mix phrases and clauses in a series, as in this sentence:

For example:
- Wrong: My roommate likes to sleep in bed and when he's in class.

The sentence is awkward because the writer has joined a phrase (*in bed*) with a clause (*when he's in class*). Here's what the writer should have written:

For example:
- Correct: My roommate likes to sleep when he's in bed and when he's in class.

Now a clause fits with a clause. (Notice also that the sentence repeats *when*, the word that signals the beginning of each dependent clause.)

5. Complete Sentences in a Series

In the earlier sample of full sentences in a series, all of the sentences are quite short, and their internal structures are exactly alike: "It had no tires. It had no brakes. It had no engine." Clearly, this is a technique you have to apply sparingly. This type of series could provide a punchy variation if it were mixed in with longer sentences. Too much of it, though, could create the type of choppy, repetitive writing you learned to avoid when you studied sentence variety in the last section. However, complete sentences in a series don't have to be so much alike. Here's another sample, this time with some variation within the sentences.

For example:
- My great-grandfather wrote that Abraham Lincoln's appearance at the caucus was striking: Lincoln's beard was short and neatly trimmed. His suit was of a dark cloth that gave him a somber but dignified air and seemed to hang on his lank frame. In his hand he loosely held a black stovepipe hat.

These sentences are of varied lengths: 7, 23, and 10 words, respectively. Obviously the internal structures are not exactly alike. Are they parallel? Well, yes, they are. In the simplest sense, they have grammatical similarity, as each is a complete sentence. More important, each provides the same type of information—a quick, descriptive example—that answers the same question: How was Lincoln's appearance striking? And even though the sentence structures are not exactly alike, the basic idea patterns are similar: his beard was... ; his suit was... ; his hand held...

6. Parallelism for Paired Ideas

One way to emphasize the connection between two ideas is to put them in identical grammatical forms. When you connect ideas with coordinating conjunction (such as *and, but, or, nor, for, so,* or *yet*) or with correlative conjunction (such as *either... or; neither... nor; not (only)... but (also); whether... or;* and *just as... so*), use the same grammatical structure for each idea. Here are sentences with such pairs:

For example:

- Many rural residents are voting on conservation issues and agreeing to pay higher taxes to keep community land undeveloped.
- General Electric paid millions of dollars to dredge the river and to remove carcinogens from backyards.
- Just as the summer saw endless rain, so the winter brought many snowstorms.

All of this may seem complicated, but it's not. You wouldn't try to compare apples and buildings, because they're not alike. Similarly, you can't expect your readers to accept a comparison of items that appear dissimilar. The principle of parallelism requires only that you make like items look alike so readers can see the similarity. Balanced sentences are not a skill you need to worry about when you are writing first drafts. But when you rewrite, you should try to put matching words and ideas into matching structures. Such parallelism will improve your writing style.

20.4 Misused Modifiers

Modifiers are words, phrases, or clauses that limit or provide additional information about other words. Word order in an English sentence often determines meaning; therefore, different word arrangements may yield different meanings. Let's see what happens if we place *only* in every possible position in "Jonathan ate the doughnut".

For example:

- Only Jonathan ate the doughnut. (No one else ate it.)

- Jonathan only ate the doughnut. (He didn't do anything else to it.)
- Jonathan ate only the doughnut. (He ate nothing else.)
- Jonathan ate the only doughnut. (There were no other doughnuts.)
- Jonathan ate the doughnut only. (He ate nothing else.)

The game's implication is obvious, isn't it? Unless you carefully place the modifiers in your sentences, you may not write what you really mean. Modifiers are terrific savers of time and space in the writing—but they also can obscure or distort the meaning, sometimes making the writing appear ridiculous. In "I never saw a purple cow", the modifier *purple* limits the discussion from all cows to only purple cows. (Modifiers that limit the definition of other words are **restrictive modifiers**.) In "Standing on the bridge, the captain watched his ship move slowly through the channel", the modifier *standing on the bridge* provides additional information about the captain—but it in no way limits the definition. (Modifiers that provide information but do not limit definition are **nonrestrictive modifiers**.) Placement problems can occur with both types of modifiers, restrictive and nonrestrictive. However, if you study the examples carefully, you'll see that the most common problems are with placing nonrestrictive modifiers. Why? Because a nonrestrictive modifier is less essential to the point of the sentence, a writer is less likely to notice that the modifier is misplaced.

1. Misplaced Modifier

Placing a modifier in a sentence requires good judgment and careful editing. No particular place in a sentence is always right for a modifier, but this much is true: A modifier tends to modify what it is close to. "Close to" may be before or after the thing modified, so long as the sentence makes sense. These sentences make little sense.

For example:
- A jeep ran over the soldier that had muddy tires.
- People stared in amazement on the sidewalk.
- The accident left neatly pressed tire marks on the soldier's shirt.

In these sentences something comes between the modifiers and the things modified. As a result, the modifiers appear to refer to the things they are closest to: *that had muddy tires* seems to modify *soldier*; *on the sidewalk* seems to refer to *amazement*; and *neatly pressed* appears to modify *tire marks*. Let's move the modifiers so they modify what they should.

For example:
- A jeep that had muddy tires ran over the soldier.

- On the sidewalk, people stared in amazement.
or - People on the sidewalk stared in amazement.
- The accident left tire marks on the soldier's neatly pressed shirt.

Notice that *that had muddy tires* works only after *jeep*, whereas *on the sidewalk* works before or after *people,* and *neatly pressed* works only before *shirt*. What matters, then, is that the modifier must be close enough to the thing it modifies to complete the thought logically. A second type of placement problem occurs when you write strings of modifiers.

For example:
- A man with red hair in a green suit crossed the street.

Both *with red hair* and *in a green suit* should modify man, but instead *in a green suit* seems to refer to *hair*. One solution is to put one modifier before and another after the thing modified:

For example:
- A red-haired man in a green suit crossed the street.
or - Wearing a green suit, a man with red hair crossed the street.

A second solution is to combine the modifiers with a coordinating conjunction:
- A man with red hair and a green suit crossed the street.
- Again, the exact position of the modifier doesn't matter if the result makes sense.

2. Dangling Modifiers

Dangling modifiers can occur anywhere in a sentence, but the most common problem is at the beginning. A modifier that begins a sentence must refer to something that follows. Because of convention, readers expect an introductory word or phrase modifier to refer to the subject of the sentence.

For example:
- Walking along the beach, Mary found a sand dollar.

Because we expect the opening phrase (*walking along the beach*) to modify the subject of the sentence (*Mary*), we know that Mary, not the sand dollar, was walking along the beach. But what if the sentence reads this way?

For example:
- Walking along the beach, a sand dollar was found by Mary.

Again we expect the introductory phrase to modify the subject of the sentence, but sand dollars don't walk. Because the modifier cannot logically modify the subject of the sentence, we say that the modifier "dangles". The following sentences contain dangling modifiers:

For example:
- Enthusiastic, the hour seemed to pass quickly.
- Finishing the game, the crowd loudly booed the home team.
- After examining the data, the steam engine appeared to be the best choice.
- To enjoy surfing, the waves must be high.
- When only nine, John's mother took him to a circus.

Was the hour enthusiastic? Did the crowd actually finish the game? Did the steam engine examine the data? Can waves enjoy surfing? Do you really believe that John had a mother who was only nine years old? Because the modifiers above have no logical connection to the subjects of the sentences, we say the modifiers dangle. You have two options to correct dangling modifiers:

The first, the most obvious, is to recast the sentence so the subject matches the modifier.

For example:
- Enthusiastic, we thought the hour passed quickly.
- Finishing the game, the home team heard loud booing from the crowd.
- After examining the data, we concluded that the steam engine was the best choice.
- To enjoy surfing, you need high waves.
- When only nine, John went to the circus with his mother.

The second method is to change the word or phrase modifier into a clause.
For example:
- Because we were enthusiastic, the hour seemed to pass quickly.
- As the game ended, the crowd loudly booed the home team.
- After we examined the data, the steam engine appeared to be the best choice.
- If you want to enjoy surfing, the waves must be high.
- When John was only nine, his mother took him to a circus.

3. The Basic Principle

You can avoid both types of problem modifiers—misplaced as well as dangling—if you keep in mind the essential relationship between modifiers and the things they modify:
- A modifier tends to modify what it is close to;
- A modifier should be close to what it must modify.

20.5 Subject-Verb Agreement

One of the most common grammar problems for students is agreement between subjects and verbs. The rule itself is quite simple: A verb must agree in number with its subject. If the subject is singular, the verb must be singular; if the subject is plural, the verb must be plural. Most errors in agreement occur because of some difficulty related to the subject of a sentence, particularly in:

- identifying the subject;
- recognizing the subject's number.

1. Identifying the Subject

Some agreement problems result from difficulties in finding the subject of a sentence. Two sentence structures make identifying the subject particularly troublesome:

- when the subject is delayed—so it isn't where we expect it to be:
- when a phrase comes between the subject and the verb—confusing us about the subject's identity.

2. Delayed Subject

We usually can find the subject if it comes in its ordinary place—just before the verb—but we may have trouble if it follows the verb. Watch for sentences that open with *there* or *here*. These words delay the subject so that it appears after the verb. You'll have to think through such a sentence because you won't know whether the verb should be singular or plural until you get beyond it to the subject.

For example:

- There *are three sailboats* at the dock.
- Here *is the box* you wanted first.

3. Phrase Between Subject and Verb

Sometimes, even when the subject comes before the verb where we expect to see it, it is still hard to identify because of a phrase between the subject and verb. Because of the intervening phrase:

- We may think a word in the phrase is the subject;
- We may think the phrase is part of the subject, making it plural.

Let's look first at an example in which a word in the phrase might seem to be the subject:

- One of the Coyne boys **has** climbed the water tower.

Here the word *boys*, though so close to the verb, is simply part of a phrase that comes between the subject and the verb. The real subject is one.

Now let's look at a phrase that might seem to be part of the subject:

- Martha, as well as her sisters, **works** in the fields regularly.

As well as her sisters seems to be part of the subject. It seems to be equivalent to *and her sisters*. But it isn't.

Confusing Prepositional Phrases

The words here are merely prepositions; they begin phrases that have nothing to do with determining the agreement between a subject and its verb:

| as well as | including | accompanied by | like |
| along with | together with | in addition to | with |

4. Recognizing the Subject's Number

The problems we just looked at occur because the subject isn't where we expect it. Sometimes, though, we can find the subject and still not know whether it is singular or plural. These rules will help you.

1) Two or more subjects joined by *and* are almost always plural. The *and* joins the items—singular, plural, or mixed—into one plural unit.

   For example:

   - That woman and her husband **look** a lot alike.

2) If *or* or *nor* joins subjects, the verb agrees with whichever subject is closer to the verb.

   For example:

   - Either Beverly or my other aunts **have** my thanks.
   - Either my other aunts or Beverly **has** my thanks.

3) *Some, all, most, part, half* (and other fractions) may be either singular or plural, depending on the phrase that follows them. We told you in the first part of the section not to let a phrase between the subject and the verb influence subject-verb agreement. However, as happens in English grammar, that rule has an exception: Many times the words in the previous list are followed by a phrase beginning with *of* ("*All of the jurors*" "*Some of the tea*"). If the main word in the *of*-phrase is plural, the verb should be plural. However, if the main word is singular or just can't be counted (we wouldn't say "one *milk*" or "thirteen *tea*", for example), the verb should be singular.

   For example:

   - Some of the grapes are still on the table. (*Grapes* is plural, so the verb is plural.)

- Some of the milk is dripping on the floor. (*Milk* cannot be counted, so the verb is singular.)

4) Relative pronouns (*who, whose, whom, which,* and *that*) may be singular or plural, depending on the word they refer to. Usually the relative pronoun refers to the word just before it:

   For example:
   - Jeannette is one of the children **who love** to read. (*Who* is a pronoun replacing *children*. Not just one child but all the children love to read.)

   Again, here comes an exception. What if Jeannette is the *only one* in the group who loves to read? Then the pronoun who refers to the word *one*, not the word *children*:

   For example:
   - Jeannette is the only one of the children **who loves** to read.

   The exception, then, is that in the phrase *the only one... who/that*, the relative pronoun refers to the word *one*, so the verb must be singular.

5) A collective noun as subject requires a singular verb when the group acts as a unit but a plural verb when the members of the group act as separate persons or things. A collective noun names a group: *audience, class, committee, family, jury, orchestra, team,* and so forth. The key is to determine whether the parts of the group are acting as a single body or as separate entities (that are doing the same thing).

   For example:
   - The jury **has** been sequestered. (The members of the collective group have been separated from the public as a single body, so the verb is singular.)
   - The jury **are** unable to agree on a verdict. (Clearly, the members of the collective group are acting as separate individuals—because they cannot agree as a unit—so the verb is plural.)

20.6 Passive Voice

Compared with active voice, passive voice has some disadvantages:
- A passive construction is wordier than an active one;
- Because it reverses the normal order of an action, passive voice is indirect;
- As its name implies, a "passive" verb lacks the vigor inherent in an active verb;
- And if the writer doesn't include the actor, the passive construction may be vague.

For example:
- There has been very little effort made by overextended police forces to attempt interdiction of drug shipments and processing laboratory destruction operations.

Although we might be tempted to start by revising the overly complex wording, an efficient editor will first solve simple problems such as faulty sentence structure. The beginning of the sentence combines a passive construction (*has been... effort made by... forces*) with a *There are* type of opening. Revising to eliminate the passive construction fixes both voice and wordiness problems.

For example:
- Overextended police forces have done little to attempt interdiction of drug shipments and processing laboratory destruction operations.

Now the editor can focus on the wordiness and lack of parallelism in the rest of the sentence:

For example:
- Overextended police forces have done little to interdict drug shipments and destroy processing laboratories.

The revision is simpler and certainly more clear. Remember to attack the simple problems in a sentence first; revising passive voice is an easy place to begin once you know how to deal with it.

1. Choosing Between Active and Passive

Though having some disadvantages, the passive is often the better choice. To choose between active and passive, you have to answer three questions:

1) Must the readers know who is responsible for the action. Often, we don't say who does an action because we don't know or readers won't care. For example, we naturally choose the passive in these sentences:

   For example:
   - The president was rumored to have considered resigning.
   - Those who are found guilty can be fined.
   - Valuable records should always be kept in a safe.

If we do not know who spreads rumors, we cannot say, and no one doubts who finds people guilty or fines them or who should keep records safe. So those passives are the right choice. Sometimes, of course, writers use the passive when they don't want readers to know who is responsible for an action, especially when the doer is the writer.

For example:

- Because the test was not completed, the flaw was uncorrected.

2) Would the active or passive verb help readers move more smoothly from one sentence to the next? We depend on the beginning of a sentence to give a context of what we know before we read what's new. A sentence confuses us when it opens with information that is new and unexpected. In th next example, the subject of the second sentence gives us new and complex information (boldfaced), before we read more familiar information that we recall from the previous sentence (italicized):

For example:
- We must decide whether to improve education in the sciences alone or to raise the level of education across the whole curriculum. **The weight given to industrial competitiveness as opposed to the value we attach to the liberal arts** (new information) will determine (active verb) *our decision* (familiar information).

In the second sentence, the verb *determine* is in the active voice. But we could read the sentence more easily if it were passive, because the passive would put the short, familiar information (*our decision*) first and the newer, more complex information last, the order we prefer:

For example:
- We must decide whether to improve education in the sciences alone or raise the level of education across the whole curriculum. *Our decision* (familiar information) will be determined (passive verb) **by the weight we give to industrial competitiveness as opposed to the value we attach to the liberal arts** (new information).

Compare the following two sentences:

For example:
- Some claim that our genes influence (active) aspects of behavior that we think are learned. Our genes, for example, seem to determine...
- Some claim that aspects of behavior that we think are learned are in fact influenced (passive) by our genes. Our genes, for example, seem to determine...

Sentences are cohesive when the last few words of one set up information that appears in the first few words of the next. That's the biggest reason the passive is in the language: to let us get old and new information in the right order and arrange sentences so that they flow from one to the next easily.

3) Would the active or passive give readers a more consistent and appropriate point of view? The writer of this next passage reports the end of World War II in Europe from the point of view of the Allies. To do so, she uses active verbs to make the Allies a consistent sequence of subjects:

For example:

- By early 1945, the Allies had essentially defeated (active) Germany; all that remained was a bloody climax. American, French, British, and Russian forces had breached (active) its borders and were bombing (active) it around the clock. But they had not yet so devastated (active) Germany as to destroy its ability to resist.

Had she wanted to explain history from the German point of view, she would have used passive verbs to make Germany the subject:

For example:

- By early 1945, Germany had essentially been defeated (passive); all that remained was a bloody climax. Its borders had been breached (passive), and it was being bombed (passive) around the clock. It had not been so devastated (passive), however, that it could not resist (active).

Some writers switch from one character to another for no apparent reason. Avoid this:

- By early 1945, the Allies had essentially defeated Germany. Its borders had been breached, and they were bombing it around the clock. Germany was not so devastated, however, that the Allies would meet with no resistance. Though Germany's population was demoralized, the Allies still attacked German cities from the air.

2. Using the Passive in These Contexts

1) You don't know who did an action, readers don't care, or you don't want them to know.
2) You want to shift a long and complex bundle of information to the end of a sentence, especially when doing so also lets you begin with a chunk of information that is shorter, more familiar, and therefore easier to understand.
3) You want to focus readers' attention on one or another actor.

3. Activating the Passive

1) Reverse the object and the subject.

   For example:

   - Passive: An example is shown in Figure 3.
   - Active: Figure 3 shows an example.

2) Delete the main verb, leaving the sentence with a form of *to be* as the only verb.

   For example:

- Passive: Your cousin is seen as the best candidate.
- Active: Your cousin is the best candidate.

3) Change the verb.
   For example:
   - Passive: Jonathan was given a new book.
   - Active: Jonathan received a new book.

These three methods will provide you with the tools you need to write simple, direct, and vigorous active sentences.

20.7 Word Choice

Choose the words carefully when you write. Always take the time to think about the word choices rather than simply use the first word that comes to mind. You should develop the habit of selecting words that are precise and appropriate for your purpose. This section covers some basic and advanced techniques for finding the good words that will make the difference between an A paper and an ordinary C paper.

1. Using Precise Words

What is a good word? Is it something really impressive, a big word that proves how educated we are? No, usually it's a word we all know. Unfortunately, even though it's a common word, it's one we rarely use because we choose an even more common word instead. *See* is one of those more general words we might slap down in a rough draft. But think of all the more precise synonyms that might work better: *glimpse, gaze, stare, peer, spot,* and *witness.* Let's take a longer example. Suppose you are reading a paragraph and run across these words.

For example:
- The man walked into the room.

The words are so general they could fit into a number of strikingly different contexts:
- The policeman, hidden behind a parked car, watched *as the man walked into the room.*

or
- The Capitol guard smiled *as the man walked into the room.*
- The class quieted somewhat *as the man walked into the room.*
- The patients gasped *as the man walked into the room.*

"What a great clause!" you say. "I can use it anywhere." The truth is, it's a lousy clause—you can use it anywhere. All the words are general, the kind of words that pop into your mind in a second. Let's try to make the words more exact. Here are some possibilities:

man: *thief, senator, English teacher, Dr. Rodney*

walked: *sneaked, hurried, sauntered, reeled*

room: *motel room, antechamber, classroom, office*

Now let's rewrite that all-purpose clause using more specific words:

For example:

- The policeman, hidden behind a parked car, watched *as the thief sneaked into my motel room.*

or

- The Capitol guard smiled *as the senator hurried into the antechamber.*
- The class quieted somewhat *as the English teacher sauntered into the classroom.*
- The patients gasped *as Dr. Rodney reeled into his office.*

Each clause is better—and certainly more interesting—because the writer took the time to come up with just the right words. Try it yourself. Look for the dull, general words in your own writing and make them more specific. This technique is one of the best ways to improve your writing dramatically.

2. Avoiding Inflated Words

Some students feel that they can improve their writing by using fancy, elevated words rather than simple, natural words. They use artificial, stilted language that more often obscures the meaning than communicates it clearly. This frequently occurs when students attempt to use a dictionary or thesaurus, but just pick words at random to replace the simpler words. Using college-level vocabulary is a way to improve the writing, but you must be careful in choosing words. Not only can certain choices sound artificial, but another problem may arise when words are chosen without enough thought. Since many words can act as nouns, verbs, adjectives, and adverbs, using the wrong part of speech often leads to obscured meaning. Here are some unnatural-sounding sentences:

For example:

- It was a marvelous gamble to procure some slumber.
- We relished the delectable noon-hour repast.
- The officer apprehended the imbibed operator of the vehicle.
- The female had an affectionate spot in her heart for domesticated canines.

The same thoughts can be expressed more clearly and effectively by using plain, natural language, as below:

For example:
- It was an excellent chance to get some sleep.
- We enjoyed the delicious lunch.
- The officer arrested the drunk driver.
- The woman had a warm spot in her heart for dogs.

3. Using Modifiers

Another basic technique, in addition to using the right word, is to use modifiers. The thoughtful use of modifiers makes the point clear and add meaning and originality to the essay. One way to accomplish this is to use powerful and specific adjectives and adverbs. Consider the difference between these sets of sentences:

- Sentence A: My grandmother put on her sweater.
- Sentence B: My grandmother put on her cashmere sweater.

- Sentence A: The football team practiced in the rain.
- Sentence B: The football team practiced in the torrential downpour.

In both cases, sentence B allows you to hear the "voice" and impressions of the writer, giving a more accurate and interesting picture of the action. The first sentences are dull, and don't give the reader much information. The right modifiers (adjectives and adverbs) can also get the message across in fewer, more accurate words. This is critical in an essay with a specified length. You don't want to sacrifice unique details, but sometimes one word will do the job better than a few. For example, *Chihuahua* can take the place of *little dog*; *exhausted* can take the place of *really tired*; and *late* can take the place of *somewhat behind schedule*.

4. Avoiding Wordiness

Wordiness—using more words than necessary to express a meaning—is often a sign of lazy or careless writing. Readers may resent the extra time and energy they must spend when you have not done the work needed to make the writing direct and concise. Here are examples of wordy sentences: Do not try to *predict* **future** events that will **completely** *revolutionize* society, because **past** *history* shows that it is the **final** *outcome* of minor events that **unexpectedly** *surprises* us more.

For example:
- We must explain **the reason for** the delay in the meeting.
- Productivity **actually** depends on **certain** factors that **basically** involve psychology more than **any particular** technology.

Omitting needless words improves these sentences:

For example:
- Do not try to predict revolutionary events, because history shows that the outcome of minor events surprises us more.
- We must explain why the meeting is delayed.
- Productivity depends on psychology more than on technology.

5. Using Comparisons

If you really want to get readers' attention, use a comparison. It may be the most memorable part of the theme. Remember: transitions are like road signs. the blueprint for the paper is like the architect's design for the structure he plans to build. These and other comparisons help readers understand an idea. This next passage reveals a truth about pleasure through a figure of speech embedded in a comparison that is itself almost metaphorical.

- The secret of the enjoyment of pleasure is to know when to stop... We do this every time we listen to music. We do not seize hold of a particular chord or phrase and shout at the orchestra to go on playing it for the rest of the evening; on the contrary, however much we may like that particular moment of music; we know that its perpetuation would interrupt and kill the movement of the melody. We understand that the beauty of a symphony is less in these musical moments than in the whole movement from beginning to end. If the symphony tries to go on too long, if at a certain point the composer exhausts his creative ability and tries to carry on just for the sake of filling in the required space of time, then we begin to fidget in our chairs, feeling that he has denied the natural rhythm, has broken the smooth curve from birth to death, and that though a pretense of life is being made, it is in fact a living death.

—Alan W. Watts, *The Meaning of Happiness*

Watts could have written this:

- ... however much we may like that particular moment of music, we know that its perpetuation would interrupt and spoil the movement of the melody... We begin to fidget in our chairs, feeling that he has denied the natural rhythm, has interrupted the regular movement from beginning to end, and that though a pretense of wholeness is being made, it is in fact a repeated end.

The two passages are equally clear and graceful. But the first illuminates music and pleasure in a way that the second does not. The metaphor of birth and the smooth, unbroken curve of life into death startles us with a flash of unexpected truth. A metaphor invites us to look at two things in a new way.

Of metaphor, Aristotle wrote:

- By far the greatest thing is to be a master of metaphor. It is the one thing that cannot be learned from others. It is a sign of genius, for a good metaphor implies an intuitive perception of similarity among dissimilars.

Comparisons have one drawback: they can be hard to think of, particularly good comparisons. We all can think of bad ones. The familiar phrases that come to mind almost automatically are clichés, and they can doom writing as effectively as original comparisons can save it. Consider this sentence:

- Although he was blind as a bat, Herman remained cool as a cucumber when he entered the arena.

See how clichés attract the wrong kind of attention to themselves? Hearing a cliché is like hearing a comedian go through the same routine time after time. After a while, nobody listens. A good rule is that if you have heard a comparison before, don't use it. But do use original comparisons. Be daring. Try one in your next theme.

6. Replacing General Ideas with Specific Samples

Here's something else to try in your next theme: When you want to use a general word that stands for an entire class of items—such as *toys* or *vehicles* or *books*—use just one item from that class instead. Let the specific stand for the general.

- Inflation means that most Americans can hardly afford to eat, but some congressmen don't seem to care how much food costs.

Let's make the sentence a little more interesting by replacing the word *food* (an entire class of items) with *a loaf of bread* (one item from that class):

- Inflation means that most Americans can hardly afford to eat, but some congressmen don't seem to care how much a loaf of bread costs.

Here are some other examples:

- As a photographer she is limited. She may be able to take pictures of nature, but she can't take good pictures of people.
- There were many expensive cars in the school's parking lot during the football game.
- You could tell spring was here because of all the flowers in bloom.
- Why do lawyers use words that mean one thing to them and something entirely different in ordinary English?

We can make the general words more interesting by changing the word *nature* to

something more specific:
- As a photographer she is limited. She may be able to take pictures of trees, but she can't take good pictures of people.
- There were many expensive cars in the school's parking lot during the football game: Mercedes convertibles, low-slung Porsches, and red Ferraris.
- You could tell spring was here because of all the flowers in bloom: tulips of all colors, yellow daffodils, and (if you want to call them flowers) even a few early dandelions.
- Why do lawyers use words that mean one thing to them and something entirely different in ordinary English (words such as *party* and *action* and *motion*)?

See the difference that quick examples make? They take general, rather abstract terms—*nature, cars, flowers, legal words*—and make them much more concrete. It's almost as though the abstract words don't really communicate, don't really find a place to lodge in the brain cells. But the more concrete words—*tree, Mercedes, tulip, party*—do. The detail instead of the generality makes the sentence livelier. Most college students neglect both of the advanced techniques in this section. And few of them get A's. If you want to learn how to write an A paper, you might start by occasionally using a comparison or a specific word instead of a general one.